A Dictionary of
ANCIENT
NEAR EASTERN
MYTHOLOGY

A Dictionary of
ANCIENT
NEAR EASTERN
MYTHOLOGY

Gwendolyn Leick

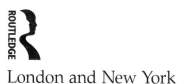

London and New York

First published 1991
by Routledge
11 New Fetter Lane, London EC4P 4EE

Simultaneously published in the USA and Canada
by Routledge
a division of Routledge, Chapman and Hall, Inc.
29 West 35th Street, New York, NY 10001

Typeset in 10½/12½ Parlament Scantext by Leaper & Gard Ltd, Bristol
Printed in Great Britain by T.J. Press (Padstow), Cornwall

British Library Cataloguing in Publication Data
Leick, Gwendolyn *1951–*
    A dictionary of Ancient Near Eastern mythology.
    1. Middle Eastern myths, ancient period
    I. Title
    299

Library of Congress Cataloging in Publication Data
Leick, Gwendolyn, 1951–
    A dictionary of Ancient Near Eastern mythology /
    Gwendolyn Leick. p.   cm.
    Includes bibliographical references and index.
    1. Mythology, Oriental – Dictionaries.   2. Mythology,
    Assyro – Babylonian – Dictionaries.   I. Title.
    BL1060.L44 1991
    299'.2 – dc20   90-39713

ISBN 0–415–00762–3

CONTENTS

ILLUSTRATIONS

ACKNOWLEDGEMENTS

To each of the following for their courteous permission to reproduce photographs, as indicated: the Trustees of the British Museum (2, 3, 6, 7, 9, 11–13, 19, 20, 23, 26, 29–32, 37–44); the Musée de Louvre (5, 24, 25, 27, 28, 33); and the Museum of Anatolian Civilizations, Ankara (14–18, 21, 22, 35).

To Francis J. Kirk, for producing the drawings (1, 4, 8, 34, 36).

INTRODUCTION

For almost two thousand years we have only been able to see the religion of the ancient Orient as a dark shadow cast by the brightness of the Hebrew God. While the Olympians and the heroes of Greece fuelled the imagination of our culture, the gods of Canaan and Babylon remained 'abominations' and utterly alien. But for the last 150 years, following the spectacular discovery of Nineveh, countless excavations have been searching for the lost civilizations of the ancient Near East. The great museums of Europe and America acquired their share of giant winged bulls, stamped bricks, stone statues, millions of pottery sherds and delicately carved cylinder seals. On shelves and drawers rest tens of thousands of clay-tablets, each one carefully numbered. While archaeologists assemble the tangible remains of villages and cities, epigraphists decipher the messages sent to people dead for more than 3,000 years; they re-read the administrative minutiae of extinct bureaucracies and reconstruct a lost literature. We now know the names of thousands of gods and goddesses, the words of hymns and litanies, the daily procedures of the Babylonian cult, as well as a growing number of mythological tales. In spite of the progress in our understanding of this ancient religion, we are only able to see part of the whole picture. We shall never be sure of the rituals performed in the neolithic sanctuaries; and the deities worshipped in the splendid cathedral-like temples of the fourth millennium BC will remain a mystery. We know nothing about the gods of the nomadic peoples at the periphery of the river valleys and very little about the indigenous religions of all those other parts of the ancient Near East that did not develop literacy.

The written testimony of the old literate civilizations is the main source of our knowledge. Several ancient languages (Sumerian, Hurrian, Hittite, Elamite and sundry Semitic dialects, including Babylonian) can now be read; although only a small amount of the thousands of tablets housed in the museum collections have been published and more are unearthed by every season of excavation. Furthermore, the texts are by no means evenly distributed in time and place. Literacy on any scale depends on a stable political and economic climate. It can only develop in highly evolved urban societies, with a sizeable 'middle class' of professional bureaucrats. When these conditions become severely disrupted for any length of time, scribal productivity declines or comes to a standstill.

There were several 'Dark Ages' in Mesopotamian history, following social and political upheavals, and outside Mesopotamia, bureaucratic urbanism developed at a slower pace and only intermittently. The impetus for the invention of writing was the demand for reliable book-keeping; with the bulk of texts always remaining economical and administrative. The growth of literary genres was actually a by-product of scribal training: many poetic, historical and mythological compositions are only known from school copies. Eventually, the centres of learning accumulated collections of many different kinds of texts, mainly magico-religious in character. The majority of myths, epics, hymns and incantations originated in these scribal centres attached to the old sanctuaries (Nippur, Sippar, Ur, Šuruppak, Babylon, Nineveh, Assur ...). These institutions were a Mesopotamian invention; when other peoples took up the medium of cuneiform to write their own languages on clay, the system of scribal training was imported from Sumer or Babylon. The Hittite, Egyptian, Canaanite or Hurrian pupil used the same educational tools as his Mesopotamian colleagues; he used the same sign-lists, he copied the same royal inscriptions, hymns, epics and myths. In this manner, the literary culture of Mesopotamia was disseminated throughout those areas of the Near East which aspired to a literate urbanism (hence the copies of Gilgameš in the capital of the Hittites, of Adapa in Amarna etc.). In turn, native scribal centres encouraged the collection of their own traditions (a good example of this process is the tablet collection of Hattusa in Hittite Anatolia). A substantial amount of the texts discussed in this volume originate from such archives.

The relationship between the scribal centres as well as the procedures of editing and transmitting texts are little known. Equally problematic is the question of how the literary tradition related to oral traditions. It has always been taken for granted that folktales and songs, minstrelsy and other courtly poetry must have existed and that it exercised some influence over the written compositions. But we only have the written works and our knowledge of poetic artifices has not progressed far enough to differentiate between a literary and an oral 'style' in all types of compositions. But attempts have been made to isolate folktale elements within literary texts, and it is now clear that many mythological texts consist of multiple layers of traditions. A well-known folktale may become attached to a historical figure, which in turn may acquire traits of one or several gods, incorporating their mythological traditions by association. This already composite text may then be reinterpreted for ideological reasons and further embellished by other folktale elements (see Gilgameš).

Myths, very broadly defined as narratives featuring divine or heroic protagonists, have a paradigmatic function. They establish connections between the known and the unknown; the past and the present; the world of the gods and the world of men. The more successful a myth, the more levels of 'meaning' it is able to allude to. Like works of art, myths can be experienced; their truth can be felt. In the absence of a 'rational' frame of reference, a Greek invention, myths also constitute a language, in the sense that the unconscious is structured as a language, according to Lacan. This language of myths extends its web of associations to all areas of literary culture; from royal inscriptions and historical annals to hymns, incantations, rituals and astronomical observations. As with all languages, mythological structures are both conservative and fluid; allowing for seemingly contradictory notions as well as conceptual continuity. Although one may attempt to explain these contradictions, one has to accept the limits of our comprehension of the language in the first place.

As to the gods and goddesses, they existed in the 'real' world of cult and worship as well as in literature, but we know more about the latter. A number of deities appear with some regularity in the mythological texts, mainly ancient deities who were credited with an important role in the formation and organization of the world. Their character is well documented, in contrast to that of many other deities, who were just as popular, or more so, and yet never became 'subjects' of the mythological repertoire. Several sources can be used to evaluate the extent of a deity's popular appeal: material evidence such as shrines, temples and votive offerings, and textual evidence in the main lists of sacrifices, dedications, references in private documents and personal names.

A number of books have been written that present a survey of ancient cults and religions (Dhorme 1949; Gese, Höfner, Rudolph 1970; Labat, Caqot, Szcnycer 1970; Ringgren 1973; Jacobsen 1976). The seminal *Wörterbuch der Mythologie*, Vol. I appeared in 1965. In the meantime, many new texts have been published, primarily in specialist periodicals. The present volume is intended as a general reference work for students of religious studies, anthropology and oriental studies and attempts to make the subject accessible to a wider academic audience. In view of the

INTRODUCTION

immense number of publications, it does not claim to be exhaustive but concentrates on the better documented deities and narratives. References to unpublished texts are not included. The entries are organized in such a way as to set the subject in a broad historical context. In some cases it is possible to trace the development of a mythological narrative or divine personality. But very often, due to the provisional state of our present knowledge, they are only documented at a specific period or place. Most entries are based on protagonists rather than content, with cross-references pointing out similar narratives. Our understanding of the texts themselves is still largely limited to their 'literal' meaning; their social and political background remains obscure, and therefore any analysis of the 'meaning' of myths will be a matter of the personal preference of translators and commentators. Consequently, the interpretation of the myths is only summarily alluded to: the reader will find references to the current state of debate in the bibliographical notes at the end of each entry.

Note: Throughout the text, words which appear in bold refer to cross-references, whilst those set in small capitals refer to sub-headings.

CHRONOLOGICAL CHART

BC	Mesopotamia	Anatolia	Syria	Elam
3000	Old Sumerian (Early Dynastic period)			
				Dynasty of Awan
2500	(Old Akkadian) Sargonic period			
			Ebla IIB	
	(Neo-Sumerian period) Ur III Dynasty Isin-Larsa	Assyrian colonies		Old Elamite period
2000	Old Babylonian Dynasty	Old Hittite Kingdom	(Amorites)	
	Kassite Dynasty	Hittite Empire		
1500			Ugarit	Middle Elamite period
	Middle Assyrian period			
	II Dynasty of Isin			
1000				Neo-Elamite period
	Neo-Assyrian period	Neo-Hittite period		Achaeminian period
	Neo-Babylonian period			
500	Achaeminian Dynasty			
	Seleucid period Parthian period			

A

Abba

(a) Babylonian goddess of probably Amorite origin. She is mentioned in the texts from Mari and a number of people there bore her name. During the Old Babylonian period she had a temple in Isin. Her personality and divine functions are unknown.

(b) In the Sumerian myth **Enki and Ninhursag** Abba is a god created by **Ninhursag**.

Ichiro 1979, 13

Adad *also* **Adda, Anda, Hadad, Addu** – Semitic **Weather-god**. (*see figures 3 and 10*)

His name is probably etymologically connected with Arabic *hadda*, 'to break' and *haddat*, 'thunder'.

In Mesopotamia, where his name was often written logographically as $^d IM$, he is attested from the pre-Sargonic period onwards. His main following was among the populations of northern Babylonia and Syria, as suggested by the onomastic evidence from towns such as Mari and Ebla. In the second millennium BC, Adad was the city god of Halab (Aleppo) but in other areas of Syria, especially in the west, he merged with other weather-gods, such as **Baal** and **Dagan**.

Adad was an important god in Assyria. Tiglath-Pilesar I built a double-sanctuary for him and **Anu** in the capital Ashur. Several kings, as well as many private individuals, had names composed with Adad (e.g. Adad-nirari). Unlike the major Babylonian deities which were integrated into the official cult of Assyria, Adad was considered to be a local deity. Together with **Aššur** he figured prominently in the royal inscriptions.

Adad is often invoked in the curses which concluded official as well as private documents. They emphasize the negative aspects of the weather-god. '*Ina beriq limuti matsu libriq*' – 'with an evil lightning he shall strike his country' is typical. He was also asked to send devastating

1

floods and storms which would turn the country into waste-land, or otherwise hold back the waters to cause a drought. In his capacity of a warrior-god he would 'break the weapons of the enemy' and 'pursue him like an evil demon'.

In some late Assyrian texts, Adad is linked with **Šamaš** as an oracle god.

Edzard, WdM 1965, 135; Roberts 1972, 13; Wyatt 1980, 375ff

Adamma

first appears as a male deity in Ebla alongside a wife called Adamtum but there are as yet no clues to the function and personality of the god. When the Hurrians incorporated Adamma into their pantheon, they associated him with **Kubaba** (Adamma-Kubaba and sometimes also in the form of a triad, including Hašintarhi). Because of this identification it seems that at this stage the deity was female. As such she also featured in a god-list from Ugarit. The main cult centre, however, was probably Aleppo.

Laroche, in Bonnefoy 1981, I, 97

Adapa

Mesopotamian myth preserved on tablets found at Amarna and Nineveh (Middle and Late Babylonian). The two versions differ in some points, but the ambiguity of the myth as to the true intentions of the gods **Ea** and **Anu** is found in both.

Adapa, one of the **Seven Sages**, was created by the god Ea as an exemplary man endowed with superhuman wisdom. He serves Ea as a priest in Eridu, where he is responsible for the food-offerings to the god. He also has to go fishing in the lagoon, usually a quiet water, where he needs neither rudder nor steering-pole. One day, however, the south wind overturns his boat. Furious, Adapa shouts a curse at the wind that should 'break his wings'. Such is the power of his words that the wind becomes immobilized and fails to blow 'for seven days' (which means a long time). The failure of the wind (which brings moisture and cool airstreams inland) does not go unnoticed by the great god Anu. His vizier informs him that Adapa was responsible and Anu demands that the culprit be sent to him for judgement. Ea, 'who knows heaven's way', decides to prepare Adapa for his journey to heaven. He tells him to put on mourning and to tell the two gods **Dumuzi** and **(Nin)giszida**, whom he will meet before Anu's gate, that he is lamenting the disappearance of the two gods from the earth. This behaviour is meant to mollify the anger of the two vegetation gods who have been directly affected by Adapa's deed. Adapa is conveyed to heaven and there he follows Ea's advice to the letter. Dumuzi and Ningišzida promise to put in a good word for him and indeed, as Ea has foreseen, Anu's wrath is appeased by their intercession. He wants to know where Adapa had acquired his wisdom and when he discovers that Ea was behind it, he offers Adapa oil, clothes and the 'Water and Food of Life', which he says will cause the sage 'to become like the gods'. However, Ea had forewarned Adapa not to accept the 'Water and Food of Death', and in the hope of escaping punishment, Adapa rejects them. At this apparent human folly, Anu breaks into 'divine laughter' and sends Adapa back to earth. The rest of the story is missing (Kramer, Picchioni, Dalley).

Kramer, in Pritchard (ed.) 1950, 101–3; Böhl 1959, 416–31; Roux 1961, 13–33; Komoroczy 1964, 31–50; Bucellati 1973, 61–6; Kienast 1973; Soden 1976, 427–33; Müller 1983/4, 75–89; Picchioni 1981; Bing 1984; Dalley 1989, 182–8

Admu

(a) In the third millennium BC, Admu appears mainly in Akkadian personal names from the Sargonic period onwards. His nature remains obscure and his name may be deified toponym, as a ^{d}Nin-admu occurs in a Ur III pantheon list.

(b) In the Mari texts (18th C BC), Admu is found mainly in Akkadian women's names and since female names are usually used with female deities it may here refer to a goddess.

Roberts 1972, 14; Ichiro 1979, 44

Allanzu – Anatolian goddess of Hurrian origin

She was mainly worshipped in Kizzuwatna. In the rock-reliefs at Yazil-ikaya she appears as the daughter of **Tešup** and **Hebat** and the female counterpart to the young god **Šarruma**. She is also mentioned as part of the female dyad Hebat-Allanzu (mother and daughter).

Allatum

Anatolian goddess; usually written as ^{d}EREŠKIGAL. She was an **Underworld** deity of Hurrian origin and during the Empire period formed part of the Hittite pantheon.

3

Amurru – Akkadian god

The name can be written syllabically or as a logogram *[d]MAR. TU* which represents the Sumerian reading.

The Amurru-people are often mentioned in Mesopotamian inscriptions as the nomadic 'people of the steppe', who would come down from the hillsides and raid the agricultural products of the settled inhabitants of Sumer and Babylon. The god Amurru is known from Akkadian texts as well as from personal names since the Sargonic period. His main epithet in Sumerian is *lú hur.sag.ga*, 'man of the steppe'. By the Ur III period his cult was well established in the larger Babylonian cities (Larsa, Isin, Dilbat, Babylon and Nippur). It has been observed that in contrast to this widespread veneration in the Mesopotamian heartland, he is absent in the texts from Syrian sites (Roberts), although he has some characteristics of a storm-god. He may therefore be a deification of a social and ethnic group, the nomadic Amurru, rather than an original West Semitic god. As these people became settled in ever greater numbers, his acceptance into the Babylonian pantheon could represent an acknowledgement of their social integration. The kinship-pattern echoes this process: Amurru is said to be the son of the great god **Anu**, while his wife is either the West Semitic **Ašratum** or the Babylonian **Bēlet-Ṣēri**, the 'Lady of the Wilderness'.

A short mythological text, THE MARRIAGE OF MARTU, describes a typical procedure of integration by a 'romantic' marriage. Martu is described with the standard epithets of an 'uncivilized' nomad, who 'eats raw flesh, has no house and will have no decent burial'. In spite of her family's remonstrations, the girl, who is said to be of a good family, the daughter of Numušda, city-god of Kazallu, accepts his proposals and the nuptials go ahead.

Falkenstein 1951, 16–17; Kupper 1961; Roberts 1972, 15f; Ichiro 1979, 53–6; Edzard, RLA VII 1989, 433–8

Anu (*see figure 10*)

The name of this important Mesopotamian god is written with the sign dingir ⸕ which means 'heaven'. It also stands for the determinative designating divinity in Sumerian, Akkadian and Hittite. In the Babylonian context the god is called **Anu**.

The antiquity of An as a divine personality is subject to controversy. His cult, like that of the goddess **Inanna**, is thought to have developed at Uruk. It cannot at present be decided which deity was worshipped there during the prehistoric Uruk IV period. It is also not certain whether the structure known as the 'Anu-Ziggurat' (Uruk V) should be associated with this god.

During the Old Sumerian period, **An** is a component of several royal names from Uruk and Ur. But due to the polyvalence of this sign this does not necessarily prove that it always stands for the god An. However, by the middle of the second millennium BC, he is mentioned in the Fara god-lists, in prayers by Urukian kings (Lugalzaggesi), as well as in royal inscriptions from Kiš (Lugaltarsi). His Sumerian title (*lugal kur.kur.ra*, 'king of the lands') points to his superior authority in the pantheon. 'Appointed priest of An' formed part of the royal titles since the Sargonic Dynasty. During the Ur III and Isin-Larsa period the popularity of the An cult is well documented by the numerous hymns and prayers. He also appears in many personal names, especially among the Akkadian population.

From the Old Babylonian period onwards Anu was usually acknowledged as one of the three most senior deities of the pantheon (with **Enlil**, **Ea** and **Ištar**), especially in official royal inscriptions and pantheon lists. But increasingly he became a *deus otiosus* who did not inspire much religious fervour; Babylonian or Assyrian hymns and prayers to Anu are therefore extremely rare. A late version of the Anu-cult occurred in Seleucid Uruk, where the theologians identified the sky-god with chthonic deities such as **Enmešarra** and **Dumuzi**.

The texts mention several consorts of An. He was coupled with Uraš or **Ki**, 'Earth', in a cosmic relationship, as well as with manifestations of the **Mother-goddess** (**Nammu, Ninmah**) or more schematically with Antum, the 'female sky'. Several royal texts from the Sargonic period describe the elevation of Inanna to the rank of An's consort. In the *Enuma eliš* An is the offspring of Anšar and Kišar (the two aspects of the horizon according to Jacobsen); he is said to be the 'father of the gods' as well as the host of **Demons**.

An's function in the mythological and theological texts is primarily one of authority (his Sumerian classic epithet is *an gal*, 'the great An'). He is represented as the apex of the divine hierarchy. His 'command is the very foundation of heaven and earth'. Several texts (such as **Lahar** and **Ašnan**) specifically credit An with the divine intelligence that conceived and sustained the universe. He was in charge of the 'divine ordinances', the *Me*, and decrees the fates. An was the ultimate source of authority; he could raise up other gods (notably Inanna, but also many other deities) to more elevated positions. On earth he conferred kingship. With the growing importance of Nippur, the cult centre of the

god **Enlil**, this 'first-born son of An', who originally manifested power
rather than authority, gradually acquired a status equal to that of his
father and was said to dispense authority and fate either with, or on
behalf of, the sky-god. The distinction between the functions of both
gods became blurred, especially when An also acquired traits of a
Weather-god, which are generally more associated with Enlil. He was
called 'Fecund Bull', which implies fertility; the sky as the source of rain
'impregnates the earth (so that) vegetation becomes plentiful'.

Finally, the sky was the realm of the constellations and planets. Astral
observation was an intrinsic part of ancient civilizations and the notion
of 'as above so below' forms the basis of all divination. In this respect
an.gal is the 'great above', the cosmic counterpart to *ki.gal*, the underworld. It is the scenario of mythic reality in which the (astral) gods eternally enact the universal drama.

Ebeling, R1A I 1932, 155–7; Jean 1950, 127–33; Edzard, WdM 1965, 40–1; Wohlstein 1976

Anat – (*see figure 1*)

West Semitic goddess; her name appears as *'nt* in the Ugaritic texts.
Etymologically it may be connected with Akkad. *ettu*, 'active will'.

Anat was a popular goddess throughout the western areas of the
Near East, including Egypt, from the middle of the second millennium
BC until the Hellenistic age.

The goddess is best known from the cuneiform texts found in Ugarit
and representations on Egyptian monuments. Her epithets *blt 'nt*,
'Virgin Anat', and *'nt hbly*, 'the destroyer' (devastratix), indicate that she
has affinities to the Babylonian goddess **Ištar**. Like her she is beautiful,
the epitome of womanhood, a passionate lover, as well as a ferocious
and bloodthirsty warrior, 'clad as men and girt as women'. In this
martial role she protects the pharaoh from his enemies. In the Ugaritic
Baal-Myths she is the daughter of the great god **El** and her relationship
with her father has parallels in Ištar's irreverent and bullying approach
to **Anu**, as it is described in the **Gilgameš Epic**. While the author of the
Baal-myths may have satirically emphasized certain characteristic traits
of the impetuous Anat in favour of the heroic Baal, it does credit to the
multifarious functions of the goddess. As her title 'virgin' implies she
remains ummarried, although the texts imply intimate relations with
Baal, her beloved 'brother' (here a term of endearment). She is always at
his side, fights with him and sometimes for him (she takes on **Mot**, the
arch-enemy of Baal after his death), she supports his wishes and pleads

on his behalf. Their sexual relationship is the subject of a number of Ugaritic texts (KTU 1.96, 10, 11), commonly known as the LOVES OF BAAL AND ANAT (de Moor). It is noteworthy that while the erotic attraction between the two gods is described at length, the actual copulation takes place only indirectly. Anat has to transform herself into a heifer, whom Baal, 'the Bull', mounts passionately. Only as a cow can she be entered and give birth to Baal's offspring, a 'young bull'. Anat is otherwise not explicitly associated with procreation and motherhood. On Egyptian monuments, however, she appears with the fertility-god Min. The Baal-Myths may also allude to her fertility aspects in the passages of Baal's Palace, when after the great blood-bath she washes herself and thus produces dew and soft rain – a clear complement to Baal's more violent wintry storms. Anat has another epithet, *ybmt limm*, which is usually translated as 'widow of the nation'. During Baal's absence she takes on the role of a widow. There may well be a ritual connection between Anat and funerary rites. Not only does she perform the mourning ceremonies after Baal's death, she also laments **Aqhat**, for whose death she was responsible. In this text she is the vengeful and terrifying goddess who kills the young hero when he refused to deliver the magic bow and furthermore refuted her divine power. Like the spurned Ištar in the Gilgames epic, she punishes the presumptuous mortal.

Dussaud 1938, 133–69; Aistleitner 1939; Albright 1941, 14–17; Cassuto 1953; Lipinski 1965, 45–73; Pope, Röllig WdM 1965, 235–41; Kapelrud 1969; Del Olmo Lete 1981, 49–63; de Moor 1987, 109–16; Colpe 1969, 37–43

Annunitum – Akkadian goddess

The name may go back to an original compound *ᵈINANNA-an-nu-ni-tum* = *Ištar-annunitum*, 'Ištar the Skirmisher'. She is often invoked by the Sargonic kings in the curse formulae of their royal inscriptions. The former epithet eventually became an independent deity. She appears as a warrior goddess in the Old Babylonian Naramsin epic. During this period she had a temple in Kisurra but her cult was also established in Sippar, Nippur, Uruk and Ur. In Ur her temple was the É-ulmaš and she was therefore known as Ulmašitum.

Sauren 1969, 19; Robert 1972, 147

Anunna(ki) – Mesopotamian collective of deities

The name was written *ᵈa-nuna*; *ᵈa-nuna-ke₄-ne*; *ᵈa-nun-na*. The term has the general meaning of 'those of princely blood; royal offspring'. It seems to denote a collective of undifferentiated but senior gods, usually counted as fifty (in an older tradition as seven and in the *Enuma eliš* sixty). At some point it may have designated the sum total of the local numina of a city (*a-nun-na-eridu^{ki}-ninnu-bi*, 'The Fifty Anunna of Eridu', in a hymn from Drehem).

The Anunna first appear in Sumerian texts in the Ur III period as protective and interceding gods. Gudea records that he 'installed them' in the É-.ninnu, the temple of **Ningirsu** at Lagash: 'the weak men are sustained by you, you prolong the life of the pious who looks towards you'. He also asked them to relay his prayers to Ningirsu. Other than that there is little evidence for a cult and they did not feature in personal names. On the other hand they appear very frequently in literary compositions, hymns and prayers, myths and epics of all subsequent periods. Their function in these texts is ambiguous. They are said to have been the offspring of **An**, or at any rate after the great gods and before the minor deities which were instrumental in the differentiation of the created world and human beings (so for instance in **Enki and Ninmah** or in **Lahar and Ašnan**). They suffered great deprivations before the world was fully organized, they had to eat grass and were always hungry (Lahar and Ashnan) and they were burdened with heavy manual labour (Enki and Ninmah, Atra-hasis; in the *Enuma Eliš* they built the city of Babylon for **Marduk**, since he was relieved from working by creating man). The composition **Enki and the World Order** mentions the Anunnaki several times, they 'do homage' to **Enki** and sing his praise, they 'take up their dwellings' in the midst of the people of Sumer, in the cities and in the countryside and twice it is said that they 'decree the fates of mankind'. The Anunnaki also appear in the **Under-world** in **Inanna's Descent** where they 'pronounce judgement'. In the late **Erra**-myth they are called the brothers of **Nergal** and are ranged against mankind. Marduk also divided the Anunnaki into three hundred 'heavenly' and three hundred 'underworld' Anunnaki (*Enuma eliš*). In other compositions, they have much less clearly defined roles. They often emphasize the prevailing mood or action of the gods in general; so, for instance, they first join in the destructive fury and are later repentant at the flood in the eleventh tablet of the **Gilgameš Epic**. In a similar manner they could serve as a poetic juxtaposition – the collective Anun-naki and the individual god or hero.

The Anunnaki are broadly synonymous with the **Igigi**.

Falkenstein 1965, 127ff; Kienast 1965, 14–158; Soden 1966, 102–11; Kinnier-Wilson 1979, 178

Anzu

In Mesopotamian mythology and iconography a creature in the shape of a lion-headed eagle. The name could be written as $^d.IM.DUGUD.MU\check{S}EN$ or *an-zu-u*.

Combined animals frequently appear in Mesopotamian art from the earliest period onwards as manifestations of demonic forces which are dangerous but not necessarily evil. The lion-headed eagle is found on numerous artefacts from the Old Sumerian period, either as an aggressor but more commonly as the central figure between two anti-thetically placed wild beasts, which suggests a protective or preventive attitude.

According to Jacobsen (1970), Anzu 'represented the numinous power in the thunderstorms' at a hypothetical stage of Mesopotamian religion, when the divine was represented theriomorphically. During the Old Sumerian period Anzu became humanized (half-bird, half-man) and eventually the animal form split from the anthropomorphic manifesta-tion (**Ningirsu**) and was finally considered to be evil.

Anzu appears fairly regularly in personal names from the Old Sume-rian period but as far as a 'cult' is concerned, it seems that Lagaš, and its dependency Girsu, with its god Ningirsu, had the strongest links, although it is difficult to prove their relationship as suggested by Jacobsen. On the famous 'Vulture Stela' in the Louvre, Ningirsu holds an effigy of the bird in his fist and Gudea reports in his inscriptions that he decorated the temple É-ninnu with the creature's statues.

Anzu appears in several literary texts. In the epic of **Lugalbanda and Enmerkar** he is said to inhabit the inaccessible peaks of the 'carneol-mountains'. He is enormous, herding wild bulls for supper. Lugalbanda, the hero, realizes that he has to approach this powerful being with great caution and proceeds to feed and actually venerate its young. He also promises to instigate a cult of Anzu in Sumer. In return, the bird rewards Lugalbanda with supernatural powers. A similar theme occurs in the JOURNEY OF NINURTA TO ERIDU where the god is led to the **Apsu** by the young Anzu, who offers his friendship and decrees his fate in return for the promise to fashion a statue and a cult. In other traditions the evil aspect of Anzu is dominant, especially in the Akkadian sources. This is evident in the iconography of Old Akkadian seals which stress the aggression of Anzu towards the 'nude hero'. In literature, the evil Anzu (or Zû) is the subject of Old, Middle and Late Babylonian mythological texts, most notably in the MYTH OF (AN)ZU AND THE TABLETS OF DESTINY (Grayson, Dalley), which is only fragmentarily preserved, as parts of the beginning and the end with the dénouement are missing (the texts are from Middle and Late Babylonian and Neo-Assyrian sources). It tells how Anzu betrayed the trust of **Enlil** and stole the Tablets of Destiny while the god was preparing for a bath. Now he has in his control the cultic institutions and the **Igigi**. This sudden shift of the cosmic order has dramatic results. In the Late Babylonian B version, the rivers dry at the source and the gods are utterly helpless. **An(u)** tries to appoint somebody to overcome Anzu, who had flown to the mountains, but neither **Adad**, nor **Girra** or **Šara**, is successful. **Ea**, the wise, is called to help the gods in their distress. He summons the **Mother-goddess**, Bēlet-Ilî, gives her pride of place in the assembly, and entreats with her to offer her son **Ninurta**, that 'his name be made great in the lands'. The goddess agrees and commands Ninurta to avenge the plight of his parents and he dutifully departs with the seven winds and a formidable (demonic) host and confronts Anzu in the mountains. His first attempt to use the 'clouds of death', his bows and arrows, remains ineffective, and with a magic spell Anzu turns back 'the arrow to the canebrake, the wood of the bow to the tree'. Ninurta returns for a second encounter, armed this time with darkness, fire and his 'divine splendour'. Ea has advised him to take an arrow for a spear and with it he lops off the pinions of Anzu and before the great bird can pronounce a spell to make them grow back, Ninurta kills him. The forces of chaos are now defeated by the representative of the gods. For this deed Ninurta is rewarded with a prominent place in the pantheon.

For the astronomical interpretation of the lion-headed eagle as a sun-symbol, see Hartner.

Jacobsen 1952, 167–27; Hartner 1965, 10; Jacobsen 1970, 3–5; Hruška 1975; Grayson, in Pritchard 1975, 17–26; Hallo and Moran 1979, 65–115; Saggs 1986, 1–19; Dalley 1989, 203–32

Apladad – West Semitic god

His name is also written $^dDUMU.U\check{S}$ ^dIM or $^dA^dIM$ which means 'son of **Adad**'. He is only known from Neo-Assyrian texts since the 8th century BC. As a young **Weather-god** he was particularly popular in North Mesopotamia and Syria – evidence for this is in the many Assyrian and Aramaic personal names. There were temples for his cult in Kannu (thought to have been located east of the Tigris) and Suhi (Middle Euphrates), later also in Dura-Europos.

Lipinski 1976, 53–74

Appu

Hero of a Hurrian tale which is recorded in a fragmentary Hittite text. Appu is a rich man but he is unhappy because he has no children. This is probably due to his lack of understanding in sexual matters, as it is said that he and his wife go to bed fully dressed and 'with boots on'. Appu decides to ask the gods for help and sacrifices a lamb to the sun-god, who promptly appears in the shape of a young man. The god advises Appu to get drunk. Then he should go to his wife and have sex with her. The sun-god next visits the **Weather-god** and probably conveys to him Appu's wish for a son. [gap in the text] Soon afterwards Appu's wife gives birth to his first child, whom for no explicit reason he names 'Bad'. A second son is called 'Good'. The boys grow up and Bad demands his share of the paternal estate. It so happens that Good receives a barren cow and Bad a good one. The sun-god however, blesses Good's cow and restores her fertility. A further fragment deals with a litigation between the brothers.

Friedrich 1949, 213ff; Schuler, WdM 1965, 158

Apsu

from Sumerian *Abzu*, which denotes the subterranean 'sweet water ocean' or groundwater, also generally the marshland of southern Mesopotamia. In this area where rainfall is rare and where the semi-floating reed-islands support a great variety of wild life, the fertile marshes were regarded as the source of abundance. In mythological terms the Apsu extended underneath the surface of the earth, into a watery depth.

Several literary texts express the creative potential of the Apsu's muddy moisture. In the Sumerian myth **Enki and Ninmah** it is the place where **Nammu** forms the first human being. The god Kullu was also made there, according to the *enuma Anu* ritual. Furthermore, an anthropomorphic Apsu is called 'the begetter of the great gods' in the cosmogonic beginning of the **Enuma eliš** (I, 59–78). In this composition the Apsu is inert and sleepy but finds his peace disturbed by the restless ways and clamour of the younger gods, the offspring of his union with another watery body, Tiamat. He decides to destroy them. The gods choose **Ea** as their champion and he puts a spell on Apsu, casting him into a deep sleep and 'killing him'. This death, however, does not annihilate the essence of the Apsu, it just renders him without any will of his own. Thereby the Apsu is contained underground and becomes the

11

dwelling of Ea Enku, the 'lord of the Apsu'.

One of the oldest sanctuaries in Mesopotamia was at the southern city of Eridu, which was apparently situated on a hillock surrounded by a lagoon. In historical times, the temple was known as É-abzu, 'the House of the Apsu', and dedicated to Enki. Other cult-centres seem to have had natural or artificial ponds or basins which represented the Apsu.

Burrows 1932, 231–56; Ebeling, RLA I 1932, 122–4; Jacobsen 1946, 139–41

Aqhat

'*Aqht*, hero of an Ugaritic story which is partly preserved on several tablets (KTU 1, 17–22) written by the scribe **Elimelek**, which originate from the archives of Ras Shamra.

King Danel laments his fate because he has no son. He asks **Baal** for assistance, who intercedes with the great god **El**. El grants the king's wish and a son, named Aqhat, is born. Some time later, the craftsman of the gods, **Kothar-and-Hasis**, arrives with a beautifully fashioned bow. Danel receives the bow in return for his hospitality and presents it to his son. After a gap, the story continues with the encounter between Aqhat and **Anat**, the combative young goddess. Anat wants the bow for herself and indeed, Kothar had originally intended it for her. She offers him gold and silver, and finally immortality. Aqhat retorts that he would rather share the common fate of men, death, and furthermore casts doubt on her ability to confer eternal life. He concludes with the taunting remark that such a bow is not fit for a mere woman and departs. Anat threatens retribution and goes straightaway to her father El, whom she bullies into his consent to her plans. (There follows a large gap in the text.) Anat enlists the help of Yatpan to effect her revenge. She flies with Yatpan in the shape of a vulture to where Aqhat is just sitting down to eat his meal. Yatpan strikes him down and Aqhat is killed. The bow, however, has been broken and falls into the sea.

Anat begins a lament over the dead body of Aqhat and the failure of the crops which are the atonement for Aqhat's spilled blood. Danel is just undergoing rituals to bring back the fertility of the fields when he hears of his son's death. He calls to Baal to break the wings of the vultures circling overhead and duly finds the remains of Aqhat in the mother bird. Danel curses the three cities near the place of the murder and returns to his palace to mourn his son for seven years. Pugat, Danel's daughter, sets out to avenge her brother and disguised as Anat –

rouged and with a sword over her dress – she finds Yatpan among the nomads. In his drunkenness Yatpan boasts about Aqhat's murder; then the text breaks off which leaves the outcome uncertain. Probably Pugat killed him. The rest of the story is not quite clear as only various fragments of the next tablet are preserved. Again Danel asks Baal for help as he cannot forget his son. Baal proposes a spiritualistic session to invoke the 'saviours' (a euphemism for the souls of the dead), inviting them to the palace and promising a great feast if they 'make Aqhat king of the Amurru'. Then follows the description of a ritual banquet. It is most unlikely that an actual 'revival' of Aqhat took place from the ritualistic context of the text. He is said to become 'the protector of your holy place'. The final pronouncements by Baal and his comfort for the grieving Danel are lost.

Gordon 1955; Driver 1956; Gibson 1978; Pope, Röllig, WdM 1965, 241–4; Hillers 1973, 71–80; Gaster 1950, 257–313; Dressler 1975, 217–21; Dijkstra 1979, 199–210; de Moor 1987, 224–73

Arali

Sumerian for 'steppe', also specifically a stretch of desert between Babtibira and Uruk. According to the mythological tradition of the area, this was the place where the shepherd-god **Dumuzi** was said to pasture his sheep and where he met his lonely death. Because of this event it became synonymous with the **Underworld**. Generally, the town-dwelling population of southern Mesopotamia considered the open semi-desert countryside to be a dangerous and lawless place, desolate and haunted by ghosts. The connection with the realm of the dead may therefore have developed independently or alongside the Dumuzi tradition.

Aruru see Mother-goddess

Asag

Mesopotamian demon; Akkadian *As/šakku*, 'the one who strikes the arm' – a demon who causes pain and disease. In mythology he is the enemy of **Ninurta** in the text *lugal ud melambi nergal*, where Asag is described as the son of **An** and **Ki**. He is a violent outlaw of justice, 'a killer of the mountain land' (Akkad. *dāik šadî*). He can appear in connection with **Anzu** and may be identical with the seven-headed serpent (Sumer. *muš.sag.inim*).

13

Asarluhhi – Sumerian god

It has not been possible so far to explain the meaning of his name. He is an ancient god, already mentioned in the texts of the Fara period. In the Old as well as the Neo-Sumerian period he formed part of the pantheon of Lagash. He also had a temple in Kuar(a), near Eridu, which is the subject of a Temple Hymn (Sjöberg, Bergmann, No. 10). This text speaks of Asarluhhi in generally martial terms; he is a 'champion' (*ur. sag*) 'who gores the rebellious land' and 'pours poisonous foam upon it' if it is not obedient. He is known as either *dumu-abzu*, 'the son of **Abzu**', or *dumu.sag.* ^{d}*en. ki. ke₄*, 'the firstborn son of **Enki**'.

In Babylonian texts of the second millennium BC he is often invoked in incantations as the 'incantation priest of the great gods', usually in conjunction with Enki. In the Old Babylonian period he was assimilated to **Marduk**, then a relatively new god.

Zimmern 1930, 255–6; Edzard, WdM 1965, 43; Sjöberg-Bergmann 1969, 25, 80–1

Ašimbabbar see **Nanna**

Ašnan – Sumerian grain goddess

Her name was written ^{d}*ŠE.TIR*. She is an ancient goddess, known since the Old Sumerian period but little is known of any cult. She is best described in **Enki and the World Order** (325–333): 'Her whose head and body are mottled, whose face is (covered with?) honey, the lady who brings about copulation, the strength of the land, the life of the black-headed people, Ašnan, the good bread, the bread of all, Enki placed in charge of them.' Her obvious connection with successful crops also stands behind her appearance as a curse-deity; Yahdunlim of Mari asks her and **Sumukkan** to starve the country of his enemy. (See also the myth **Lahar and Ašnan**.)

Ebeling, RLA I 1932, 168

Ašratu – West Semitic goddess

During the Old Babylonian period she was known as the 'Mistress of abundance and fertility', as well as the wife of **Amurru**. She was integrated into the Babylonian pantheon as the 'daughter-in-law of **Anu**'. This goddess is probably identical to **Ašart** in Syria.

Aššur (*see figures 3 and 4*)

Assyrian god, the eponymous deity of the capital Aššur who became the national god of Assyria.

The origin of the name is unknown. He seems to have been a local mountain god of the Semitic population of northern Mesopotamia (*bēl* *šadu*abeh) and known as such from texts since the Ur III period. With the rise of the political power of Assyria, Aššur was promoted to a supreme rank among the gods, taking on the characteristics of several other gods, such as **Enlil**, **Anu** and **Šamaš**. This process recalls the elevation of **Marduk** in Babylon. An Assyrian version of the ***Enuma Eliš*** replaces the name of Marduk by Aššur, who was at the same time equated with **Anšar**. The worship of Aššur survived in northern Mesopotamia until the third century AD.

The Assyrian monarch had a special relationship to this god whom he served as the first priest of Aššur and who was directly responsible for the exercise of kingship, in analogy to the role of Anu and Enlil in Babylon.

Aššur seems to have had no official consort before the reign of Sennacherib (7th C BC), when **Ninlil** appears as his wife. On the other hand, **Ištar** of Aššur or of Nineveh are also mentioned as wives of the great Assyrian god.

His iconographical image, which appears on various Assyrian reliefs and obelisks, shows a winged sun-disc containing a bearded deity holding a bow.

Tallqvist 1932; Ebeling, RLA I 1932, 196–8; Dhorme 1969

Aštar/Aṭṭar – Ugarit. *'ṭṭr*, West Semitic god

He was the personification of the male aspect of **Venus** as the morning star. In Southern Arabia he was also worshipped, there uniting both the aspect of morning and evening star.

In Syria he is the son of **Aštart**. The name has etymological connections with Arab. *'ard 'atur*, 'irrigated land'. This may account for his subordinate role in the **Baal-Myths** which reflect an agriculture based on rainfall. In the absence of Baal he is unable to fill his throne (in Baal and Mot, I, 46f) and in Baal and Yam he is told by **Šapaš** that he cannot have a palace like the other gods because he is not married or betrothed. There is no evidence of a cult of Aštar in Ugarit but a Greek text of the 5th C AD mentions Aštar in connection with child-sacrifice among the Bedouin tribes in Sinai.

Caquot 1958, 46–60; Gray 1949, 46–60; Röllig, WdM 1965, 249–50

Aštart/Astarte – Ugar. *'Aṯtrt*; West Semitic goddess (*see figure 2*)

She was also known as 'Lady Asherah of the Sea'. Aštart was well known and worshipped throughout the Near East (including Egypt) from the middle of the second millennium BC onward. In Babylonian texts she appears as **Ašratu** and is married to the nomad-god **Amurru**. She was integrated into the Mesopotamian pantheon as the daughter-in-law of **Anu**.

In South Arabia she may have had solar characteristics.

In the Old Testament Astoret is a goddess of the Sidonians and Phoenicians. The veneration of her cult-symbol, the Asherah, was condemned by the prophets.

In Ugarit her name appears in offering lists, sacrificial texts, rituals and god-lists, although not apparently in personal names. This prominent role is less evident in the Ugaritic myths, where she seems diminished in favour of **Anat**, the lover of **Baal**. Astart is the wife of **El** in the Palace of Baal (see **Baal-Myths**). However, she lives apart from her husband, 'by the sea'. She is 'the mother of all the gods', including Baal, although she seems to prefer some of her other offspring to him, as in Baal and Mot, when she rejoices over Baal's death. Another epithet is 'wet-nurse of the gods', which also points to her capacity of a **Mother-goddess**.

Perlman 1978; Hermann 1969, 6–55; Lipínski 1972, 101–19; Patai 1965, 35–52; Pope-Röllig, WdM 1965, 245–7; de Moor 1986, 225–31

Atra-hasis see **Flood-myths**

Aṯtart-šem-Baal – Canaanite goddess

Her name means 'Astart Name of Baal'. In the **Baal-Myths** she appears as a manifestation and consort of Baal. Her character resembles that of **Anat**, as a goddess of war and the chase. Her fertility aspect is more pronounced in the Old Testament, where she is called Ashtoreth. In an Egyptian papyros from the XIX Dynasty she is 'the bride claimed by the tyrant sea'.

Gibson 1978, 4n.6; Gardiner 1932, 74–85

Ayya

Written $^{d}A\text{-}A$, Ayya is an ancient Semitic goddess, well attested in numerous personal names since the Old Sumerian period. She seems to have been a primarily astral deity, according to her Sumerian epithets: ^{d}sud-aga$_2$ = nur šamê, 'heavenly light', but she is also connected with sexuality and fertility, as another epithet is Akkad. *kallatum*, 'the bride', and *bēlet-ulṣazu unat*, 'Mistress adorned with voluptuousness'. As the wife of the sun-god **Šamaš** she was greatly venerated in Sippar and during the Old and Neo-Babylonian periods, less in her own right than in her capacity to intercede with her husband. She is also found among the treaty-gods of Hatti.

Ebeling RLAI 1932, 196–8; Roberts 1972, 14f

B

Baal (*see figure 5*)

Title of several West Semitic gods; *b'l* means 'lord, master'. Most of the gods bearing this name were **Weather-gods** and have very similar characteristics. They can be distinguished from one another by their epithets which refer to individual cities or mountains, the traditional dwellings of weather-gods. **Baal-Zephon**, for instance, lived on the Jebel el-Aqra in Syria. He had temples in Ugarit and was worshipped in XIXth dynasty Egypt. **Baal-Karmelos** was the god of Mount Karmel in Palestine and is mentioned in the Old Testament (1 Kings 18, 19–40). When the Phoenicians colonized the Mediterranean, they brought their Baal-cult with them – most notably **Baal-Hammon**, who was a major deity in North Africa (cf. Hannibal!). Best known from mythological texts is the Ugaritic Baal, also known as **Baal-Hadad**, or Hadad, since he became identified with the Mesopotamian **Adad**. He was the central deity of Ugarit; most Ugaritic personal names contained the actual name Baal, or one of his epithets, and at least two temples were dedicated to him. As a weather-god, Baal is one of the most important deities for the western parts of the Near East. As *rkb 'rpt*, 'the rider of the clouds', he is manifest in the storms which herald the autumn season with thunder and lightning, the rain-swollen clouds and the coastal breeze. He symbolizes the life-giving principle of fertility in crops, animals and people. Baal battles valiantly against the unruly waters of the sea and the scorching heat of summer. Like Baal-Zephon he has his abode on the cloudy summits of Jebel el-Aqra. Another epithet is *zbl*, 'prince', the origin of the corrupted 'Baalzebub' of the Old Testament. The father of Baal was another weather-god, **Dagan**, although he sometimes also addresses El as 'my father'. It is not certain whether this is a merely honorific address or a reflection of a different tradition. The relationship between Baal and El in the Baal-myths has provoked much comment. It seems that El represents the chief of a patriarchal pantheon, embodying the principle of supreme authority, whereas Baal is fundamentally a cosmic deity. Like the natural phenomena he represents, he is an elementary but unpredictable and unstable power which is difficult to integrate in a structured hierarchy.

Kapelrud 1953; Cassuto 1962; Schmidt 1963, 1–13; Pope, WdM 1965, 253–64; de Moor 1971; Ziyl 1972

Baal-Myths – Ugarit *Ib'l*

Were recorded on clay-tablets in the Ugarit cuneiform 'alphabet' by the scribe **Elimelek** (texts KTU 1.101, 1, 1–6) (c. 1500 BC). The texts form a cycle of interrelated narratives, all of which illustrate the nature and actions of **Baal**, specifically Baal-Hadad, and which seem to relate to a 'mythological prototype of the normal agricultural and cultic year of the people of Ugarit' (de Moor 1987, 1). The tablets are not in a very good state. of preservation, with beginnings and ends missing. The exact sequence of the various tablets is therefore still to some extent hypothetical and the translation of many passages uncertain (see also **Ugaritic mythology**). The following synopsis follows the recent translation by de Moor (1987).

The cycle begins with a banquet held by Baal to celebrate his victory over **Mot**, 'Death' (KTU 1.101, 1, 3). Baal is surrounded by his daughters Pidray, 'the girl of the honey-dew', and Tallay, 'the girl of the mist', while a minstrel sings to the sound of cymbals. [gap of some 40 lines] Then follows a section that is also known as THE PALACE OF BAAL. It begins with the description of the goddess **Anat**, who adorns and scents herself before she goes down into the valleys to fight 'between two cities', where she smites the people of the seashore. She causes havoc among the population and decorates herself with the heads and hands of slain victims. Not satisfied with these violent deeds, she turns her household furniture into an army and wades knee-deep in blood and gore. Having satisfied her lust for battle, she restores the *status quo* and 'she scooped water and washed herself with the dew of heavens, oil of the earth, the rain of the Rider of the Clouds'. [gap] Baal sends messengers to Anat, summoning her to Mount Zaphon so that he may disclose 'the word of trees and a whisper of stones, the groaning of the heavens to the earth, of the Flood to the stars'. Anat is worried about Baal and asks anxiously what enemy could be threatening him now that she has dealt with all his foes. The messengers reassure her that Baal is safe and invite her to join their master. From her distant cave, she swiftly heads for Zaphon, where Baal receives her hospitably. [gap] Baal complains to Anat that he alone among the gods has no house or court. Anat takes up his case and rushes to her father El. She demands that he does something about Baal's house, since Baal is now 'our king, our judge, nobody is over him'. El seems to prevaricate [gap] and somebody, maybe **Aštart**, El's wife, decides to send for **Kothar-and-Hasis**, the Clever Craftsman, who dwells in Egypt. [gap] According to col. II of the second tablet KTU 1.1, Anat is in trouble because other, envious gods seem to harass her. El promises to put a spell on them and tells her to come with a 'list of lapis-lazuli, a list of gold'. [gap] Fragment III contains the commission for Kothar-and-Hasis, who promptly departs from Egypt. [gap] In column IV, Baal is in difficulties. Somebody (Aštart?) has been plotting against him and now El decides to support **Yam** instead of Baal and offers him the palace. [gap] Column V is badly damaged, it seems to contain a vision or premonition of Baal's, that he is to bound 'between the stones, between the stones of the stream-bed'. The third tablet (KTU 1.2) is usually called BAAL AND YAM and it records the fight between the two gods. Yam, the deified stormy waters, also called *zbl jm*, 'Prince Sea', sends envoys to El, the supreme god of heaven, where they are to deliver the following message: 'Give up the one whom you protect (...), give up Baal and his attendants, the son of Dagan, whose gold I am to inherit'. El is quite ready to hand over Baal, but Baal seizes his weapons to attack the messengers and is only restrained by the intervention of Aštart. [gap] Yam, having defeated Baal, takes possession of his adversary's unfinished residence on Mount Zaphon. But according to the remainder of column III, he does not fit into it (he is too big), and Kothar-and-Hasis is told to build him a new palace. The god **Aštar** challenges Yam's right to a palace and they begin a quarrel. [gap] Kothar-and-Hasis manages to get away and talk to Baal, who is in a miserable state, 'cowering under the chair of Prince Yam'. He announces that the time has come to fight Yam and claim 'his eternal kingdom'. He has brought two magical weapons (*ṣmdm*: clubs?) called 'Driver' (*Igrš*) and 'Chaser' (*aymr*). Baal hits Yam on the shoulder and 'Chaser' strikes him on the skull. Yam is defeated and Baal wants to slay him for good, but he is stopped by Aštart. Yam is taken captive. [gap] The next tablet (KTU 1.4), takes up the account of the rebuilding of Baal's palace. Baal departs with Anat to enlist the support of Aštart, the Lady Asherah of the Sea, in order to persuade El to allow the building of Baal's palace to proceed. They ask Kothar-and-Hasis to produce suitably lavish gifts to soften her mood. Aštart, who lives in a distant place 'by the sea', is just engaged in some ritual by the shore, when Anat and Baal arrive. She is frightened when they appear, assuming they have come to kill her sons in revenge. However, she is comforted by the rich presents they have brought. [gap] Baal and Anat persuade Aštart to saddle an ass and to visit her husband El, in order to plead on Baal's behalf. El is pleasantly surprised to see her and finally gives his consent for the building of Baal's palace. Aštart reminds him that now is the right time for Baal's rains, who 'will sound his voice in the clouds, let loose the lightnings of the earth'. Anat brings the good news to Baal who instructs Kothar-and-Hasis upon the design of the palace, insisting that it should have no windows. Building materials are brought from the Lebanon, silver, gold and cedar wood, and the construction begins. A magic fire turns the precious metals into bricks and stone and the palace is finished. Baal is glad and prepares a feast to celebrate the completion of his house with his relatives. [gap] Baal returns from the sack of ninety cities and orders Kothar-and-Hasis to install a window in the house and 'through a rift in the clouds he gave forth his holy voice' until the earth shakes. Baal is enthroned in his palace and rejoices in his power. But even at this very apex of his might he is aware that his destiny is to descend into the 'gullet of Mot'. He sees his enemies (the dry dust-storms which cause the vegetation to wither) and he sends messengers to the underworld, inviting 'Death' to his palace. Mot's answer is hostile; he resents the fact that he is never invited to the banquets of the gods and threatens Baal. The next tablet (KTU 1.5) describes the encounters between BAAL and MOT. Gapan and Ugar, Baal's messengers, return from the underworld with Mot's message: 'I will eat you in red lumps of two spans, you will go down in two cubits chunks, into the throat of Mot, son of El, into the gullet of the beloved of El, the hero.' [gap] The gaping jaws of Mot are described: 'one lip to the earth, one lip to the sky'. Baal sends a message back, accepting his fate: 'Hurry to meet me, o Mot, I am your slave, yours forever'. [gap] Someone, maybe the sun-goddess **Šapaš**, gives Baal secret advice about his journey into the underworld. [gap] During a banquet in the palaces of El and Baal, the latter's absence is noticed and laments begin. [gap] In column V, Baal receives further instructions on how to escape from the underworld. He is to take Tallay and Pidray, and go towards the two mountains of the tunnel in the west, where the sun descends into the underworld. On his way he sees a heifer in the steppe and copulates with her 'seventy-seven times, eighty-eight times'. This results in the birth of his 'twin-brother', an ox. [gap] Two messengers arrive before El and report that they have found the corpse of Baal. (It is probably the body of this 'twin' whom Mot devoured instead of Baal.) The death of Baal is announced in heaven. El comes down from his throne to lament him. Anat too performs mourning rites, lacerating herself, and then goes in search of Baal, Tablet VI (KTU 1.6). When she finds what she considers to be her lover's dead body, she calls to Šapaš, the sun-goddess, to lift the corpse of Baal on her shoulder in order to bury with him due oblations on Zaphon. Then she proceeds to El, exclaiming bitterly that Aštart and her sons will now rejoice because Baal is dead. El does indeed call for Aštart and asks her to appoint one of her sons as the successor to Baal. Aštart answers that it should be one 'who is able to moisten' and proposes Aštar, who mounts Baal's throne. However, 'his feet did not reach the footstool, his head did not reach the headrest'. He has to descend from the throne unable to fill Baal's place. [gap] Anat goes in search of Baal ('like the heart of a cow for her calf, like the heart of a ewe for her lamb, so was the heart of Anat after Baal'). She descends to the underworld, the very domain of Death. Mot admits to having eaten Baal and for a long time Anat entreats with him. Finally she seizes Mot, 'she splits him with a knife, sieves, burns, grounds and mills him' and finally 'sows him in a field, (where) the birds eat his flesh'. [gap] El is asked to perform a dream-oracle; should he dream that 'the heavens rain oil and the wadis run with honey', it will be clear that Baal is still alive. El does indeed dream in this manner and he rejoices and sends Anat to Šapaš in order to enlist her collaboration in the further search for Baal. In his message to Šapaš, El describes the parched and cracked fields that await the harrowing (wetting) by Baal. The sun-goddess instructs Anat to pour 'sparkling wine into the wine-skins' and bring wreaths. [gap] Somebody is predicting the actions of Baal after his return, how he will kill the sons of Aštart (those who rejoiced over his death) and how he will resume his seat of the throne of his dominion. Seven years pass uneventfully, then Mot (who is by now revived as well) sends a challenge to Baal. He orders one of Baal's brothers to atone for the wrongs done to him by Anat. Baal pretends to do as bidden, but he intends to outwit Mot by offering him 'brothers of Mot' (also sons of El and Aštart – maybe boars, the usual sacrifice to chthonic gods in Ugarit). When Mot discovers that he has eaten his own kin, he returns to Zaphon and they begin to fight in earnest, bitterly, but neither can defeat the other. Šapaš finally intervenes and warns Mot that El will take away his kingship over the underworld if he continues to fight Baal. Mot retreats. [gap] The final passages of the text contain a hymn-like conclusion, entrusting Baal with 'eternal kingship', inviting the other gods and Šapaš to partake of a feast. The sun-goddess is asked to rule over the spirits of the dead with Kothar-and Hasis' assistance.

Ginsberg 1935, 327–33; Montgomery 1935, 268–77; Gaster 1937, 21–32; Gordon

1949; Driver 1956; Aistleitner 1959; Pope, WdM 1965, 258–69; Ginsberg, in Pritchard, 1955, 129–55; Caquot, Szyncer, Herder 1974; Grabbe 1976, 57–63; Gibson 1978; Margalit 1980; Caquot, Sznycer 1981; Stolz, in Assmann, Burkert, Stolz 1982, 83–118; de Moor 1987, 1–101

Baba – Sumerian goddess (*see figure 6*)

Her name could be written $^{d}ba\text{-}ba_{s}$, $^{d}ba\text{-}ba$, later $^{d}ba\text{-}bu$.

She is one of the very ancient Sumerian goddesses, well attested in texts since the Fara-period, especially in personal names. Kings mention her in their royal inscriptions (Uruinimgina, Entemena). As a manifestation of the **Mother-goddess**, she was responsible for the fertility of human beings and animals, the very 'Lady of Abundance' (*SAL šág.ga*). As the wife of **Ningirsu** she formed part of the Lagaš pantheon; her temple there was the É-urukuga. At the New Year festival the city celebrated a **Sacred Marriage** between her and Ningirsu. But there was also a temple of Baba at Uruk, at least from the time of Uruinimgina onwards. She is the recipient of numerous votive offerings, especially during the Neo-Sumerian period (Gudea). At this time Baba became known as the daughter of **An** and the planet **Venus**. During the Old Babylonian period she became identified with the goddess of healing, **Ninisinna**, and with **Inanna**. Towards the end of the second millennium BC she also appeared in connection with magic, equated with **Ningirim**, the goddess of incantations.

Jean 1931, 81–5; Ebeling RLAI 1932, 432–3; Edzard, WdM 1965, 45

Babylonian mythology (*see figures 7 and 9*)

What we define here as Babylonian myths are a number of texts which were written in Akkadian during the second millennium BC (some may be older and the **Erra-Epic** is from the first millennium). Most of these compositions, however, are preserved on tablets that were found in the great Neo-Assyrian and Neo-Babylonian archives, notably those of Nineveh, Uruk, Ur and Babylon. We know from colophon entries and other reports that the majority of the texts were copies of older material. Peripheral sites from the middle of the second millennium BC, such as Amarna in Egypt, Boğazköy in Anatolia and Sultantepe in Syria, also yielded versions of Babylonian mythological material, amongst other cuneiform sources. The oldest editions of some texts date from the Old Babylonian period. During the Kassite rule (Middle Babylonian period), while some new compositions were made, other genres of cuneiform literature underwent a process of 'canonization'. The majority of Sumerian myths seem to have been 'weeded out' as they were apparently not passed on beyond this time. Other texts were edited into 'standard versions' which entailed considerable homogeneity of textual transmission over several hundreds of years. During the Neo-Assyrian and Neo-Babylonian periods, when the collections for the royal archives were being made, literary texts from different scribal centres were copied and occasionally amended to reflect contemporary attitudes (see for instance the **Gilgameš Epic**, which was given a new ending by the addition of another tablet).

The Babylonians inherited the culture and religious structures of the Sumerians. The scribes of the Old Babylonian period copied and translated a number of Sumerian mythological texts (see **Ištar's Descent**, the **Flood-myths** and parts of the Gilgameš epic). But there is also much that owes more to Syrian or Amorite concepts than Sumerian tradition (see the myth of **Harab**, the rise of **Marduk** and **Nabû**). While hymns and prayers and other 'proto-philosophical' compositions developed the concept of morality, justice and personal piety, 'mythography', the writing of new myths, though certainly not a new genre in Mesopotamian literature, was used to explain and dramatize the modification of the official pantheon (**Nergal and Ereškigal**; to some extent *Enuma eliš*). The Babylonian myths also reflect the political and economic instability which was symptomatic of much of the second millennium BC. Unlike Sumerian myths, which construct a basically sound and optimally organized universe, they are set in a more unpredictable world and pose questions which remain unanswerable: how can man cope with the unexplicable moods of the gods (**Flood-myths**: Atra-hasis, **Adapa**), how to face death and suffering (**Gilgameš**). The only text which suggests a revival of the old trust in a perfectly ordered universe is the *Enuma eliš*. In the divine personality of **Marduk** and his celestial monarchy, authority and power combine for the ultimate benefit of the world.

Jacobsen 1976, 145–221; Bottéro 1985

Bēl(um)

Akkad. 'Lord', correlative to Sumerian *En* which defines the status of a city-god as the Lord of the town. By extension this title could be used for cosmic deities; thus **Enlil** became the 'lord' of the Universe; so did **Marduk**. In the latter case the appellative became synonymous with the name Marduk, especially during the Neo-Babylonian period. The female equivalent was **Bēlet** (Sumerian *Nin*).

Bēlet-ēkallim – Babylonian goddess

Her name was usually written $^dNIN.É.GAL^{(lim)}$, 'Lady of the Great House'. She is well known from personal names and greeting formulae dating from the Old Babylonian period, especially in Mari, where she appeared as the patroness of the royal family with the epithet *bēlet ḫaṭṭi*, 'Lady of the Sceptre'. She also had temples in Larsa, Ur and Qatna. Her husband was Uraš, the city-god of Dilbat.

Ichiro 1979, 103ff

Bēlet-ṣēri – Babylonian goddess

Her name means 'Lady of the Steppe'. She was the wife of the nomad god **Amurru**. In view of the conceptual connection the Babylonians made between the steppe and the **Underworld**, the goddess was also associated with the realm of the dead, where she functioned as a scribe. Bēlet-ṣēri was identified with the Sumerian goddess **Geštinanna**.

Edzard, WdM 1965, 46

Berossus

A Babylonian priest who lived under the reign of the Seleucid king Antiochus I (3rd C BC). He is known as the author of a volume called *Babyloniaca*. It was written in Greek. Only fragments of some mythological accounts are preserved, mainly in the form of quotations by later Greek writers.

Schnabel 1923; Burstein 1978

C

Canaanite mythology see **Ugaritic mythology**

Cosmogonies

Although the considerable amount of secondary literature on this topic seems to suggest otherwise, cosmogony was not in itself a literary genre. Most 'cosmogonies' are to be found in Mesopotamian sources in connection with a variety of subjects, such as incantations, rituals or other literary compositions. The reference to a primordial state of affairs lent weight and authority to the text and it also connected the origin of the spell, ritual or institution to the evolving structure of the world. In the most famous 'Epic of Creation', the Babylonian *Enuma eliš*, the elevated position of the god **Marduk** is justified by his decisive actions *in illo tempore*.

There is great variety in the narrative sequences, even the divine personalities involved. However, there seems to be one concept which underlies most cosmogonic texts. It is the notion that there is a dynamic tension between chaos and order. Chaos is unformed, unnamed, inert. Yet it is pregnant with the possibility of order and has to give birth to a successively more differentiated system which finally constitutes 'civilization'. According to the ancient cyclical notion of time, this process is not unilinear but subject to repetition. It is therefore not surprising to find that these passages were recited on 'dangerous' dates, such as at the inauguration of a new temple, or New Year festivals. It also explains why the Canaanites for example 'have no cosmogonies' – their mythological texts already express the very same concerns.

Sumerian Cosmogonic references are found in a number of Sumerian incantations, disputatious texts, myths, rituals and god-lists. In the so-called 'Eridu-theology', the 'primordial matter' is composed of the mingled sweet and salty waters of **Apsu** and Tiamat. Together they produce a third, creative element, Mummu, out of which **An** and **Ki** (Heaven and Earth) arise. They in turn beget the great gods.

The 'Nippur theology' contrasts an embryonic, androgynous universe presided over by **An** (*an.en.né*) with a fully fledged civilized world, led by **Enlil**, which began with the separation of An and Ki (Heaven and Earth), followed by the creation of the heavenly bodies, the **Anunnaki** etc.

The role of the 'creator', who by the power of his command called the given phenomena of the world into existence, was assigned to different deities, most prominently in the extant texts, to **An**, Enlil and Enki (Eridu). The **Mother-goddess** is sometimes credited with the creation of people and animals. The texts usually proceed to describe the more detailed organization of the Sumerian civilization; see **Enki and the World Order**, **Enki and Ninhursag**, **Enki and Ninmah**, **Lahar and Ašnan**.

Kramer 1944, 52f; van Dijk 1964, 39ff; Pettinato 1971; van Dijk 1976, 125–33; Cassin, in Bonnefoy 1981, 228ff

Babylonian Various late Babylonian temple rituals and incantations with cosmogonic sections follow the Sumerian precedents. The incantations series *enuma Anu*, for instance, begins with 'When Anu created the heavens, Nudimmud (Enki) created the Apsu, his dwelling, Ea in the Apsu took clay and fashioned Kulla (the brick god) for the restoration of temples'. Another much longer text, intended to be recited for the purification of a temple in Borsippa, ascribes to **Marduk** the creative acts hitherto associated with Enki and is indeed based on the Eridu system: 'The holy house, a house of the gods in a holy place had not been built, no reed, no brick nor brick-mould, no house, no city, no living creature' – (...) 'only the sea existed and its midst was a source.' There Eridu was built and its temple became the prototype of the temple É-sagil in Babylon. On Apsu Marduk created a hillock out of a reed-frame and populated it with human beings and animals, and fertilized the dry land with the waters of the Tigris and Euphrates which were specifically created for this purpose (Heidel). The longest and most coherent creation-story occurs in the ***Enuma eliš***. It is again Marduk who plays the decisive role in the process of creation and embodies the active principle of order pitted against the archaic, inert, creative powers personified by Tiamat, Mummu and Apsu. The poem also dramatizes the dichotomy between the 'generations' of old and young gods. Marduk sets in motion the process of creating and organizing the universe in a manner experienced by mankind (i.e. the separation of heaven and earth out of

Tiamat's slain body, the defining of space and time, the creation of man for the purpose of serving the gods etc.).

Heidel 1942; Labat 1959; Brandon 1963; Edzard 1965, 121–4; Labat, in Labat, Caquot, Sznycer 1970, 75–7; Cassin, in Bonnefoy 1981, 228–35; Bottéro 1985, 112–62

Anatolian Very few cosmogonic references can be found in ancient texts from Anatolia. The Hurrian ideas contained in the **Kumarbi**-myth seem influenced by Mesopotamian thought. Heaven and earth formed a whole which had to be separated with a metal implement by some previous generations of gods.

Creation of man See **Lahar and Ašnan**, **Enki and Ninmah**, *Enuma eliš*, Atra-hasis (**Flood-myths**).

D

Dagan/Dagon – West Semitic god

His name (Ugarit. *dgn*, Akkad. *ᵈdagan*) means something like 'the rainy one', although the precise etymology remains uncertain.

Dagon was one of the many manifestations of the **Weather-god** and was worshipped especially in the Middle Euphrates region. He headed the pantheon of Ebla and was very prominent in Tuttul and Mari. The Sargonic kings also acknowledged the divine assistance of Dagon. During the Ur III period he was integrated in the official cult and had an important sanctuary in Puzriš-Dagon, the livestock centre of Nippur. During the Old Babylonian period he also had a temple in Isin. During the latter half of the second millennium BC, the cult of Dagan spread to Western Syria and Palestine. He had temples in Ugarit and people were called after him. However, he does not feature in the mythological texts of this city, except for Baal's appellative 'son of Dagan'. During the Iron Age he was very popular with the Philistines (cf. city-names, such as Beth-Dagon). At the same time he became assimilated to other weather-gods, such as **Adad** and **Baal**. The origin of this god is uncertain. It may be Akkadian rather than Amorite (Caquot, Sznycer).

Dagan has also chthonic associations; and as the *bēl pagrê*, 'lord of corpses', he received sacrifices for the dead in Mari and Ugarit.

Schmöckel 1928; Forterose 1957, 277–9; Edzard 1965, WdM, 49–50; Ichiro 1979, 111–51; Wyatt 1980, 375–9; Caquot, Sznycer 1981, 13ff; Lebrun 1984, 35

Damkina

Sumerian goddess, 'the rightful wife'; she was also called *ᵈdam.gal*, 'great wife (of) the exalted'. She was probably one of the manifestations of the **Mother-goddess** as her name is used synonymously with **Ninhursag** in **Enki and Ninhursag**. She is known since the Old Sumerian period, had temples at Nippur and Adab and received offerings at

Umma and Lagash. In the Old Babylonian times she became primarily known as the wife of **Enki**, who lives with him in the **Apsu**, her Akkadian epithet is accordingly *Šarrat apsû*, 'queen of the Apsu'. This is where according to the *Enuma eliš* she gave birth to **Marduk**.

Edzard 1965, WdM, 50

Damu – Sumerian god

He is documented since the Ur III period and had a cult in Isin where he was called the son of the local tutelary goddess **Ninisina**. Like her he was a healing deity.

In a number of liturgical texts Damu is the subject of laments similar to those of **Dumuzi**. In these laments he is mourned by his mother and his sister (the physician Gunuru), as 'the child who disappeared in the marshes or the river'. Jacobsen saw in Damu 'the god of the sap that rises in trees and vegetation'.

Kramer 1969, 158n.15; Jacobsen 1975, 67, 85–6; Kramer 1982, 141–6; Alster, in Hecker, Sommerfeld 1986, 19–29

Demons (*see figures 11, 12 and 13*)

are probably older than the gods, and many totemistic societies acknowledge the existence of non-human beings ('spirits') endowed with a force to influence the lives of people and animals. This is inevitable in a world-view which does not differentiate between animate and inanimate, between a human and a 'supernatural' conscience. Features of the landscape, weather phenomena, the beasts of prey and those of the hunt, as well as human beings, are all part of one interconnected system of 'numinous' power. The psychological and physical well-being of people is constantly threatened by forces outside their control; disease and quarrels, misfortune and death are the work of malignant forces. They can therefore only be averted by participating magic which sends the evil back.

The Ancient Near East has sometimes been described as fear-ridden and obsessed with demons and evil spirits. The great number of apotropaic objects and the long and complicated rituals of the incantation priests (*ašipus*) seem to support this assumption. However, one has to bear in mind that the polytheistic religion which appears already formulated in the earliest texts (beginning of the third millennium BC) had to some extent re-interpreted the relationship between man and the 'numen', now experienced as the 'gods'. It became the task of priestly theologians for the next three thousand years to refine and delineate the sphere of divine influence in ever greater detail. However, the power ascribed to demons and spirits seems to fluctuate; while they are sometimes described as being beyond the influence of the gods, the second millennium Babylonian prayers rely on the gods to subdue them. Such speculation was surely restricted to professional theologians; for the majority of the population (even at the present day) it must have been safer to ward off the evil influence of demons by special apotropaic amulets and other preventive measures.

The concept of the friendly, protective spirit (cf. *genius*; angel), who is attached to the individual, stands between the 'great gods' and the human being (see **Lama**).

See also **Asag**, **Galla**, **Lamassu**.

Ebeling, RLA I 1932, 113–15; Edzard, WdM 1965, 46–9; Black, Green 1990

Dingir-Mah[meš]

A group of Hittite goddesses, sometimes envisaged as a triad, with the goddesses Allinalli and Iyaya, or Zukki and Anzilli. They are also mentioned in connection with the *Gulšeš* goddesses. According to some texts they created man (Siegelová) and they sit by rivers, wells, or by the seashore. They decide the fates on every human being and are present at birth. Dingir-Mah in the singular stands for the mother-goddess **Hanna-hanna**.

Siegelová, Otten 1970, 32–8; Haas, 1977, 54

Dumuzi – Sumerian god

His name, usually written as *ddumu.zi*, means literally 'rightful son'; Jacobsen prefers 'the Quickener of the Young [in the Mother's Womb]'. In Hebrew and Aramaic: TAMMUZ

Dumuzi first appears under this name in economic texts from Šuruppak (Old Sumerian period). In the god-lists and in personal names from the same time, however, he is known as *dama. ušum.gal. (an. na)*, 'the mother (is) a (heavenly) dragon'. The Sumerian king-list mentions two Dumuzis, one as the 'shepherd' who became the king of antediluvial Babtibira, the other as 'a fisher', who eventually ruled over Uruk. Unfortunately, there are no other historical references to these kings. Dumuzi as a divine figure was associated with Babtibira, as well as

Kullaba (within the district of Uruk). This is documented by the Temple Hymns and other cultic texts from Uruk. During the Neo-Sumerian period the god was frequently mentioned in votive inscriptions, hymns and other literary and religious texts. The kings of the Third Dynasty of Ur showed a predilection for the religious and literary traditions of Uruk and seem to have identified themselves with Dumuzi in his role of **In-anna**'s husband (see below). After the Old Babylonian period Dumuzi appears only rarely in Mesopotamian texts outside incantations and **Eršemma**s. His cult, however, enjoyed considerable popularity throughout the Ancient Near East until and beyond the Hellenistic time, when Tammuz merged with other **Dying Gods**, such as Adonis. For the Neo-Assyrian interpretation of Dumuzi as a god who takes disease and affliction with him into the underworld, see Farber (1977).

In the mythological texts Dumuzi features primarily in connection with the steppe (Sumerian *edin*) and the goddess Inanna. In DUMUZI AND ENKIMDU, she has to decide between the shepherd Dumuzi and the farmer Enkimdu. Both praise the products of their profession, the 'sweet milk' and the 'abundant grain'. Inanna, as the tutelary goddess of a Sumerian city, prefers the farmer, but eventually accepts Dumuzi after her brother, the sun-god **Utu**, intercedes for him (Jacobsen 1946, 14–15; Falkenstein 1950, 325–7).

Various compositions celebrate the love of Inanna for Dumuzi: 'The people will set up my fruitful bed, they will cover it with plants (the colour of) lapis-lazuli, I will bring there my sweet-heart, I will bring there Amaušumgalanna, he will put his hand in my hand, he put his heart to my heart, his putting of hand to hand – its sleep(?) is so refreshing, his pressing of heart to heart – its pleasure is so sweet' ... 'My lord, the "honey-man" of the gods, my favoured of the womb(?)' (Kramer, in Pritchard 1975, 195–204). The ritual context of these texts is still unclear, although it has been proposed that they formed part of the so-called **Sacred Marriage** ceremonies. According to other texts, the happiness of Inanna and Dumuzi was doomed. Dumuzi, the shepherd, did not integrate into the urban Sumerian pantheon. He remained the 'shepherd' and continued to live in the steppe with his herds. It is there that he dies and disappears. Several Sumerian compositions explain how his death came to pass (see also **Inanna and Belili**). In **Inanna's Descent**, he is chosen by the goddess as a substitute to take her place in the underworld because he alone failed to mourn her. Inanna points him out to the **Galla** demons who pursue their victim. In spite of the various metamorphoses he undergoes with the help of Inanna's brother, the Sun-god, the demons eventually find him in his 'holy stall' in the steppe and seize him. His sister **Geštinanna** tries to save her brother by offering herself as a substitute. Somebody (it is not clear whether Inanna or **Ereškigal**, the queen of the underworld, is speaking) thereupon decides: 'You half a year, your brother half a year should sojourn in the underworld.'

Another Sumerian text with the modern title, DUMUZI'S DREAM (Alster), concentrates on the psychological condition of the doomed hero. Dumuzi has left the city and wanders in the lonely steppe, the lawless **Arali**. He is overcome with foreboding and addresses the very landscape with all its inhabitants to inform his mother of his death, since without the customary burial rites his soul would never find peace. In the second part of the text we find Dumuzi in the sheepfold of his sister Geštinanna. There he lies down to sleep. He awakes panic-stricken, having just had four frightening dreams which he relates in great detail to his sister. The dreams involve a series of destructions, affecting uncultivated plants such as rushes, trees and reeds and the vital tools of the sheepfold. He also saw four birds of evil portent. Geštinanna explains that the destruction will be performed by the demons and that it will concern Dumuzi himself. She advises her frightened brother to hide among some plants and promises not to betray his hiding place. The demons arrive to attack Dumuzi and only find Geštinanna. They seize her and although they offer her a 'river full of water and a field full of grain', she refuses to lead them to Dumuzi. The demons then go to his friend (a shepherd) and succeed in bribing him to betray Dumuzi. They proceed to catch him like some wild animal, by stalking and netting. They bind his arms and legs, but as in Inanna's Descent (see above), Dumuzi in his desperation utters a prayer to Utu who grants his wish to be changed into a gazelle. Dumuzi escapes but the demons again catch up with him. This time he asks **Utu** to help him escape to the 'old woman Belili's' house, whom he asks for a meal. When the demons find him he wishes to be at his sister's place. Geštinanna sees her brother, pursued by the demons. She screams and scratches her body in despair. The demons then enter the fold and, fulfilling the dream, wreck it completely. The sheepfold is destroyed and Dumuzi is dead. Although this composition is so far the longest, there exist various others, especially among the **Eršemma**-texts, which describe events surrounding the death of Dumuzi. They contain lengthy references to burial rites and other rituals, as well as lamentations. The order of events can vary and Dumuzi's mother, Şirtur, takes part in the searching and the mourning. One *eršemma* (Cohen) includes an etiological 'mini-myth' which explains why flies are found in alehouses, fruit containers and around cattle. Inanna and Geštinanna were looking for the vanished Dumuzi, Inanna because she wants to hand him over to the demons, and the loyal sister because she wants to save him. Both goddesses approach the fly and offer her rewards, and since Geštinanna can also offer the 'superb calves' (being a herding-deity), she is able to bring various healing plants and food to her brother. (Alster 1972; Kramer 1980, 5–13; Cohen 1981, 71–92).

Dumuzi is one of the most complex figures in Sumerian mythology. As a mortal being ('the shepherd') his fate is death, the lonely and frightening death in the steppe, devoured by wild animals and evil spirits. This may explain Dumuzi's essential passivity; he can only try to escape and turn to prayer. By wooing and winning Inanna, he enters into intimate relationships with the great gods, and the joyful consummation of their union was one of the unique features of Sumerian religion. Dumuzi, in spite of his passivity, is a great dramatic figure because he is the means of expressing a whole range of tensions, as Alster has noted. Deified, he stands between man and the gods, between life and death, even between the desert and the city. On yet another level, and probably most enduringly, Dumuzi is the archetypal **Dying God**. His fate is identified with the annual death and resurrection of vegetation outside the irrigated land. For a few months the desert blooms, the crops flourish and the animals multiply, until the scorching sun dries it all up again. This seasonal connection is confirmed by the astronomical position of Dumuzi. The Bull of Heaven (= Dumuzi, = Taurus) disappears for six weeks below the Sumerian horizon (from January to March, the beginning of the Sumerian year). As we know from various cultic calendars, the partial disappearance of Dumuzi was also celebrated in a ritual journey which seems to have lasted half a year. Dumuzi started from the Elamite mountains, proceeded to Lagash and via Apisala to Enlil in Nippur. After a stop-over in Umma, he went on to Ur and presumably Eridu until he reached the temple of Geštinanna in Zabalam (Sauren).

Falkenstein 1954, 41–65; Hartner 1965, 1–16; Sauren 1969, 230f; Alster 1972, 14; Jacobsen, in Frankfort et al. 1977, 198–9; Alster, in Hecker, Sommerfeld 1986, 1–13

Dumuziabzu – Sumerian goddess

The name means 'true child of the **Apsu**'. Gudea, the famous ruler of Lagash during the Neo-Sumerian period, called her the Lady of Kinirsha, a district of his territory. According to Jacobsen she stands 'for the power of fertility and new life in the marshes'. In the regions around Eridu, however, she was viewed as a male deity, and formed part of the entourage of **Enki**. Any connections with the god **Dumuzi**, apart from the first element of the name, are spurious.

Edzard, WdM 1965, 53; Falkenstein 1954, 45; Jacobsen 1970, 23

Dying Gods

As gods are generally distinguished from men by their immortality, this category seems a logical contradiction. However, one must bear in mind that death as a complete annihilation is a modern concept and that all ancient and 'primitive' peoples believe in the continued existence of the 'soul' (in Egypt *ka*). As a 'spirit' or 'shade' it will live on in the **Underworld**. The communication between the two spheres was unilateral; whoever entered the underworld had to stay in it for ever ('The Land of No Return'). As all rules have exceptions, there are cases in which former inmates of the underworld contrived to get out – even if only temporarily (for a brief emergence see the dialogue between Gilgameš and Enkidu in the twelfth tablet of the **Gilgameš Epic**, also Odysseus and Saul). In Sumerian mythology there are several interrelated accounts of dying gods:

(a) **Inanna's Descent** and the fate of her husband **Dumuzi**. Inanna, the 'great queen of heaven', decides to go to the underworld and gains admission on the pretext to join in the mourning for the husband of **Ereškigal**. But Ereškigal then 'fixes the eye of death' upon her and she becomes a lifeless corpse, caught in the underworld and unable to be buried. Eventually, by a ruse, this process is reversed, and sprinkled with the 'water of Life', the goddess is revived. This is the only case of a complete and irreversible resurrection in Ancient Near Eastern literature. Her exit from the underworld, however, is only granted by her promise to provide a substitute. The **Galla**-demons accompany her and finally make off with Inanna's husband, Dumuzi. As a mortal, or at any rate, far less divine than Inanna, his death sentence can only be alleviated to a part-time arrangement with his self-sacrificing sister **Geštinanna**. In the Akkadian version of the same tale, the effects of Inanna/Ištar's disappearance are vividly described: 'since **Ištar** has gone down to the Land of No Return, the bull springs not upon the cow, the ass impregnates not the jenny, in the street the man impregnates not the maiden.' – fertility amongst animals and people is seriously disrupted and only restored upon Inanna's return. Other compositions describe the effects of Dumuzi's absence on milk production. The substitution theme also occurs in the myth of **Enlil and Ninlil**, where **Enlil** is banned to the underworld as a punishment for the rape of Ninlil. In a series of further sexual encounters he engenders four other deities, three of whom end up in the underworld as his substitutes. (See also **Damu** and **Nergal**.)

(b) In Ugarit, **Baal** (see **Baal-Myths**) is eaten by **Mot** and with him vanish the dew, the rain and the storm. He too is mourned by all the gods, who in vain try to find someone who would take his place in heaven (a variant of the substitution motive?). Although **Anat** does battle with Mot, Baal reappears as a matter of course, after a certain time.

In Hittite mythology, gods are not said to actually die, but their temporary absence amounts to the same results. The tale of **Telepinu** records how the disappearance of this god brought on general calamity and famine. He has removed himself, being angry and when found, has to be pacified by rituals. His reappearance brings back fertility.

The majority of myths featuring dying gods seem to be anchored in seasonal rituals. These were of great importance to the ancient agricultural communities, as the transfer from one part of the annual cycle to the next was always fraught with expectation and uncertainty. Although an eschatological dimension of salvation through the dying god does not seem to form a prominent part in the myth, its message is reassuring: it makes sense of the annual or sabbatical fluctuation in fertility, the change of the seasons and confirms the beliefs in the ultimate cosmic balance.

Colpe 1969, 23–44; Soden 1955; 1952

E

Ea – also 'Ay(y)a; Akkadian god (*see figures 10, 32, and 39*)

The name of this god is probably Semitic, although no reliable etymology has yet been found. Ancient Babylonian scribes derived it from Sumerian *É.a*, 'house of the water'.

In the texts from the Old Sumerian and Sargonic periods Ea/Ayya occurs mainly in Akkadian personal names. The pronunciation Ea (Ay-a) is attested since the Ur III period.

The original character of this god is impossible to assess because of his syncretism with the Sumerian god **Enki**, which probably occurred as early as the Sargonic period. Ea's functions in the Babylonian and Assyrian tradition are therefore essentially the same as Enki's. He is a water-god (*Bēl naqbi*, 'lord of the Spring'), a creator (*bān kullati*, 'creator of everything'), a god of wisdom (*bēl uzni*, 'lord of wisdom'), the supreme master of magic (*maš.maš ilāni*, 'incantation specialist of the gods'), the protector of craftsmen and artisans. He remained amongst the 'great gods' of Mesopotamia until the end of cuneiform sources, as official inscriptions, legal documents, religious texts and personal names testify.

In the Akkadian myths, Ea is the god who is appealed to in difficult situations because of his cunning and wisdom (as in Atra-hasis (**Flood-myths**, the **Gilgameš Epic**, 11; **Nergal and Ereškigal**). He is ever ready to help those in trouble and protects the persecuted. In the story of **Adapa**, Ea's real intentions towards the hero are unclear and in the ***Enuma eliš*** Ea is shown to be less capable than **Marduk** in dealing with Tiamat and her host.

During the Middle and Late Babylonian period, Ea was often invoked in special prayers against evil portents, as part of a triad consisting of Ea, **Šamaš** and Marduk (Seux, passim).

Roberts 1972; Seux 1976; Galter 1981

El/Ilu

el or *il(u)* are the general appellatives for 'god' in practically all Semitic languages (cf. Allah!). The etymology of this term is still much debated; Albright proposed *'wl*, 'to be first; leader'. It first appeared among the Semitic personal names of the Old Sumerian period and finally in Hellenistic times, when El was identified with Cronos.

If the deity written as ^dBE in the Ebla texts is taken to stand for El, his cult was established in Syria during the mid-third millennium BC.

In Ugarit he was with **Baal** one of the most important deities and he plays a prominent part in most of the **Ugaritic myths**, especially in **Aqhat**, **Keret** and **Šahar and Šalim**. El, like the Mesopotamian **An**, represents divine authority and the creator of the world. He represents the principle of order on a cosmic and political level. His epithets reveal the range of his competence: as *'ab šnm*, 'father of the years (or the exalted?)', he is the father, the patriarch of all the gods (with the exception of Baal who is consistently called 'Son of **Dagan**'). As *mlk*, 'king', he rules over the world of men as well as gods. He is the source of royal power and therefore the king on earth is called the 'Son of El' (e.g. Keret). *Tr 'el*, 'Bull El', refers to his procreative power and his function of dispensing fertility – Baal in comparison is called the 'bull-calf'. The sexual vigour of El has been the subject of much academic interest, as some myths seem ambiguous about his potency (Šahar and Šalim). The epithet *'b 'adm*, 'Father of Men', probably embraces both the physical and the social implications of this relationship. It is interesting in this context that most of the early verbal-sentence names composed with El seem to have allusions to childbirth and infancy. *ltpn il dpid*, 'merciful and kind El', refers to his equanimity; in contrast to Baal he is passive and not easily moved to anger.

The iconography shows the god with a long beard and seated, while Baal strides and throws a bolt of lightning. El's relationship to Baal has been investigated by many scholars, as the various mythological texts seem to suggest some tension between the two gods. This may be due to the generation-gap between the old El and the young Baal, different strata of religious development, or as pointed out by L'Heureux, due to different sociological groups within Ugaritic society, wherein El stands for the tribally structured, pastoral Amorites and Baal for the urban population and the court.

Eissfeldt 1951; Pope 1953; Lokkegard 1953, 219–35; Gray 1957, 115ff; Pope, Röllig, WdM 1965, 279–83; Oldenberg 1969; Roberts 1972, 31–43; Gibson 1978, 52; L'Heureux 1979

Elimelek/Ilumilku

is the name of the scribe who was responsible for the transmission of three major texts of **Ugaritic mythology**, the **Baal-Myths, Aqhat** and **Keret**. In several colophons he calls himself 'The Shubanite, pupil of Attanu, majordomo, high priest, high shepherd, officiant of Niqmepa, king of Ugarit'. While it is very likely that Elimelek as a literate and highly trained priest was familiar with any orally transmitted liturgical and mythological material, it does not necessarily follow that he merely committed these to writing. Although the current understanding of poetic artifices in Ugaritic is still patchy, it has also been shown that he was an original author with a distinct style and language. There are several structural similarities in all his works, as well as a coherent theology which links the different narratives, cross-references and a standardization of characterization and epithets which are also typical of the Homeric epics.

De Moor 1987, passim

(El)qunirša – West Semitic god

The name is derived from the Semitic *qn'rṣ*, 'creator of the earth'. A Canaanite myth partly preserved in a Hittite text tells of Elqunirša's troubled marital relations with Ašertu (= **Aštart**). The goddess, in sexual frustration, attempts to seduce the weather-god (**Baal**) who proves not only unwilling but informs her husband. Elqunirša decides to 'humiliate' his wife by asking the weather-god to sleep with her. **Baal** seems to comply but he upsets Ašertu by telling her about the death of her children, for which he is somehow responsible. The goddess begins a long period of mourning which affects the whole country. After a lost passage, the married couple are apparently reconciled and together they plot the punishment of the weather-god. The goddess **Ištar** overhears their discourse in the shape of a cup and a bird. The following passages are still unclear, but it seems that the weather-god is in difficulty or has disappeared. Ištar then departs to find and heal him.

Schuler, WdM 1965, 162

Enbilulu – Sumerian agricultural deity

In **Enki and the World Order**, he is called 'the inspector of canals' (1.272-3) and charged with the supervision of the Tigris and the Euphrates.

In the Babylonian godlist An=*Anum* he appears among the **Weather-gods** of Babylon. He was also considered to be a son of **Ea**.

Edzard, WdM 1965, 56

Enki – Sumerian god (*see figures 39 and 43*)

The name can either be taken to mean 'Lord Earth', but *KI* also stands for 'Below' in regard to a two-tiered cosmic structure with *AN* (Heaven) as the 'Above'. Certainly the character of Enki ever since the earliest documents from the Old Sumerian period is formed by his association with water, most notably in the ground-water or **Apsu**. The Apsu is his dwelling-place and in the figure of Enki, the creative potential of the fertilizing humidity is given a dramatic expression (see **Enki and Ninhursag, Enki and Ninmah, Enki and the World Order**). One of his literary epithets is *nudimmud* – 'who creates', while the appellative *nagbu* means directly 'source, groundwater'.

Enki is also the god of 'wisdom', a term which embraces the practical skills (Enki is also a god of crafts and arts), intellectual faculties, the ability to 'decree a fate' (most pertinently described in Enki and Ninmah) and the command of magic powers (he was the most important god for incantations and the patron of incantation priests). He is closely linked with the differentiation of (Sumerian) civilization (see Enki and the World Order, **Enmerkar and the Lord of Aratta**). In some Sumerian myths (see below) he collaborates as well as competes with female deities. It seems that Enki's creative potential, like that of the Apsu, is inert and has to be activated by the goddesses. He is cursed by Ninhursag as well as Ninmah for his intellectual arrogance and directly challenged by Inanna (see also **Inanna and Enki**), to whom he is otherwise well-disposed.

Enki was one of the major Mesopotamian gods and this is also reflected by his official position in the pantheon. In most god lists he occupies the third rank after An and **Enlil**, his only rival being the **Mother-goddess**.

He is well attested in personal names and seal-inscription, since Enki was considered to be the most approachable among the 'great gods'.

His main cult-centre was the lagoon-based Eridu, where he was worshipped in the temples É-abzu and É-engura, but as one of Mesopotamia's most prominent deities he also had numerous temples elsewhere (Assur, Babylon, Isin, Kisurru, Lagash, Larsa, Mari, Nippur, Ur, Uruk etc.). A long poetical text describes the building of the É-engura by Enki himself, which was celebrated by the gods with a great banquet (Falken-stein and Soden 1953, 136). Many year-names refer to the renovation and dedication of temples to Enki, particularly during the Ur III and the Old Babylonian periods. Enki was identified with the Semitic god **Ea**.

In the divine genealogy, Enki/Ea is the offspring of **An** and **Nammu**; his wife is **Damkina** and the most prominent among their children are **Marduk** and **Nanše**.

His symbols include the goatfish, the tortoise, a ram-headed staff, a ship and a vessel with overflowing water.

Ebeling, RLA 2 1932, 374–9; Galter 1981

Enki and Ninhursag

Sumerian myth; preserved on UR III and Old Babylonian tablets. It is a highly complex text and various different translations and interpretations have been proposed. This summary of the plot follows Rosengarten's French translation.

The story is set in a mythical place called Dilmun (the actual Dilmun was a busy trading-post in the Persian Gulf). It is a potential, not yet 'real' world described by negative statements: the girls did not perform lustrations, sickness was non-existent, lions and wolves did not behave like lions and wolves and most notably there was no sweet water. The **Mother-goddess**, who appears in the story under different names or appellatives, asks Enki to procure some water. Enki first creates the rivers and canals. With the help of the god Ud, he brings water from the depth of the earth and makes basins and cisterns for their storage. The fields are thus able to produce grain with the 'water of abundance'. Quays and waterways, essential for profitable trade, are also erected; Dilmun is now a desirable place. The goddess Nin-tud, called *ama kalam.ma*, 'mother of the land', appears and Enki creates the marshland where he unites himself with Damgalnunna, who from this moment of conception on is called Ninsikil, 'the pure lady'. After a pregnancy lasting nine days, she gives birth to Ninmu. Enki unites himself also with Ninmu, who bears him Ninkurra, 'the lady of the land' = under-world?, who in turn becomes impregnated by Enki and delivers Uttu, 'vegetation'. Ninhursag now intervenes. She advises Uttu to avoid the advances of Enki. In order to achieve a union with Uttu, Enki now extends the water well into the dry zones, to the great delight of the gardener. When Enki arrives at Uttu's dwelling, laden with the horticul-tural products that have just been brought into existence – apples,

41

cucumbers and grapes – Uttu rejoices and lets Enki sleep with her. Ninhursag, however, removes or just transforms the seed of Enki to create eight plants (corresponding to the eight basic plant-groups). Again Enki desires the plants, he wants to 'know' their nature. He needs to be ferried from his domain, the **Apsu** (here probably the marshes), to the garden where the plants grow and proceeds to eat them one by one. This causes the anger of Ninhursag, as it is she alone who should 'know' them or decree their fate. She curses Enki who becomes afflicted in eight different parts of his body. She furthermore threatens not to 'look at him with the eye of Life', which would entail his death. It is only at the inter- cession of the fox that she consents to restore Enki's well-being. To this purpose she seems to take the ailing god on her lap (or in her lap; the passage is still unclear) and talk to him 'like a brother'. In order to heal him, she gives birth to eight divine beings, one for each afflicted part (this involves a number of Sumerian puns) and decrees their fate. **Abba** becomes the lord of the plants, Ninsikila the lord of Magan, Ninkirutu the spouse of **Ninazu**, Ninkasi the 'wish-fulfiller', Nazi the husband of UmunDara, and Ensag the lord of Dilmun.

Kramer 1945; Lambert, Tournay 1949, 105–36; Rosengarten 1971; Alster 1978, 15–27; Attinger 1985, 1–52

Enki and Ninmah – Sumerian myth

The text is not fully preserved; it is reconstructed on the base of some Ur III tablets and a Neo-Assyrian bilingual copy.

It seems to begin with a prologue *in illo tempore*. The **Anunnaki** have been born, and the process of engendering the other generations of gods has been set in motion by marriages between gods and goddesses. Every deity has an assigned task to keep the land well-tended and irrigated; some are basket-carriers and the 'great gods' are the supervisors. The hard labour, however, does not suit them at all and they complain loudly to Enki, who in his wisdom is supposed to come to their rescue. Enki seems the only one not working, he is fast asleep in his **Apsu**. **Nammu**, the mother-goddess, decides to wake Enki and tells him that he ought to get up and create man. Enki awakes but delegates the job to Nammu, instructing her to take some of the Apsu's fertile clay, to nip it off and shape it, assisted by some helpers. Ninmah is one of these companions, it is her duty to impose hard work upon mankind. After a gap in the text, we find the gods enjoying a banquet, where Enki is praised for his knowledge of how to create mankind. Enki and Ninmah drink more than the others and become intoxicated; Ninmah is in a competitive mood and proposes to fashion some other creatures. Enki complies but insists on deciding their fate himself. Ninmah sets to work and makes six human creatures, who all suffer some defect. The nature of their deformities is difficult to understand. The first seems to have something wrong with his arm, so Enki appoints him to be a certain type of court official. The second being has a 'tic' – his eyes are constantly blinking; he is to be a singer. The third is crippled, but Enki also finds a 'good fate' for him, although we don't understand what it is. The fourth man has uncontrollable ejaculations and Enki cures him with a ritual bath. The fifth is a barren woman and she is assigned a place in a 'harem' (probably a priestly function). The last creature seems to lack sexual organs of any kind and Enki appoints him to be a court official. Enki now changes roles with Ninmah; he will create human beings and she will 'pronounce their fate'. The text becomes almost unintelligible at this point. Enki fashions two creatures; one seems to be a fertile woman (?), the other is called Umul (from Sumerian u_4-*mu-ul*, 'my day is remote'). He is very sick, suffers from headaches and his eyes and neck, heart, lungs and bowels are afflicted. He cannot feed himself, his arms and legs are weak. He is unable to walk. Enki now approaches Ninmah and asks her to decree a good fate for Umul. Ninmah questions him but he is unable to answer. She brings bread and he cannot stretch out his hands to take it. Unable to do anything useful to this creature, Ninmah announces: 'The man you have created is not alive and not dead, I am not able to raise him up.' Enki taunts Ninmah with his success at decreeing a good fate for the people she created and – here the text is damaged again – seems to arouse the anger of Ninmah. She curses him: 'on earth you shall not dwell', thus confining him to the subterranean regions of the Apsu. [gap] Enki admits that Ninmah's word 'cannot be altered' and then gives her more advice. She is to hold Umal (who is probably the first baby) on her lap, his penis must be praised (?), her own actions more restrained, his house (Enki's temple?) must be built. This final passage seems to summarize the creation of human beings, and explain their neotany, procreation and duties towards the gods.

Benito 1969; Alster 1978; Draffkorn-Kilmer 1976, 265–71

Enki and the World Order

Sumerian text preserved on Old Babylonian tablets. The structure resembles that of a certain type of incantation and is divided into four sections. The first part contains the praise of Enki, including a self-glorification, the homage of the **Anunnaki** and a description of the various rituals performed by priests (lines 1–160). Then follows the blessings of Enki. In this boat he travels through all of Sumer and her neighbours and blesses the cities and countries (161–249). Having filled the rivers Tigris and Euphrates with overflowing water, he appoints various gods to be in charge of these areas (251–385). The last and longest section (386–466) concerns **Inanna**'s request for more power. The goddess complains that she has been overlooked and, unlike other goddesses, had not received an office and the suitable **Mes**. In a long speech Enki tells her that she already has considerable amounts of *Mes*. Enki also seems to accuse Inanna of upsetting the peace and harmony of his world by giving in to her love for battle. As the last twenty lines are lost, the outcome of this dialogue is uncertain.

Benito 1969; Alster 1973, 107–8

Enkidu (*see figure 37*)

In Mesopotamian mythology, the companion of **Gilgameš**. The name means 'Lord of the Good Place'. In the Sumerian forerunners to the Akkadian epic, he appears in **Gilgameš and Huwawa** and, more prominently, in **Gilgameš, Enkidu and the Netherworld**. In these texts he is the slave (Sum. *ìr*) of Gilgameš. In the Akkadian versions their relationship is more explicitly defined. In tablet 1, **Ninsun**, the mother of Gilgameš, announces the arrival of Enkidu as an equal to her son, who is to be 'a strong companion, one who helps a friend in need'. In fact, it is stated earlier in the text that Enkidu was specifically created by the **Mother-goddess** Aruru in response to the prayers from the suppressed people of Uruk, the town of Gilgameš. He is one of the most intriguing figures of Mesopotamian mythology – the archetypal non-civilized wild man who runs with the beasts of the steppe. His body is covered in shaggy hair, 'he eats grass with the gazelles, with the game he presses on to the drinking-place' (1, col. ii, 40–41). This intimate relationship with the animals is shattered by his encounter with the 'harlot'. He first tastes sex, then bread and beer and when she takes him to town, he has become a man, an enemy in the eyes of the beasts. The people of Uruk cheer when they see him: 'For Gilgameš an equal, like a god has arisen'. He meets Gilgameš face to face and the gate posts tremble under the impact of their collision. Having tested each other's strength, they become friends and this friendship becomes legendary. It is Enkidu who now advances the pursuit of heroic adventure, who urges the young king into dangerous exploits. And it is he who is punished for his rashness; Enkidu has to die. Gilgameš himself takes up the former existence of Enkidu, roaming the steppe and running with the beasts. His lamentations and agonies for the dead friend find a later parallel in Achilles' grief for the slain Patroclus. In both cases it is their refusal to accept the death of their friend which forms the basis of their own undying 'fame'.

Wolff 1969

Enkimdu – Sumerian agricultural god

He is the unsuccessful suitor of **Inanna** – in a text where **Dumuzi**, the shepherd, and Enki(m)du, the farmer, compete for her hand. In **Enki and the World Order**, he is called 'the farmer of Enlil, the man of ditch and dike' (lines 322–324) which underlines the importance of irrigation techniques in south Mesopotamian agriculture.

Enlil – Sumerian god, in Akkadian: Ellil

One of the 'great gods' of Mesopotamia. His name (usually translated as 'Lord Air', but see below) appears in the earliest Sumerian texts (Jemdet-Nasr period) and already in a prominent place in the Old Sumerian pantheon lists (Fara). This is probably connected with the political importance of Enlil's city, Nippur, during the Early Dynastic period. Although this city was never the actual seat of a ruling dynasty, according to some Ur III texts, which may record earlier practices, the king of Sumer was proclaimed or confirmed by the 'divine assembly' at Nippur. Enlil was said to bestow the divine authority, given to him by his father **Anu**, to the legitimate leader of the country. This function is acknowledged in many royal inscriptions. In Akkadian texts (from the Old Babylonian period onwards), the concept of Enlil's authority was known as *ellilū'tu*, 'Ellil-ship'. Like Anu, Enlil could promote other deities by conferring Ellil-ship upon them (thereby sanctioning the elevation of 'new' gods, such as **Marduk** and **Aššur**).

Apart from royal inscriptions, Enlil (or his epithets or temples) features prominently in the personal names from all periods of Mesopotamian history. He is the subject of numerous Sumerian liturgical hymns (e.g. Falkenstein-Soden 1953, 76, 77, 87) and Babylonian prayers (e.g. Seux 1976, 145, 147, 149, 271, 274).

45

The main sanctuary of Enlil was the É-kur at Nippur. As one of the great gods, however, he was worshipped in many other cities, even outside Mesopotamia (Elam), and had several other important temples (in Assur, Babylon, Uruk-Kullaba etc.).

The personality of Enlil is very complex. It is not certain what the Sumerian element *lil* originally stood for; later bilingual lists denote a relationship with *erṣetu*, 'country, earth', *ṣeru*, 'steppe, desert', and *zâqîqu*, 'wind, dust-storm'. Some of his epithets reveal aspects of a **Weather-god**; such as Sum. *kur.gal*, 'great mountain' (see the name of his temple, É-kur 'The House (is a) Mountain)' and *lugal a.ma.ru*, 'king of the storm'.

Ab.ba dingir.re.ne, 'father of the gods', is an ancient title, already used by Entemena of Lagaš. He is often called *nun.a.mir*, 'the well respected', and from about the 1st Dynasty of Larsa, Enlil is 'the one who decides the fate' (*na. me nam. tar. ri*), a function he shares with **Enki**, the mother-goddess or **Inanna**. In the myth of **Anzu** he is in possession of the Tablets of Destiny. His name could also be written with the sign for the number fifty (Sumerian *ninnu*). On a cosmic level, Enlil's domain is the earth and the sphere of the winds and the weather above (Sum. *kur*), while Enki's realm is 'below' (the **Apsu**) and An rules 'above', in heaven. Enlil is responsible for all aspects of life, fertility and prosperity, as well as famine and catastrophes. On the one hand he is the 'lord of abundance', 'whose word – it is plants, it is grain', who maintains the well-being, peace and fertility of the land; on the other hand a considerable number of myths and religious compositions concentrate on his negative influence. In the lamentations and other cultic songs, the catastrophes are always ultimately his work. He seems ever ready to utter 'his angry word' which brings all manner of calamities over the land. Although his wrath is often called upon to be turned against the enemies of Sumer or Babylon, he is no reliable partisan of his country. The **Flood-myths** always cast Enlil in the role of the irate god who wants to destroy humanity. Prayers and hymns on the other hand also portray Enlil as a wise and kindly god, who protects his people (this aspect was also much in evidence in the Akkadian personal names).

Enlil is the firstborn son of An (who was mentioned in prayer by Lugalzaggesi of Uruk), but other texts quote a descent from Enki and Ninki or even self-propagation from the mountain (Tallqvist 1938, 296f). His relationship with An has provoked much comment, since it seems to reflect typical generational tensions. Some texts very carefully delineate Enlil's actions as being carried out on behalf of his father, or in accord with him, while others freely ascribe to Enlil the authority and functions of An (such as the decreeing of fates, the promotion of other gods, judgement etc.). The subject is further complicated by the inherent bias and purpose of these texts, which is not always transparent. Enlil's son **Ninurta** is also said to carry out his valorous deeds at the behest of his father, and the various poetic compositions exalting Ninurta echo the father-son relationship between An and Enlil.

Enlil's wife was first one of the mother-goddesses, then, since the Old Babylonian period, **Ninlil**. His other sons are **Sîn**, **Nergal** and **Namtar**.

Nötscher 1927; Edzard 1965, WdM, 59–61

Enlil and Ninlil

Sumerian myth originating from Nippur. The text of some 150 lines has been reconstructed from tablets dating from the Old and Middle Babylonian period, plus a Neo-Assyrian copy. The Sumerian catalogue-title is *uru na.am*, 'There was/is a town'.

The story begins with a description of the town Nippur, its rivers and quays, wells and canals. Then the leading characters are introduced: 'Enlil is her young man, Ninlil is her young girl, Nunbaršegunu is her wise old woman' (lines 1–12). Ninlil begins by asking her mother's advice; she seems to have reached the marriageable state. Nunbarše-gunu informs her daughter that the women of Nippur purify themselves in the river. She warns her, however, not to go near the canal Inunbirdu, where Enlil will see her, get her pregnant and leave her. Ninlil seems to go straight down to this canal, where Enlil sets eyes on her and wants to kiss her. Ninlil resists his advances, telling him that she is too young and inexperienced in kissing. She also warns him, that if her mother found out, she would punish her and if her father found out, he would punish Enlil. In the next passage (35–43) Enlil discusses the situation with his vizier **Nusku**, who procures a boat for Enlil. In this boat he seems to sail to a certain place (unintelligible) and there he has intercourse with Ninlil and 'pours the seed of Suen-Ašimbabbar' (the moon-god, see **Nanna**) into her womb. Enlil then walks about the courtyard of his temple É. kur, when the 'fifty great gods and the seven fate-deciding gods' seize and expel him, because he has become 'impure' (Sum. $ú.zug_x$). He leaves town but Ninlil follows. Enlil stops at the city-gate and commands the gate-keeper not to disclose his whereabouts to Ninlil. When the goddess arrives and asks for this information, Enlil, in the guise of the gate-keeper, answers evasively. Ninlil then makes a proposition, emphasizing her present condition. Enlil makes a 'pronouncement of fate', which anticipates the outcome of his next move: 'May my royal seed go to heaven, may my royal seed go down to the earth/underworld' (lines 85–86). Thereupon he goes with Ninlil into a chamber and impregnates her with **Nergal**-Meslamta'ea. This whole scene, beginning with Enlil's dialogue with the gate-keeper, is repeated twice more, resulting in the conception of two further gods, **Ninazu** and **Enbilulu**. The text then ends in a paean for Enlil as the lord of abundance 'whose decrees cannot be altered', and a doxology praising 'mother Ninlil' and 'father Enlil'.

The message and context of this myth is subject to some controversy. Behrens proposes a ritual background: the yearly boat-journey from É.kur to the Tummal sanctuary in Nippur which would have had dramatic passages acted out. Others (Cooper) have argued against this and favour a sociological interpretation, the sanction of Enlil's rape of Ninlil by the great gods which seems to banish him to the underworld. The fruit of the rape is the moon-god and the subsequent three acts of intercourse provide substitutes for Enlil ('let my royal seed go down to the earth/underworld'). Both these views neglect the role of Ninlil who seems far from a passive victim. From a nubile girl she develops to the well-known figure of 'mother Ninlil' who bears Enlil many children. She seems aware of her condition in any of the successive episodes and is in all respects a match for Enlil. His impurity which causes the anger of the god may be due to his haste, omitting ritual purification, rather than a moral one.

Behrens 1978; Cooper 1980

Enlil and Sud

Sumerian myth, reconstructed from an Old Babylonian version from Nippur, plus a Middle Babylonian fragment and a bilingual text from Neo-Assyrian Nineveh. The unmarried Enlil is looking everywhere for a suitable wife. In Ereš he meets the beautiful young goddess Sud on the road and makes advances to her. He is indignantly rejected. Thereupon Enlil promises to marry her and demands a kiss. Sud disappears into her parents' house and Enlil returns to Nippur. He proceeds to send **Nusku**, his vizier, to Sud's mother Nanibgal to officially ask for her daughter's hand. He promises the usual gifts and a rich dowry for the future wife. She is also to share his exalted position as the ruler of the gods. The mother too will be assigned an influential position, she will have control 'over the life of the people'. In addition, Nusku is told to slip Sud a personal present of Enlil's in secret. Nusku accomplishes his mission, Enlil's offer is accepted, and Nanibgal asks Enlil to send his sister Aruru 'to explain the young bride the house'. He sends Aruru (though now she is called **Ninmah**) with an enormous caravan bearing his gifts (there are wild and domestic animals, milk products, honey, fruit, metals and jewels). After a gap in the text, Sud is led to Enlil's temple in Nippur. She is told of the happiness she will find in Enlil's love. Upon her arrival, someone (Aruru?) pours oil over Sud's face, then she consummates the marriage on the 'shining bed'. Afterwards Enlil decrees her fate and assigns her various divine functions. He calls her **Nintu**, 'the Lady who gives Birth', **Ašnan**, 'Grain', and finally she is **Ninlil**, the great wife of Enlil, queen of Nippur.

Civil, in Sasson, 1984 43–64; Lambert, in Sasson 1984, 64–6; Wilcke 1987, 179ff

Enmerkar and Enšuhkešdanna

Sumerian literary composition from the Ur III period, featuring Enmerkar, a historical king of Uruk, the goddess **Inanna**, and the lord of Uruk's great rival city, Aratta. It forms part of the so-called 'Geste d'Uruk', which also includes **Enmerkar and the Lord of Aratta**, the story of **Lugalbanda** and **Gilgameš and the Akka of Kiš**.

The text begins with a description of the wealth and beauty of Uruk, which is said to be greatly superior to Aratta's. The lord of Aratta, however, challenges Enmerkar to surrender to him. He declares himself to be the 'true bridegroom' of the goddess Inanna. When the message is brought to Enmerkar, he is furious and swears that only he, as the king of Uruk, has a legitimate right to Inanna. When Enšuhkešdanna hears this reply he assembles a council in order to decide how to proceed against Enmerkar. A 'sorcerer' (*maš.maš*) volunteers, and is dispatched to Ereš (near Uruk), where he dries up the milk supply in the 'holy stables of **Nisaba**'. As a result, the milk production stops and the distraught shepherds leave the folds and ask the sun-god **Utu** for help. The *maš.maš* then goes down to the river. But a wise old woman from Ereš, called Sagburru, arrives and the two specialists in the magic arts begin a contest of transformations. Each throws a metal object into the river. The sorcerer pulls out a carp, whereupon the woman pulls out an eagle which seizes the carp. Next he brings forth a ewe and its lamb, she produces a wolf that devours them both. This pattern is repeated three more times, with Sagburru's predators carrying off the domestic animals produced by the *maš.maš*. The magician admits defeat. The old woman

49

reprimands him for his interference with the goddess's milk supply and throws him into the river to kill him. When Enšuhkešdanna hears about the outcome of the contest, he sends a message to Enmerkar, declaring that he acknowledges his superiority. The text closes with the doxology 'Nisaba be praised'.

Alster 1973, 101–10; Berlin 1979

Enmerkar and the Lord of Aratta

Sumerian 'epic', preserved on some twenty tablets dating from the Old Babylonian period which originate from Nippur. It is a difficult text and several interpretations exist which differ quite markedly from each other. The following synopsis follows Alster.

The first thirty lines are badly broken; they seem to contain a preamble about the origin of Uruk. Lines 30–32 seem to summarize the outcome of the story; '(But) (Inanna) did not favour him like (she favoured) the lord of Kullab./ The people of) Aratta [brought down] stone for É-anna, /built the ... for the pure Inanna.' The actual narrative begins with a speech by Enmerkar, the king of Uruk (he is also called the 'son of **Utu** and the 'brother of **Inanna**'). He wants the people of Aratta to come to his city, with lapis lazuli, jewels and 'stones from the mountains', and to build him temples and chapels in Uruk, as well as the **Apsu**-temple in Eridu. Inanna graciously consents to help him and announces that all will be as he wishes. She advises him to send a messenger across the mountains and deserts to Aratta. There he is to prostrate himself and deliver a message which is partly an overt threat (l. 120, 'I will surely destroy this place like it has never been destroyed'), partly a spell (the 'spell of Enki'; 135–150). [gap] The 'word-wise' herald duly crosses the seven mountains and delivers his message before the Lord of Aratta. This ruler, who is not called by any name in this text, rejects the summons to Uruk, saying that he too has a special relationship with the goddess Inanna. The herald replies that while this may well be the case, Inanna had been made the 'queen of É-anna' at Uruk and had promised its king Enmerkar that Aratta would submit. This causes some shock to the Lord of Aratta, but he declares that the use of warfare should be avoided and that the two rivals should have recourse to a contest. He sets him some tasks which are seemingly impossible to perform. Should Enmerkar succeed in solving them, he would readily submit to him, as it would prove that Inanna had indeed forsaken him. He first asks Enmerkar to send him large amounts of grain, transported solely on donkeys in sacks with large meshes. Enmerkar solves this problem by making the holes smaller with wicker-work and sends his herald to Aratta with the grain. He also gives him a sceptre, which he is to present to the Lord as a sign of vassalage. The famished people of Aratta are delighted with the grain and ready to go to Uruk, but the Lord of Aratta demands to have carnelian delivered to him and a sceptre that 'is not made of wood and not called a sceptre'. The herald goes back to Uruk and Enmerkar consults the omens. He plants out some reed which he cuts down after 'five, ten years' have passed. He then sends his herald out again with the sceptre, which was presumably fashioned from the reed. Once in Aratta, the herald just holds it aloft and its sight inspires fear, convincing the Lord that Inanna favours Uruk. Nevertheless, he is not ready to yield, for he challenges Enmerkar to send a fighting dog (or man?) without any natural colours, to do battle with one of his own. Upon his arrival in Uruk, Enmerkar accepts the challenge and sends back his herald with a threefold message, which he inscribes on a tablet of clay, since the herald is unable to remember it (Enmerkar is here credited with the invention of writing!). Firstly, so the message goes, he agrees to the combat trial, secondly, he demands again the silver, gold, precious stones and lapis lazuli for the goddess in Uruk, and thirdly, he repeats the threat of total annihilation should Aratta not comply and send its people to build his shrines. The herald delivers the tablet safely. Then something unexpected happens; the rain-god **Iškur** heaps up 'wheat growing of itself' in the courtyard of Aratta. This greatly cheers the Lord of Aratta and he exclaims that this is proof that the goddess Inanna had not completely abandoned him and his city. The rest of the story is obscure because of the damaged state of the tablets. A champion (or dog) appears covered in a cloth without natural colours. The rites of **Dumuzi** are mentioned and a young maid dressed in white is brought out. The rest is even more fragmentary, but the conclusion, according to the initial 'synopsis', seems to be that the people of Aratta will bring the desired stones and gems and build the temples in Uruk and Eridu, thereby establishing the fruitful exchange of goods between the two cities.

Kramer 1952; Alster 1973, 101–9; Berlin, in Sasson 1984, 17–24

Enmeš and Enten

'Summer and Winter', Sumerian myth in the form of a 'disputation'. The text is only fragmentary due to the poor state of preservation of the Ur III tablets.

When the great god **Enlil** had conceived the 'idea' of making the earth fertile with plants and animals, he created two brothers, Enmeš and Enten, to bring it to completion. Enten caused 'the ewe to give birth to the lamb, the goat to give birth to the kid, cow and calf to multiply, fat and milk to increase'. He populated the steppe with wild donkeys, sheep and goats, filled the sky with birds and the rivers with fish. He planted palm-groves, fruit-trees and laid out gardens. Enmeš took over from there, he 'made wide the stalls and sheep-fold', 'caused abundant harvest to be brought in the houses' and finally founded 'cities and habitations' and caused houses to be built as well as 'temples high as mountains'. Having accomplished their tasks, the brothers come to Nippur and present gifts to Enlil, which symbolize their achievements. Enmeš brings wild and domestic animals and plants, Enten offers precious metals and stones, trees and fish. They start to quarrel and present their case to Enlil. The final verdict is that Enten, who is in charge of the irrigation, the basis of Sumerian agriculture, can justly call himself 'farmer of the gods'. The brothers acknowledge this decision, Enmeš bends his knee to Enten and then they exchange gifts and pour out libations to Enlil.

Kramer 1961, 49–51; 1963, 218–20

Enuma eliš, Akkad. 'When above'.

Initial line and title of a long Babylonian text (see **Cosmogonies**). Modern translations of the *enuma eliš* are based on Neo-Assyrian and Neo-Babylonian tablets found at Aššur, Nineveh, Kiš and Uruk, but the text probably goes back to the Second Dynasty of Isin (c. 12th C BC).

The recitation of the *enuma eliš* formed an integral part of the New Year ceremonies at Babylon, and by extension, in Assyria, where the god **Aššur** was the main protagonist. Although it has been called 'A Babylonian Genesis' (Heidel), the main portion of the composition is taken up with the deeds and glorification of **Marduk** and his city, Babylon. The theological purpose of the text was to justify Marduk's position as the 'greatest' among the great gods. Traditional mythological concepts and narratives, which originally concerned other deities (most notably **Enlil** and **Ninurta**) were re-worked to form a coherent sequence of events which culminate in the divine sanction for Marduk's pre-eminence.

The first lines describe the primordial time 'when above the heaven had not (yet) been named/ below the earth had not (yet) been called by name, the primeval **Apsi**, their begetter,/ MUMMU (and) Tiamat, who gave birth to them all/ (still) mingled their waters'. The combination of the sweet and salty waters is the creative 'material' for all subsequent generations of gods, which become successively stronger and more differentiated (Lahmu and Lahamu – Anšar and Kišar – then **Anu** who creates **Enki/Ea**). The young gods are restless, 'moving and roving about' incessantly. This disturbs the passive quiet of their ancestors, especially of Apsu, who decides to destroy his noisy offspring, while Tiamat counsels him to be more tolerant. Mummu, the 'vizier' of Apsu, however, supports the idea and proceeds to devise a plan which should annihilate the troublesome gods. But Ea, 'the wise', divines their intentions. He draws a magic circle around them all and recites such a powerful spell over Apsu that he falls into a deep and eternal slumber. Ea removes the tiara and the 'divine splendour' of his fallen enemy and turns to subdue Mummu, who offers no resistance. Ea then installs himself in the watery depth that Apsu had become and this is where his wife **Damkina** gives birth to **Marduk**, 'the wisest of the gods'. He is not only wise, but exceedingly powerful, with gigantic limbs, four heads and 'clothed in the rays of the sun'. However, 'he causes waves and disturbs Tiamat'. The other primeval gods reproach her for not having lifted a finger to aid Apsu and she herself complains about the restlessness of the younger gods, who disturb their sleep. Tiamat consents to do battle this time and they prepare for it by creating monsters, serpents and dragons 'crowned in awe-inspiring glory'. She appoints Kingu, her first-born, to be their leader. Tiamat's activities do not escape the vigilance of Ea and he reports it to Anšar, who commissions Ea to do something about it. The text is here too damaged to allow a translation, but Ea has not been successful since Anšar now charges Anu to talk to Tiamat. Anu does not manage to get near enough to the angry goddess and the assembled gods are dejected: 'No god whatever can do battle/ and escape with his life from the presence of Tiamat'. Ea now calls his son Marduk and reveals to him in private that it is his destiny to overcome their enemies. Marduk joyfully consents, but he stipulates that in exchange for this deed he shall have supreme command of the gods, that his utterance shall determine the destinies henceforth and that his creations shall be unaltered. His exaltation has to be agreed by the first generation of gods. Lahmu and Lahamu consent in view of the impending destruction by Tiamat and her host. Marduk tries out the power of his command on a piece of garment, which he conjures up with his word, destroys with a command and restores again. The gods then give him irresistible weapons: a bow and arrows, a club, a net and the seven winds. With these winds he raises up a terrible storm and a flood. He then harnesses his chariot with a team of four, 'sharp of tooth, bearing poison', and approaches the raging Tiamat. At first he too is dismayed by her awesome appearance and his helpers are stunned at the sight. But then he raises the rain flood and addresses Tiamat, challenging her to a single combat. She screams in fury, recites an incantation and then they close in upon each other. 'Marduk spreads out his net and enmeshes her/ the evil wind, following after he let loose on her face./When Tiamat opened her mouth to devour him/ he drove in the evil wind, in order that (she should) not (be able) to close her lips./The raging winds filled her belly.' He then looses an arrow which pierces her heart, casts down her carcass and stands upon it. Her monstrous army disperses, but Marduk catches them all in his net, including Kingu. From him he takes the 'tablets of destinies' and fixes them to his own breast, legitimized by his seal. Then he turns on Tiamat, his vanquished enemy. He crushes her skull with his club, severs her arteries and then splits open her body, 'half of her he set in place and formed the sky (therewith) as a roof'. He posts guards, commanding them not to let her waters escape. He measures the Apsu and establishes its heavenly counterpart, the *ešarra*, the residence of Anu, Enlil and Ea. Marduk also creates the stars and the signs of the zodiac, thereby dividing the year into twelve months. He fixes the moon in the zenith of the sky and determines its monthly cycle in relation to the sun. Then he turns his attention to the earth, which he makes from the lower body of Tiamat, plus some dust created by Anu. He fashions a great mountain of her head and out of her eyes run the Tigris and the Euphrates. Her nostrils become reservoirs and her breasts a range of hills. The tail of Tiamat he turns into a knot, which serves as a plug for the Apsu, thus preventing the waters of the deep from flooding the earth. He fixes solid pillars between heaven and earth and then turns to Anu, to hand over to him the 'tablets of destiny' for safe-keeping. The gods salute Marduk as their king and the official investiture follows. After a short gap the narrative continues. He calls for the guilty god to be delivered up to him and the gods produce Kingu, whom they charge with having encited Tiamat to her revolt. They bind him and cut his arteries and Ea creates mankind out of his blood mixed with earth and 'imposes the services of the gods (upon them) to set the gods free'. Marduk then proceeds to divide the **Anunnaki**, assigning three hundred to Anu in heaven and three hundred on earth (i.e. the underworld). In gratitude for having been relieved from their heavy work, the Anunnaki propose to build Marduk a suitable sanctuary which he graciously accepts, naming it 'Babylon'. The Anunnaki immediately set to work and in a year they complete the temple É-.sagila and the ziggurat, as well as shrines for themselves. The gods then sit down to celebrate and solemnly decree the destinies and omens. The remainder of the text is a recitation of the 'fifty names of Marduk' – which establish the comprehensive responsibilities of the god.

Translations: Heidel 1942; Speiser, in Pritchard 1955, 60–72; Dalley 1989, 228–77; articles: Lambert 1965; Labat, in Labat, Caquot, Scznycer 1970, 36–70; Cassin, in Bonnefoy 1981, 230–4; Bottéro 1985, 113–63; W.G. Lambert, in Hecker, Sommerfeld 1985, 65f

Ereškigal – Sumerian goddess of the Underworld

Her name means 'Lady of the great place' (a euphemism for the realm of the dead). It is already mentioned in Old Sumerian offering lists, and temples dedicated to her are known from the Ur III period, such as the *ki* [d] *babbar.è* and the *ki.nam.tar.ri.da*, 'place of the fate' at Ur.

While hymns and prayers to the goddess are rare, and her cult was probably not as important as that of the chthonic god **Nergal** (certainly in the second millennium BC), she plays a significant role in several mythological narratives. In **Gilgameš, Enkidu and the Netherworld**, Ereškigal receives the underworld as her share following the creation of the world. In the myth of **Inanna's Descent** she is the sole and terrifying ruler of the dead, who fastens the 'eye of death' on those who enter her domain. She is **Inanna**'s sister and counterpart, in some ways a negative mirror-image of the Sumerian goddess of procreation. She is therefore liable to frustration – her husband **Gugalanna** seems to be dead, and the special creatures fashioned by Enki have to commiserate with her on her 'labour-pains'. Her sexual deprivation is even more pronounced in the Akkadian version, **Ištar's Descent**, where she falls for the eunuch Asušunamir, who thereby obtains the body of Inanna, 'having made her happy'.

During the Old Babylonian period, Ereškigal was proclaimed as the wife of Nergal; several religious texts refer to the couple as 'the **Enlil** and **Ninlil** of the Netherworld'.

The myth NERGAL AND EREŠKIGAL is preserved on Middle Babylonian tablets (from Amarna), as well as some Neo-Assyrian ones found at Sultantepe. It describes how Nergal came to be the lord of the underworld. This myth too makes use of Ereškigal's sexual and emotional vulnerability; it becomes a reason for her loss of authority.

The beginning is lost, but it probably describes a banquet held in heaven. **Anu** would like to invite Ereškigal, but as according to the laws of the underworld, she is unable to leave her realm, he sends Kaku, his messenger, to bring her down some food. Kaku descends the long stairway to the underworld and is well received by Ereškigal. She in turn sends up her vizier, Namtar. There is another lacuna in the text, which resumes with **Ea** admonishing Nergal for not having shown enough respect to Namtar. It seems that Nergal was summoned to Ereškigal for this lack of civility. Ea helps him to prepare for the journey; he gives him a magic staff and furthermore he is warned to avoid giving any more offence (for the taboos of the underworld, see **Enkidu, Gilgameš and the Underworld**). Most of all, he is not to 'do what is normal for man and woman', when confronted with the goddess. Nergal descends and is admitted to the underworld, where he passes through the seven gates. Nergal turns down any offers of rest and food as advised by Ea, but when Ereškigal reveals her body to him after her bath, he succumbs; 'passionately they get into bed' and spend 'seven days and nights' together. Nergal seeks for a pretext to go back to heaven and manages to obtain Ereškigal's permission. Upon his arrival in heaven, Ea realizes what has happened and foresees that Ereškigal will be looking for Nergal. He therefore changes the god's appearance into that of an old man. Indeed, Ereškigal is in the throes of love ('I was not sated with his charms and he has left me') and she commands Namtar to ascend to heaven again, to fetch her lover back. She gives him a message to relay to Anu: 'Since I, thy daughter was young, I have not known the play of maidens (...) [That god whom] thou didst send and who had intercourse with me, let him lie with me'. She goes on to plead with the great gods of heaven to return Nergal to her, as she is not able 'to determine the verdicts of the great gods of the underworld' in her state of sexual impurity. And as a threat she adds that should they fail to deliver the god, she will 'send up the dead that they devour the living'. When Namtar first goes up to heaven he does not recognize Nergal in his changed form, but Ereškigal sees through Ea's trick and asks for the old and lame god to be sent. Finally, Nergal has to obey. He is led down and through the underworld, where he has to deposit an article of his attire at each gate (see **Innana's Descent**). When he enters the courtyard, he laughs, determined to assert his authority. He drags Ereškigal off the throne by her hair, before passionately making love to her for another seven days. Meanwhile Anu has made his decision. He sends Kaka down again with the decree that Nergal is to stay with her for ever. (Speiser, Dalley).

The Akkadians assimilated their own Semitic underworld goddess,

Allatum, to Ereškigal (first mentioned in Old Babylonian god-list). In the first millennium BC the goddess is sometimes referred to as Laz (^{d} la-az).

Speiser, in Pritchard 1975, 5–17; Lambert, in Alster (ed.) 1980, 62f; Dalley 1989, 165–81

Erra Akkadian god

He is well known since the Sargonic period and his name is probably related to Akkad. *erēru* 'to be dry, to become dried up'. As such he seems to be originally a personification of various phenomena associated with the scorching sun – parched fields, spontaneous fires in the steppe, famine as a result of drought etc. He is also a warrior god (one of his most common epithets is *qarrâd ilî* – 'warrior of the gods'), but he tends towards anarchy and rebellion, bringing pestilence as the by-product of warfare. On the other hand, he has some traits of a **Weather-god**, since he controlled floods and mountain streams and as such affected the fertility of the land; especially the steppe. All these functions are also typical for chthonic gods and indeed Erra was first identified with the Sumerian **Šulpa'e** and then with **Nergal**. He was worshipped in the great centre of the Underworld-cult, Kutha. The Babylonian god-lists cite **An** as his father, and his consort is the underworld goddess **Ereškigal** or **Mamitum**.

The Akkadian **Erra myth** was recorded in the 8th century BC (tablets come mainly from Nineveh, Assur and Sultantepe). The colophon mentions a scribe called Kabti-ili-Marduk, who eports that the god **Išum** had dictated him the text in a dream. The text was also perserved on tablets found in Babylon, Ur and Tell Haddad; extracts were furthermore written on amulets to ward off evil. It is an example of a literary composition, which uses the structure of a myth to convey a theological explanation for disastrous historical events (probably the 'dark age' at the beginning of the first millennium BC) (Lambert 1984). The lack of dramatic tension, however, and the structure which is basically a succession of monologues, may point to oral performance (Dalley). The characterization of the gods, especially Erra and even **Marduk**, has traits of satirical exaggeration.

The text beings with a poetic introduction, introducing Erra and his entourage, his 'captain' **Išum** and the dangerous 'Seven' (**Sibitti**). Then these Seven speak up and address the retired Erra, who lives comfortably with his wife in the underworld. They wax nostalgically about the comradeship of the soldier's life, reminding him that his weapons have become rusty. As the god of war, he ought to be true to his nature, otherwise everyone will make fun of him. In short, it is time he started to fight again, since mankind is getting too noisy and disturbing the peace of the **Anunnaki**. Erra decides to comply with their wishes and ignores the pleas for moderation issued by Išum. In a long speech he decides to go and find **Marduk**, who 'has neglected his word and does as he pleases'. Once before Marduk, in his temple É-sagila, Erra expresses astonishment over the lacklustre state of the great god's statue and tiara. Marduk answers that he would have to procure various rare and precious materials in order to restore them to their proper splen-dour, but that he was unable to quit his residence. Last time he had done so, his absence had provoked a flood and all sorts of terrible calam-ities had befallen the earth. Erra cunningly offers to keep order in the universe during Marduk's departure and Marduk trustingly departs. The text becomes broken here, but it appears that Marduk is now divested of his 'radiance', i.e. his divine powers, and the usual order of things is upset ('darkness covers the day' etc.). Erra goes to see **Ea** in the **Apsu** and again the fragmentary state of the text makes it impossible to decide exactly what happens there; Erra seems to obstruct the craftsmen who are trying to restore Marduk's regalia. [gap] Disorder also affects the heavens; Erra's star (the Fox Star) is waxing bright, it portends evil for mankind. **Ištar** tries to placate Erra but he persists in his 'anger'. Erra launches into another monologue which reads like an evil incantation: '. . . I shall cover the face of the Moon in the middle of the night (. . .) I shall finish off the land and count it as ruins (. . .) I shall destroy moun-tains and fell the cattle (. . .) I shall fell people and leave no life (. . .) I shall let a [barbarian] enter a god's shrine where evil men should not go (. . .) I shall let a bad omen occur to devastate a city (etc.)'. It all adds up to a comprehensive description of the horrors of war as the exact oppo-site of the desirable state of affairs in times of peace and prosperity. Išum, who had listened to Erra's speech, feels compassion: 'Woe to the people against whom Erra rages' and addresses the god. He summarizes the catastrophic results of Erra's rule, but at the same time he flatters the god's vanity: even the great gods were afraid of him and in Babylon he caused civil war, inciting the 'lawless rabble' to violence and bloodshed, filling the river with corpses. (The speech includes several passages of direct speech, very much like the chorus responses in Greek drama.) He devastated other Babylonian cities, Uruk, Sippar and Dêr in a similar manner, severely disrupting the cult. Išum's 'eulogy' seems to work, since Erra now turns away from 'Akkad' (southern Mesopotamia) and lets Išum direct his destructive force towards the country's numerous enemies. Eventually, his anger subsides, and in the company of the great gods, he justifies himself by saying that it is in his nature to act as he did ('When I am enraged, I devastate people'). He praises Išum for his equanimity and accepts his vizier's suggestion that he should rest now. It is Išum who then utters a blessing over the devastated lands, making them again populous and fertile, as well as assuring the pre-eminence of Babylon (Bottéro, Cagni, Dalley).

Lambert 1957/58, 395–401; Cagni 1969; Roberts 1972, 21–9; Edzard, RLA IV 1976, 166–70; Cagni 1977; Bottéro 1977/78, in Bottéro 1985, 163–221; Lambert, in Sasson 1984, 211–16; Machinist, in Sasson 1984, 221–6; Dalley 1989, 282–316

eršemma

A type of Sumerian religious text of which many examples are known from the Old Sumerian down to the Neo-Assyrian period.

Eršemma compositions were written in the *emesal*, 'the woman's tongue' dialect of Sumerian, maybe because they were originally recited by female cult-personnel. From the Old Babylonian period onwards, *gala*-priests chanted them on certain days of the month 'as a constant vigil to prevent the anger of the gods over acts unknowingly committed by the king' (Cohen 1981, 6). The texts were part of a liturgy and therefore became embedded in the cultic tradition of the Babylonians, when other genres of Sumerian religious texts had become obsolete. *Eršemmas* can be lamentations over catastrophes such as the destruction of temples and the ensuing national calamities, or hymns of praise, and some incorporate mythological narratives. These deal mainly with **Dumuzi** and **Inanna**, although texts featuring **Nergal**, **Ninisina**, **Geštinanna** and Iškur are also known.

Cohen 1981

Eštan

Hattian sun-deity; Hittite Ištan: written logographically as (Sumerian) *ᵈutu*. The Hittite king refers to himself as 'my sun' (*ᵈUTUˢⁱ*) and on the rock-relief of Yazilikaya, near the old Hittite capital Hattusas, the sun-god of the sky is represented with a winged cap. In various texts, however, Eštan/Ištan appears with feminine adjectives or appellatives, e.g., *ᵈUTU-i SAL.LUGAL*, 'Oh sun-goddess, queen'. It is therefore uncertain whether this deity was a distinct god or just another name for the great **Sun-goddess of Arinna**. The Hurrian sun-god **Šimigi** was male and appears in various mythological compositions, such as **Kumarbi**, **Appu** and the Sun-god, the Cow and the Fisherman (see **Telepinu**).

Schuler, WdM 1965, 196–201; Neu 1974, 126ff; Fauth 1979, 227–63

Etana (*see figure 36*)

According to the Sumerian king-list, Etana was the twelfth post-diluvian king of Kiš, the 'Shepherd who Ascended to Heaven'. This seems to allude to an Akkadian myth which was transmitted from the Old Babylonian period onwards. There is also a Middle as well as a Neo-Assyrian version which is the most complete. The following synopsis is based on the recent translation by Dalley.

A prologue *in illo tempore* contains an account of the creation of Kish by the **Igigi** and **Anunnaki**. But the city still lacks a king. The goddess **Ištar** is 'searching high and low for a king'. **Enlil** looks 'for a throne-dais for Etana'. [gap of about 120 lines]. At the source of a river by a great tree, a serpent and an eagle have made their nests. The eagle offers his friendship and because the serpent does not trust the eagle, he insists that they swear an oath of loyalty before **Šamaš**. The object of their partnership is an equal distribution of food procured by hunting. All goes well, their respective young prosper, until one day the eagle plots to eat up the young of the serpent. His own offspring warn him against such sacrilege, but the eagle replies that he will just keep to the sky and the tree-tops, and proceeds to devour the young snakes. When the serpent comes back in the evening and discovers the empty nest, he cries out to Šamaš. The god hears his lament and tells the serpent of a ruse to ensnare the eagle. He is to kill a bull on the mountainside and hide inside the cadaver. When the greedy eagle alights, to pick at his favourite bits, the intestines, the serpent will be able to grab him, pluck his feathers and throw him in a deep pit. The eagle sees the tempting carcass and flies down to eat it, in spite of the warnings of his clever son who sees through the trick. The eagle is caught, and no appeals to either the serpent or Šamaš are of any avail. The sun-god only declares that the eagle has to bear the punishment for his wickedness, but he also tells him that he will send a man who will help. Etana (by now king of Kish) is still without an heir. Daily he prays to Šamaš, reminding the god how well he always fulfilled his sacrificial and ritual duties. He implores him to show him the Plant of Birth. Šamaš tells him of the imprisoned eagle, announcing that the bird should be able to help him. Etana sets out and discovers the eagle languishing in his pit. For 'seven months' he patiently feeds the creature until it regains its strength and can get out of the pit. But by that time the eagle has presumably grown new wings and is able to fly again. [gap] The bird asks Etana what it could do to help his friend. Etana mentions the Plant of Birth and the eagle sets out to look for it in the mountains. Since it is not to be found there, he volunteers to fly up to heaven, to consult **Ištar**, the mistress of birth. Etana gets on his back, holding on to the quills of the eagle's wings and up they go. The sight of the ever-diminishing countryside below makes Etana giddy and three times he slips off the back of the eagle, who always manages to catch him just before he falls to the ground. [gap] The first attempt obviously failed. Back in Kish, Etana as well as his wife dream about the Plant of Birth. The king describes how in his dream he and the eagle went through the gates of the great gods. In a house with open windows they saw a girl with a crown and the snarling lions under her throne sprang at him and he awoke. (The girl is obviously Ištar.) The eagle declares that the significance of this dream is clear to him and offers to carry Etana up to heaven again. This time he ties him on securely and they begin their ascent. Just as they enter the gate of **Sîn**, Šamaš, **Adad** and Ištar, the text breaks off. It seems likely that they did obtain the Plant of Birth from the goddess. There are as yet unconnected fragments, which concern the wife of Etana and their son Balih, who is also mentioned in the king-list, as well as the death of Etana, maybe in retribution for some crime.

Kinnier-Wilson 1985; Dalley 1989, 189–202; Farber 1989, 155

Exaltation

A type of theological text which exalts a deity above all others. The earliest literary example is the *Nin me šar.ra* or the Exaltation of **Inanna** (Hallo and van Dijk). It is said to have been written by Enheduanna, daughter of Sargon of Akkade, high-priestess at Ur (24th C BC), but may date from the much later Isin-Larsa period. The goddess is said to have become 'superior to An'. Other texts name **Nergal** (van Dijk 1966) as exercising the *ellilutu* (see **Enlil**) at Uruk, **Ninurta** in *lugal.e ud me.lam.bi nir.gal* (Lambert 1961) and most notably **Marduk** (*Enuma eliš*). It is tempting to see historical events behind such exaltations. The political success of a city was generally ascribed to the exertions of its local gods. Likewise, the founder of a new dynasty promulgated his personal, tutelary deity as the supreme god/dess of his realm as it substantiated his own claims for being chosen to lead. In this manner Sargon of

Akkade, for example, promoted the Semitic **Ištar** in a syncretism with the Sumerian **Inanna** as the patroness of his newly founded empire, and his educated daughter may well have supplied some of the theological *apologia*.

van Dijk 1966, 61f; Lambert, M. 1961, 185; Lambert, W.G. 1964, 3–13; Hallo and van Dijk 1968

F

Flood-myths

are part of the folklore and mythological repertoire of many cultures all over the world. Although the earliest written versions are from the Ancient Near East, it cannot be postulated that all deluge-myths originated there.

Calamitous floods, probably following earth tremors, were certainly a reality in Mesopotamia, as we know from the so-called 'flood-deposits' in the remains of ancient cities such as Ur. The Sumerian king-list is divided into ante- and post-diluvian stages; after the flood 'kingship came down from heaven again'. Among all the other catastrophes, such as drought, foreign invasions and pestilence, the deluge was considered the most devastating. It was the ultimate method of destruction ordained by the gods.

The SUMERIAN DELUGE-MYTH is the prototype of a number of later Akkadian stories. The main text dates from the late Old Babylonian period and is fragmentary, the beginning is lost. It may have contained a cosmogonic prelude and an account of the creation of mankind. Enki is speaking about the threatened destruction of mankind, but he plans to prevent this becoming reality. He wants the people back in their dwellings, the **Me**-endowed cities[1], with their restful shade. [gap] Column II describes the institution of Sumerian civilization, kingship, city-states and irrigation. [gap] **Nintu** and **Inanna** are said to weep for the people and **Enki** decides to save the situation, although the gods are formally bound by an oath to **Anu** and **Enlil**. Ziusudra is described as a humble and pious king. He is singled out by Enki to receive a secret revelation, announcing the 'unalterable decision' of the gods to send a flood. A further gap probably contained instructions on building a seaworthy craft. The text resumes with a flood raging for 'six days and seven nights'. But then the sun-god **Utu** appears in his boat to Ziusudra, who prostrates himself and offers sacrifices. [gap] The gods apparently re-populate the earth and when Ziusadra, 'who protected the seed of mankind . . . of destruction', does homage to An and Enlil, they grant him 'eternal life, like a god' and transport him to Dilmun, 'the place where the sun rises'. The rest of the text is missing. (Civil, in Lambert, Millard 1969, 138–45; Kramer 1983, 115–21.)

The broken state of the Sumerian text obscures the reason for sending the flood. This is explained at length in the Myth of Atra-hasis. This text, which is known from several fragments from the Old and Neo-Babylonian period, as well as from Neo-Assyrian tablets, is written in Akkadian. The Old Babylonian version is reputed to be the work of a scribe called Nur-Aya, from Sippar. The story begins *in illo tempore* when the 'toil of the gods was great' and the **Igigi** had to work for the great gods, the 'seven **Anunnaki**'. Enlil, 'the counsellor of the gods', faces a serious revolt by the Igigi who protest that their heavy workload is killing them. Enki intervenes and asks Bēlit-Ilî, the **Mother-goddess**, to fashion a man (called *lullû*), so that he may 'bear the yoke' and 'carry the burden of the gods'. The goddess answers that she is unable to create, as only Enki has the right skills. Enki addresses the great gods and reveals that he will institute purification rites on certain days of the month. He orders that 'one god be slaughtered so that all the gods may be cleansed in one dipping. From his flesh and blood let Nintu mix clay, that god and man may be thoroughly mixed in the clay' (208–213). The mother-goddess then proceeds to knead that special clay and the great gods spit into it for good measure. Then she announces the successful completion of her task and, assisted by Enki and the assembled birth-goddesses, she recites incantations and creates seven pairs, male and female. She decrees the right procedures for pregnancy, delivery and marriage and mankind is thereby able to reproduce itself and take over the tasks of providing food and labour for the gods. The flood-story proper begins after a break. 'Twelve-hundred years had yet not passed' and mankind had multiplied so quickly that their 'noise and bustle' disturbs the peace of the great gods (the same motif is used in the first tablet of the **Enuma eliš**). Enlil sends first a plague, then famine, in an attempt to decimate the number of people. But his plans are foiled by the subterfuge of Enki, who relays Enlil's intentions to his protégé Atra-hasis, 'the exceedingly wise'. He also informs him of the means to counteract the threat with appropriate measures (mainly by bringing special offerings to specific gods). Furious, Enlil decides to put an end to it all by sending a great and devastating flood, which would kill every single human being. He makes the gods swear a solemn oath of secrecy but Enki, anxious for the survival of 'his creation', appears to Atra-hasis in a dream, where he speaks to a reed-wall, thereby circumventing Enlil's prohibition by a trick. He tells Atra-hasis to build himself a boat and load it with his family and various species of animals. The flood is released, but Atra-hasis is safe in his boat. The gods are in distress, especially the mother-goddess, who bemoans the fate of her creatures. [gap] The smell of Ziusudra's first offering after the subsiding of the flood announces his survival. Enlil is furious at the betrayal, but Enki speaks up and points out that Enlil would have gone too far and that henceforth he ought to limit his acts of revenge on the criminals who disobey his commands. However, he proposes certain measures to limit the population. Again assisted by the mother-goddess he creates, or rather 'decrees', the existence of sterile women, special classes of priestesses barred from having progeny, as well as infant mortality personified by the child-snatching demon pašittu. Atra-hasis, like Ziusudra, is given eternal life and a place 'among the gods'. (Lambert and Millard 1969; Moran 1971, 51–61; Draffkorn-Kilmer 1972, 160–77; Oden, 1981, 21–37; Moran 1987, 245–56; Dalley 1989, 1–38.)

The ELEVENTH TABLET OF THE EPIC OF GILGAMEŠ (on the Ninivite recension), contains the longest and best known version of the flood-story which has several parallels in the Biblical account of Genesis. The story is told in the first person by the flood-hero Utnapištim. He tells **Gilgameš** that he was a citizen of Šuruppak, when he received a message from Ea through his brick-wall that the gods were about to bring on a deluge. The gods told him the exact measurement of the boat he was to build and even what excuse he was to use for his inquisitive fellow citizens, namely that he intended go to and 'live with Ea in the **Apsu**'. When the vessel was finished, he loaded it with gold and silver, his family and the species of all living creatures. The appointed time came, the rain started to pour down, the dams burst, the ground-water swelled up and the 'horror-cloud of **Adad** passed over the heavens', obliterating all light. The storm was so fierce that even the gods 'cowered like dogs and crouched at the outer defences of Anu's heaven'. After the seventh day, the flood subsided and Utnapištim opened a vent to look outside. He realized that his ship had grounded on Mount Nisir and after a week he let fly a dove which, finding no resting place, returned to the ship. The swallow fared no better, but when he released the raven, he 'ate and flew about and did not return'. Utnapištim then brought copious offerings, poured out libations and burnt sweet incense. 'The gods smelled the savour, the sweet savour, the gods gathered like flies about the priest and his offering.' The **Mother-goddess** arrived in great distress and vowed never to forget what had happened. She blamed Enlil for the almost total destruction of 'her people'. Enlil was furious that one human being did escape, but Ea managed to soothe him, chiding the great god at the same time that he ought to have sent the 'wolf or the lion to diminish mankind'. He also revealed that it was he himself who had communicated the plan of the gods to Utnapištim and engineered his escape. Enlil, assuaged, blessed the flood-hero and his wife and granted them eternal life.

Heidel 1954; Parrot 1955; Simoons 1974, 17–35; Dalley 1990

G

Galla – Sumerian underworld demons

The Galla appear in **Inanna's Descent** and the accounts of **Dumuzi**'s Death, where they are described as ruthless beings, who have none of the attachments and habits of living people and who make sure that nobody destined for the underworld can escape.

Geštinanna – Sumerian goddess

Her name means 'Lady of the Grape-vine'. She is part of the city pantheon of Lagash, where she is first mentioned by Eannatum, then also by Ur-bau and Gudea, who calls her the 'wife of **Ningišzida**'. She does not feature in any known personal names. Since the First Dynasty of Isin, the goddess was also known as *ga.ša.an dub.sar*, 'the scribe of the underworld', possibly by assimilation to the Akkadian **Bēlet-Ṣeri**. There is some evidence that during the Old Babylonian period she was one of the chief deities of Karāna (Tell al Rimah).

In mythological texts, Geštinanna appears as the sister of **Dumuzi** in **Dumuzi's Dream**, **Inanna's Descent** and related compositions. She is said to dwell in the steppe where she has a sheep-stall. When her brother is pursued by the underworld demons, she shelters and protects him there. At the very last, when he is finally captured, she offers herself to be taken instead of him. This act of unselfish love converts Dumuzi's death-sentence into a half-year sojourn in the underworld, with Geštinanna serving the other half. Her involvement with Dumuzi makes Geštinanna a very important figure in the Sumerian as well as Babylonian cult-literature, where she plays a prominent part among the mourners. She was called Belili and her most common epithet in this context is 'she who weeps continually'.

Carroué 1981, 121–36; Alster 1985, 219–28

Gibil – Sumerian god of fire, in Akkadian **Girra/u**

A very ancient deity, he appears already in the god-lists of Fara. Later he is mainly invoked in incantations and magic rituals as the purifying power of fire. He was called the son of **Enki**, himself a great god of exorcism. An Old Babylonian myth GIRRA AND ELAMATUM describes the fire-god as an exalted champion of the gods. He fights on their behalf against the 'woman of Elam' (a common designation for a witch), who is held responsible for a famine and the infertility of the herds. Girra overcomes her and **Enlil** decrees that Elamatum's body is to become a celestial feature. There is a festival to commemorate the event.

Edzard 1965, 68–9; Walker 1983, 145–52

Gilgameš (*see figure 44*)

A Sumerian king of Early Dynastic Uruk; he was later deified and became the hero of Mesopotamia's eponymous epic. His name (written as *ᵈgiš.bíl.gín.meš, ᵈgiš.bíl.ga.meš, ᵈgiš.bíl*) has been interpreted as 'the old man is (still) a young man', but that may be a late etymology referring to the Plant of Youth (see below). The Sumerian king-list calls him the son of the goddess **Ninsun** and mentions that his father was *lillu* (an 'unknown mortal'?) who later became a 'high priest of Kullab'. In the epic, **Lugalbanda** is his father.

Gilgameš appears as the recipient of ritual offerings in Old Sumerian texts from Lagaš. During the Ur III period he became known as a 'king of the underworld', 'who pronounces judgement and gives final decisions' on behalf of the sun-god **Šamaš**. The close relationship between Gilgameš and the sun-god might have led to an eventual solar interpretation of the hero himself. He was worshipped as a god at Nippur, Umma and Drehem.

There are five extant Sumerian compositions concerning Gilgameš. They were probably written down during the reign of the Isin kings, who had dynastic connections with Uruk and were interested in the heroic past of that city. The different versions of the various stories betray their origin in oral traditions, although there are some indications that literary versions existed as early as the Fara period (Bing 1977), 1–4.

Gilgameš and Agga

Sumerian title: *lú.kin.gi₄ra*, 'The man of Sumer'. As far as the plot is concerned, this text stands apart from the other Gilgameš tales by its affinity with the so-called 'Geste d'Uruk' (see **Enmerkar and the Lord of Aratta, Enmerkar and Ensuhkešdana, Lugalbanda**). These compositions are mainly concerned with political rather than mythological subject-matter: warfare, international trade and diplomatic negotiations. The text describes how Gilgameš, as king of Uruk, dealt with the aggressive Agga of Kish, who came to besiege him in his city. It seems that the Kishites had the advantage initially, but by some trick or subterfuge, involving one of his men, Girišhurduru, who distracts the besiegers' attention, Gilgameš is able to get hold of Agga. In the end, however, he pardons his adversary and sends him home, declaring that he is returning a favour once received by Agga.

Romer 1980; Cooper 1981, 224–41; Heimpel 1981, 242–3; Klein, in Sasson 1984, 201–4; Katz 1987, 105–14

Gilgameš and the Land of the Living

Translates the Sumerian title: *en.e.kur.lú.ti.la.šè*, it is also called **Gilgameš and Huwawa** and **Gilgameš and the Cedar Forest**. The text is preserved on tablets from different sources, mainly Nippur and Uruk, with considerable variations.

The summary follows the translation and interpretation by van Dijk. Gilgameš, accompanied by his servant **Enkidu** and fifty warriors of Uruk, sets out to the 'Land of the Living', which in the later epic is referred to as the Cedar Forest. Although this is not spelled out in the text, it is a place of dread, and sacred to the great god **Enlil**, who has placed his creature Huwawa in charge of it. The motives given for this expedition are the desire to win fame ('to make a name for myself') and to declare the loyalty to 'the gods'. Gilgameš' god is the sun-god **Utu** and it is him whom he asks for guidance. They cross 'seven mountains' and reach the forest. Enkidu hesitates to enter, but Gilgameš presses on. He commands his men to cut down the trees in spite of the terrible rays of the sevenfold 'divine splendour' (*melam*), which Huwawa sends against them. In the end they capture Huwawa, who pleads for his life in a very personal and moving manner, appealing to the generous heart of Gilgameš, who is prepared to spare him. Enkidu, however, advises Gilgameš not to trust Huwawa and when the captive speaks of him in a dismissive tone, he is so overcome with fury that he cuts off the creature's head. The next thing the two heroes do, is go to Enlil (in Nippur presumably). Defiantly they present to him the severed head and the enraged Enlil pronounces a curse on the offenders. He fashions the

69

seven *melam* of the slain Huwawa into agents of revenge and danger to persecute Gilgameš and Enkidu.

van Dijk, in Garelli 1960, 69–81; de Jong Ellis 1982/83, 123ff; Shaffer, in Sasson 1984, 307–13

Gilgameš and the Bull of Heaven

The text is still only known from some small fragments and seems to contain most of the story later told in full on Tablet VI of the Epic (see below). The goddess **Inanna** makes advances to Gilgameš, but quite unlike other epic kings of Uruk, such as **Enmerkar** or **Lugalbanda**, he rejects her offers with insults. The spurned goddess sends the giant Bull of Heaven to avenge this blatant lack of respect, but Gilgameš kills the Bull. (Since the $gu_4.an.na$, the Bull of Heaven, was the name for the constellation of Taurus, this may be an etiological account of the zodiacal sign and its position.)

Kramer 1944, 15

Gilgameš, Enkidu and the Netherworld

Also called 'Gilgameš and the Huluppu-tree'. Relations with Inanna are markedly different in this tale. The text begins with a prologue referring to the 'days remote', when light and everything else was first created. A *huluppu*-tree grew at the banks of the Euphrates, but as the south wind was constantly tearing at its branches, the goddess Inanna took it away to replant it in the gardens of her shrine in Uruk. She tended it well because she meant to have a bed and a chair made from its wood. When the tree is matured, Inanna wants to cut it down but finds herself unable to do so as the tree is now inhabited by three demonic creatures. At the base lives a serpent 'who knows no charm', the **Anzu**-bird has its nest in the crown and the 'maid of desolation', Lilit, lives in the middle. Inanna is bitterly disappointed and goes to her brother **Utu** for help. Utu, however, says he can do nothing for her and the goddess relates her tale again to Gilgameš, who agrees to assist Inanna. He promptly dons his heavy armour and with his mighty battleaxe kills the snake, whereupon Lilit and the Anzu-bird take flight. The tree is cut down and presented to Inanna for her ritual furniture. Of the base of the *huluppu*-tree the goddess makes an object called *pukku* and of the crown another called *mukku*. The following twelve lines describe what Gilgameš does with these implements, but their translation is far from certain. It may have something to do with the dead or their spirits, for the text states that 'because of the cry of the young maidens' the *pukku* and *mukku* fall into the underworld. Gilgameš is disconsolate over their loss and his servant Enkidu, who has heard his master's laments, offers to fetch them. Gilgameš is overjoyed but he warns Enkidu of the dangers involved, and gives him detailed instructions on how to behave in a place where all the rules applying to the world of the living are changed into their exact opposites. Enkidu, however, does not heed this advice and manages to break every single taboo of the underworld. As a consequence he has to remain there for ever. Gilgameš, greatly troubled, goes to Nippur to consult **Enlil**, who in turn refers him on to **Enki** in Eridu. Enki orders Utu to open a hole in the ground, and there emerges Enkidu's shadow, who tells Gilgameš about the underworld. Those with only one son are badly treated, those with three 'have water to drink' and those with seven 'are close to the gods', while those whose bodies lie unburied 'can find no rest'.

Kramer 1944, 33–7; Schott, Soden 1958, 101–6; Kramer, in Garelli 1960, 66–7; Liagre-Böhl, in Oberhuber 1977, 254

The Death of Gilgameš

is a title devised by Kramer for several very fragmentary texts which may belong to a very extensive text of some 450 lines. It is still doubtful whose death is actually meant; it may well be Enkidu's.

Kramer, in Pritchard 1950, 50–2

The Gilgameš Epic (*see figure 37*)

As it is presented in modern translations (Pritchard, Penguin Classics, Soden, etc.), the epic is composed of a variety of sources. The most extensive text (some 1,500 lines) is the so-called Ninivite recension from Ashurbanipal's 'library', which is divided into twelve tablets. It goes back to a Middle Babylonian text, usually ascribed to the scribe Sin-leqqe-unnini, except for the twelfth tablet, which is only found in the Ninivite version.

The second most important edition and also the oldest written in Akkadian, is the Old Babylonian (c. 470 lines). Then there is a Neo-Babylonian version preserved on various fragments (c. 40–50 lines), and a Neo-Assyrian one slightly older than the Ninivite text, also in several fragments. In addition to these texts which come from Mesopotamia, several tablets with some small portions of text are known from the cuneiform archives found in Boğazköy (the ancient Hittite capital Hattusa), the Syrian site of Sultantepe, and Megiddo in Israel – these are all from the middle of the second millennium BC.

The text still offers great difficulties and even the plot is far from certain in many respects. More than any other literary text of the Ancient Near East, the story of Gilgameš served also as a vehicle for certain religious and proto-philosophical concerns which motivated the scribes of the various epochs of the epic's transmission. It was further modified by the re-telling of the narrative in an independent oral tradition which must have produced a variety of modifications. The tenor of each version, as it was written or told in the different parts and epochs of the ancient Near Eastern world, was therefore quite distinct and any modern 'composite' translation obscures the original intent and 'flavour' of the individual compositions.

Garelli 1960; Tigay 1982

The following synopsis is based on the Ninivite recension, then follows a brief account of the Old Babylonian one.

Tablet 1. The introduction (1–12) describes the mission of Gilgameš, who is described as 'he who saw everything, experienced everything', who went on a long journey and engraved all his 'toil' on a tablet. He built the wall of É-anna in Uruk which 'no future man can rival'. The story proper begins on col.II. Gilgameš, who is 'two-thirds god and one-third man', is the lord of Uruk. He oppresses his citizens by his insistence of seigneurial rights in respect to the 'young maids and the young men'. The people's complaints are heard by **Anu**, who instructs the **Mother-goddess**, Aruru, to fashion a match for Gilgameš and she creates **Enkidu**, the wild man of the steppe, 'who knows nothing of people or land'. A huntsman observes the strange man covered in hair, who eats grass with the beasts and sets the trapped animals free. He asks advice of his father, who sends him to Gilgameš with a message about the strength and valour of Enkidu. He also tells him how to deal with the wild man by sending out a prostitute called Šamhat, 'the Voluptuous', to charm him. The huntsman does as bidden and relates all to the king of Uruk, who dispatches him with the prostitute. They reach the watering place, she takes off her clothes and when Enkidu draws near, she embraces him and they make passionate love for six days and seven nights. The effect of this sexual encounter is as predicted by the hunter's father: he has become alienated from his previous companions, the wild animals. The prostitute consoles him by telling Enkidu of Gilgameš, who at this moment is dreaming of him. The scene switches to Uruk, where Gilgameš relates his dreams to his mother, **Ninsun**. In the first dream Gilgameš sees a heavy object fall from the sky which he is unable to lift. He experiences a powerful sexual attraction towards it. The second dream is virtually the same, except that it is an axe (for the significance of these objects as a punning reference to homosexuality, see Draffkorn-Kilmer 1982). Ninsun explains that what he saw was a man, who was to become his best friend and companion in need.

Tablets 2, 3 and 4 are very fragmentary. They contained the story of the expedition against Humbaba (Huwawa – see also the Sumerian '**Gil-gameš and the Land of the Living**', above). Gilgameš and Enkidu decide to go to the cedar-forest, 'to slay the fierce Humbaba', whom it was said previously was under Ellil's special protection. The elders advise caution and the two friends proceed to the temple É-galmah, to ask Ninsun to intercede with **Šamaš** on her son's behalf, as the aim of their journey is to 'destroy from the land all the evil which Šamaš abhors'. Ninsun offers incense etc. and then the text breaks off again. (A Late-Babylonian fragment describes the long journey.)

In tablet 4 the heroes have arrived at the gates of the cedar-forest. The gates are guarded by a magic spell and Enkidu's hand withers as he touches them.

Tablet 5. 'They beheld the cedar-mountain, the dwelling-place of the gods, the throne of Irnini (Ištar?)'. Again the text is mutilated. It probably contained three dreams by Gilgameš which Enkidu interprets (some of these dreams and the encounter with Humbaba are preserved on tablets from the Hittite archives). With the help of Šamaš and the winds, the two heroes overcome Humbaba. Enkidu cuts off his head although, as in the Sumerian version, the defenceless Humbaba pleads for his life and Gilgameš is inclined to spare him. Humbaba curses Enkidu and has his head cut off, which the heroes bring to Uruk.

Tablet 6. The victorious friends are back in Uruk. Gilgameš puts on his festive robes, his crown and the goddess **Ištar** appears. She asks him to be her consort and promises him success in warfare and fertility for his herds. In an extraordinary retort, Gilgameš rejects her offers, quoting a number of appropriate proverbs and finally enumerating various famous human and animal lovers of the goddess, who all had to suffer a tragic fate. Surely she would treat him like them, he concludes. The furious goddess rushes to her father Anu and threatens to smash down the door of the underworld unless he creates for her the Bull of Heaven. Anu demands that she provides enough food and grain for the next seven years and finally accedes to his daughter's demand. The mighty Bull of

Heaven descends, killing hundreds of people with each snort of his nostrils. Enkidu and Gilgameš, however, overcome the great beast; they tear out his heart which they offer to Šamaš. Ištar appears again to curse the two men who had killed the Bull. Enkidu pulls off the right 'thigh' of the dead beast and tosses it before her, exclaiming that he would serve her the same way if he could. While Ištar and her maids lament, the two friends are cheered by the inhabitants of Uruk and retire to celebrate.

Tablet 7. Enkidu has an ominous dream. It reveals that he is to be sentenced to death by the great gods for his part in the killing of Humbaba and the Bull of Heaven (only preserved on the Hittite version). At any rate, Enkidu falls sick and reviewing the fateful stages of his life, he invokes Šamaš to curse the agents of his present doom, from the door at the gate of the cedar-forest which lamed his hand, to the prostitute and the hunter who first saw him in the steppe. Šamaš points out the glorious aspects of his friendship with Gilgameš and tells him how his friend will mourn him by donning the skin of a lion and roaming the steppe. Enkidu, appeased, turns his curses into blessings.

Tablet 8. But he is still haunted by dreams, he has visions of the under-world and its denizens, which he recounts to Gilgameš. When he dies, Gilgameš is overcome with sorrow and addresses the elders of Uruk with his lament, recounting the happy days he had spent with Enkidu and their shared adventures. (The mourning ceremony and burial are lost.) Gilgameš, as in Enkidu's dream, throws off his princely robes and puts on a lion-skin, and brings offerings to the sun-god (the remainder of the tablet is destroyed).

Tablet 9 begins with the first of several identical speeches by Gilgameš, which he will address to various people in the course of his lonely wanderings, giving the reason for his journey and unusual appearance. 'When I shall die, shall I not be like Enkidu?' 'I am afraid of death and roam over the desert' in order to reach Utnapištim, the well-known Babylonian flood-hero, to whom the gods have granted eternal life. With the help of the moon-god, Sîn, he is able to overcome his fear of lions and he traverses many strange countries. The Mašu-mountains which he reaches first are watched over by terrifying scorpion-people. But when they hear of his quest, they let him pass and he crosses their land in utter darkness, maybe in a sort of tunnel. He emerges eventually in a beautiful garden of precious stones, where Siduri, the 'ale-wife', lives by the sea. She is frightened by the approach of Gilgameš and bars the doors. He then tells her his story at great length, voices his anxiety about death and asks her for the way to Utnapištim. She warns him about the dangers facing him and points out that only Šamaš is able to cross the waters of death. But she does give him some advice, although exactly which is unclear because of a break in the text.

Tablet 10 begins with a dialogue between Uršanabi, the ferryman of the deadly waters, and Gilgameš, who again relates the reason for his quest. Uršanabi asks him to cut down some 120 'punting-poles' and similar equipment. They board the ship and Gilgameš propels the craft forward with the punting-poles, using them up one after the other. Utnapištim sees them coming and is astonished at the stranger ferrying the boat. Once landed, Gilgameš has to tell his tale once more, and Utnapištim answers with a series of proverbs which express the transience of all things in life. He tells Gilgameš that the gods allot life and death and 'reveal not the day of death'.

Tablet 11. Gilgameš is surprised that Utnapištim is a man like any other and asks how he managed to attain eternal life. As an answer, Utna-pištim tells him the story of the Flood (see **Flood-myths**), which he and his wife alone had survived, because Ea helped them. He concludes that it was in the face of this momentous destruction that he was given eternal life but who, he asks, would assemble the gods again for Gilgameš to grant him the same. But as a test he tells Gilgameš to refrain from sleep for six days and seven nights. Gilgameš promptly falls asleep and Utnapištim's wife places a freshly baked loaf of bread at his side; one for every day that he sleeps. The first loaf has gone mouldy when he finally awakes. Dejected, Gilgameš realizes that his quest has failed and Utnapištim, after banishing Uršanabi for having brought a mortal across, tells him to wash himself in the river and gives him new clothes instead of the old lion-skins, clothes which will not show any sign of wear until he reaches the end of his journey. Just as the two are about to depart in their ship, Utnapištim's wife, feeling sorry for Gilgameš, asks her husband to grant him one last favour. In response, he reveals to Gilgameš the secret of a magic plant, which would help him to 'find new life'. Gilgameš puts stones as weights on his feet and dives to retrieve the plant, which he intends to bring back to Uruk, as it will make the 'old young again'. On their way home, when Gilgameš stops to have a bath in a cool pond, a serpent smells the plant and snatches it away, leaving its old skin behind. Gilgameš sits down and weeps when he realizes that the 'earth-worm' has stolen the only boon he managed to get for himself. He decides to leave the ship there and then and after some days arrives with Uršanabi in Uruk. Gilgameš tells him to climb the wall of Uruk and look about, to inspect its brickwork of burnt brick and the cultivated and uncultivated lands of his city.

Tablet 12 is a late addition (only found in the Ninivite recension) and follows closely the Sumerian story of Gilgameš, Enkidu and the Nether-world, taking up the story when the *pukku* and *mukku* have fallen into the underworld. The narrative, which contains a description of the various classes of souls in the underworld, ends abruptly after the account of the miserable fate of one whose body was left unburied in the steppe, has been described.

Speiser, in Pritchard 1950, 72–99; Heidel 1954; Soden and Schott 1958 and 1982; Draffkorn-Kilmer 1982, 128–32; Lambert 1987, 37–52; Dalley 1989, 50–135

There remains some doubt as to whether a unified OLD BABYLONIAN GILGAMEŠ story ever existed in written form. The surviving fragments, the Pennsylvania and Yale tablets augmented by texts from Ishchali (Greengus 1979) and Sippar (Millard 1964), could almost be described as the epic of **Enkidu**, for much of the events focus on him. His arrival is announced by two dreams of Gilgameš (called *giš* here), which are ident-ical to those in Tablet 2 of the Assyrian version. The prostitute initiates him into a civilized life, she clothes him with one half of her garments and takes him to the sheepfolds, where she gives him bread to eat and wine to drink. After a visit to the barber, who shaves his shaggy mane, he takes up weapons and slays lions, being now firmly on the side of the shepherds as their very protector. He has become fully human and a fitting match for Gilgameš whom he seeks out in Uruk. The people see him and rejoice, he is like Gilgameš and he is his rival. Then follows the fight between the two heroes, which Gilgameš seems to win, but he praises Enkidu as an equal. The Yale tablet is taken up with a lengthy and some-times obscure description of the preparations for their campaign to the cedar-forest. Another important fragment is the speech by Siduri (cf. Tablet 10 of the Assyrian version), preserved on the so-called Meissner-fragment (Millard 1964). The ale-wife tells Gilgameš that 'when the gods had created mankind, they allotted death to mankind, life they retained in their keeping'. She advises him to be merry and enjoy the simple life of human beings, song and dance, clean garments, the joys of parenthood and marriage.

Jastrow 1920; Dalley 136–53

The HITTITE texts offer fragments of a maybe fuller version; they cover parts of the journey to the cedar-mountain, the aftermath of the slaying of Humbaba, where Ellil accuses Šamaš of being in league with Gilgameš. In the story of the Bull of Heaven (cf. Tablet 7), the dialogue with Ištar is markedly different. The goddess seems to anticipate the *carpe diem* advice given by Siduri in the Old Babylonian version. It is also noticeable that the dreams figure prominently in the Hittite as well as the Akkadian fragments from Boğazköy.

Friedrich 1930; Stefanini 1969, 40–7

Gugalanna – Sumerian god

His name means 'wild bull of **Anu**'. He is quoted in some god-lists as the husband of **Ereškigal**. In the same capacity he is mentioned in **Inanna's Descent**, where **Inanna** says that she has come to the underworld in order to mourn for Gugalanna, her brother-in-law. He was identified with **Nergal** by the time of the Old Babylonian period.

Gula – Babylonian goddess of healing. See **Ninisina** (*see figure 10*)

Gulšeš – Hittite goddesses of fate.

The interpretation and reading of their name is related to the Hittite word 'inscribe'. They are underworld deities and much invoked in incantations, where they have either a benevolent or a hostile character. They also have affinities to childbirth. There does not seem to have been a local cult for the Gulšeš. In the rock-relief of Yazilikaya they are described as **Hutena and Hutellura**. This name corresponds to Hurrian *hut*, 'to write'.

Laroche 1948, 113–36; Otten, RLA 4

H

Halmašuit – Anatolian goddess

The name ^{d.} ^{GIŠ}*Halmašuit/Hanuašuit/DAG* seems to derive from the Hattian word *ha-nua(š)*, 'to sit'.

In the Hittite inscriptions, notably in rituals conected with the purification of the palace, she appears as the personification of the royal throne. She invites the king to come to the mountains, the traditional seat of the **Weather-god**, and divides the areas of their respective influence, entrusting the king with the rule 'over the land'.

Szabo 1971; RLA 4 (1972), 62

Hannahanna

Hittite name for an Anatolian, probably proto-Hattian, goddess. *Hanna* meaning 'grandmother', the name could be rendered as 'Granny-granny'. The logographic version is *^dMAH/NIN.TU*. In the myth of **Telepinu** she is the only one among the gods who is able to find the vanished fertility god by sending out the bee, an animal which has a traditional association with mother-goddesses.

von Schuler, WdM 1965, 170; Beckman 1983

Harab or the Theogony of Dunnu

Babylonian myth which is only partially preserved. It probably dates from the beginning of the second millennium BC.

It concerns the foundation of Dunnu, a central Babylonian town and the genealogy of its gods. The gods form a succession of incestuous and patricidal relationships which became gradually more normal. It also follows the sequence of the agricultural year and probably relates particular events to seasonal festivals.

Harab ('Plough') and **Ki** ('Earth') are the first parents. They cultivate the land, establish Dunnu and beget the **Šakkan**, the Cattle god. Earth desires her son and marries him, having killed the father, Harab. **Šakkan** takes over from his father, whom he buries at Dunnu. He then marries his sister, Tiamat, who in turn slays her mother, the previous wife of Šakkan. Their offspring in turn marry each other and kill the mother. The next generation consists of Gaiu?Lahar? and the River-goddess; they kill both parents and again bury them in Dunnu. Their children, a Herding god and goddess, increase the fertility of the pastures. He installs some cult and does away with his parents, taking the dominion over the land himself. Harhanum, their son, marries **Bēlet-Şeri**, their daughter; the parents are killed and buried. On New Year's Day, Hayyašum, his son, marries his sister, takes over the rulership but does not kill his father, he merely imprisons him. The rest of the composition, which also mentions **Nusku**, **Ninurta** and **Enlil**, is only very fragmentarily preserved.

Lambert, Walcot 1965, 64ff; Jacobsen 1984; Dalley 1989, 277–81

Hattian gods

The term 'Hatti' was used by the Indo-European Hittites to describe the language and people of the central Anatolian plateau, an area roughly circumscribed by the river Kizil Irmak (the ancient Halys). The Hattians had their own little known religion and some mythology, which the Hittites to some extent took over. They certainly translated Hattian rituals and mythological texts which have partly survived in the archives of Boğazköy. Due to the formalizing tendencies of the Hittite scribes, they organized local gods into 'families' and 'courts' (*kaluti*) and assigned to them functional categories. It is difficult to determine the original character and relationship of the Hattian gods. As elsewhere in Anatolia, the female deities are much in evidence, first of all the **Sun-goddess**, Wurunšemu, then her daughter **Mezulla**, as well as **Inara**. The warrior-god **Wurunkatte** may have belonged to the circle of the **Weather-god**. Another well-known deity is Tahattanuitiš, whose Hittite epithet *Wattarašannaš* means 'mother of the springs'. She appears in the myth of **Telepinu**. Wašizzil was also called *UR.MAH.LUGAL.aš*, 'Lion-king'; Tašimetiš was known as *SAL.LUGAL.aš*, 'the queen'; she is the mistress of **Tešub** in the myth of **Kumarbi**.

Laroche 1947, 187–215

Hattian myths

are only known from Hittite sources and are preserved generally in connection with rituals. A common theme is the disappearance of an important god, the ensuing crisis and attempts to discover and placate the hidden god, often with the help of a mortal as well as another deity by specific rites (see **Telepinu** and **Illuyanka**).

Hoffner, jr., in Goedicke, Roberts 1973, 136ff

Hauran/Hawran/Horon – West Semitic god

His name is connected with the Arabic word *hôr*, 'bottom of a well, cave', and could be read as 'the deep one'. He appears in personal names from the beginning of the second millennium onwards to about 600 BC, mainly in Syria and Palestine, as well as in Mari. He was also worshipped in Egypt (XVIII and XIX dynasties).

Horon is a primarily chthonic god, like the Mesopotamian **Nergal** and the Canaanite **Rešef**. He is mentioned in a magical text from Arslan-Tash. In the Ugaritic **Keret**-myth, the king curses his son by asking Horon to smash his skull in. There is also a ritual narrative, seemingly against the effects of a snake's bite (KTU 1.100), which involves Horon and a goddess in equine form, who is threatened by a venomous serpent. She has appealed for help to eleven gods and only Horon is left. He agrees to come to her rescue and first performs a ritual with a date-cluster. Inflamed with desire, he asks to be admitted to the presence of the goddess, who first demands a (subdued?) snake as a wedding-gift. The end is missing but the consummation of his passion may be implied.

Horon is one of the terrifying gods who were popular because of the degree of harm they could inflict on one's enemies; hence the context of incantations.

Albright 1936, 1–12; Pope, in WdM, 288; for KTU 1.100: Young 1979, 839–48; Bowman and Coote 1980, 135–9; Dietrich and Lorenz 1980, 153–70

Hebat/Hepat – Anatolian goddess, worshipped by the Hittites and the Hurrians.

She first appears in the pre-Sargonic texts from Ebla, later in numerous feminine names from the archives of Boğazköy, Alalakh and Ugarit during the second millennium BC. The etymology of her name is so far unknown; the Hittite inscriptions call her *NIN.SAL.LUGAL.šamê*, 'The Lady, Queen of Heaven'.

Hebat first appears in the Hurrian pantheon during the Mitanni period, as the city-goddess of Halab (Aleppo). At Alalakh she forms part of the triad **Tešub**, Hebat and **Ištar**. The southern regions of Anatolia were strongly influenced by Hurrian culture. Hebat, in association with the weather-god Tešub and her son **Sarruma**, became a widely worshipped deity with sanctuaries in many places (Kummanni in Cappadocia, Uda, Lawazzantiya etc.). During the thirteenth century BC the Hurrian pantheon became incorporated into the official Hittite state religion. Hebat was identified with the **Sun-goddess of Arinna**, the traditional protectress of the royal couple. As such she is depicted on the rock-reliefs of Yazilikaya, where she stands on a leopard-like animal. Her entourage includes, apart from Sarruma, Allanzu, Takiti and the **Gulšeš**, Hutena and Hutellura.

Hebat's role in mythology is limited to her appearance as Tešub's worried wife in **Kumarbi**.

The nature of Hebat is that of a **Mother-goddess** and the origin of her worship may well go back to the ancient Neolithic female deities, which are known from Çatal Hüyük and Hacilar.

Laroche 1948, 113–36; Danmanville, in RLA IV 1975, 326–9; Laroche, in Bonnefoy (1981) II, 487

Hedammu

Hurrian myth, partly preserved in a Hittite translation found among the archives of Boğazköy. It seems to belong to the cycle of **Kumarbi** which describes the conflict between Kumarbi and the **Weather-god**.

The beginning is lost; we find Kumarbi asking for the daughter of the sea-god in marriage. Their offspring is probably Hedammu, a dragon-like monster, who lives in the sea and daily devours vast quantities of domestic animals and people. The goddess **Ištar** discovers Hedammu and reports back to the weather-god, who sheds tears at the news. After a gap in the text, the goddess prepares for her encounter with Hedammu. She bathes and anoints herself, puts on her jewellery and goes down to the water. When Hedammu sees the goddess, he wants to eat her too. [gap] She goes down to the water again and this time she resorts to magic and changes the sea-water into a sleeping potion. Hedammu succumbs and, enticed by her charms, leaves the water. The end of the story is unclear due to the fragmentary nature of the texts, but it would seem that the weather-god eventually triumphs over his adversary.

Güterbock 1946; Friedrich 1949, 230–54; Siegelová 1971, 35ff

Hendursanga – Sumerian god

Also written logographically as *dPA.sag.(ga)*; the etymology is still unclear.

The god first appears in the Fara god-lists, then in various sacrificial and ritual texts from the Old and Neo-Sumerian periods. Gudea calls him the *nimgir kalam.ma*, 'herald of the Land (Sumer)', and in the Hendursanga hymn (Edzard and Wilcke) he acts as an adviser to **Utu**. In the incantation series 'Evil demons', he is called *nāgir sūqi šaqummi*, 'the herald of the quiet street'. It seems that he was primarily a benevolent and supportive, if minor, god.

The genealogy of Hendursanga is rather obscure; in one text he is said to be the (illegitimate?) son of Utu and **Ninlil**. His wife is the little-known ancient Sumerian goddess Ninmuga. By the Old Babylonian period Hendursanga became identified with the Semitic **Išum**.

Edzard, in RLA IV (1975), 324; Edzard and Wilcke 1976, 142–76

Hittite gods (*see figures 16 and 17*)

There are numerous texts written in the cuneiform or hieroglyphic versions of Hittite, which deal with religious matters. There are cultic calendars, descriptions of rituals, incantations, god-lists and also political documents, such as treaties and proclamations with references to the gods of the land. The great variety of divine names in these documents is striking in comparison with Mesopotamian or Ugaritic sources. The Hittites called them 'the Thousand Gods of Hatti' to summarize the totality of divine numina. This proliferation can be explained by the fact that the Hittites were only one among several peoples in Anatolia, all of whom had their own religious traditions and local gods. But as the political influence of the Hittites expanded, these cults were incorporated into the Hittite system, usually maintaining their original language. This attitude of religious tolerance furthered the integration of conquered areas and also contributed to the divine powers protecting the state. Only on rare occasions was there any interference with the local or national cults, which on the whole remained unchanged and followed the Anatolian age-old tradition of worshipping the divine force manifested in nature (mountains, rivers, springs), as well as the ubiquitous **Mother-goddess** and her consort, the **Weather-god**. The 'state-religion' of the Hittite Empire, however, in its attempts to transcend the local cults, is highly complex in comparison, and subject to change due to historical development. Initially the Hittite kings venerated the Indo-European sky-god Siu (Greek *Zeus*, Latin Iu(piter)). The concept seems preserved in the self-appellation of the Hittite ruler as 'my sun'. Then the **Hattian** weather-god rose to prominence with his important cult-centre of Nerik in North Anatolia. The greatest expansion of the official pantheon occurred after 1400 BC when **Hurrian** and Luwian deities were introduced. The scribes of the imperial capital attempted to bring some order into this confusing array of divine names and they proceeded by certain patterns, which are discernible in the various lists of gods found in state documents. They often grouped several gods into functional categories, loosely identified by a Sumerian logogram, such as ^{d}KAL for 'protective deities', etc. In addition, gods of diverse origin are assembled into extended groups, known as *kaluti*, which can include parental and marital relationships. Hittite divine names are sometimes included as a possible reference to the functional aspect of gods, rather than attempts at a straightforward syncretism (Laroche). In addition, the lists are hierarchically structured with the most important deities at the beginning. A typical late treaty-list would therefore incorporate, first the royal and national deities, the sun-god of Heaven and the sun-goddess of Arinna – 'the King and Queen of the Lands'. Then come the various weather-gods (designated by the cult-centres), the ^{d}Kal gods, some important Babylonian gods (such as **Allatum**, **Ea** and **Damkina**, **Marduk** etc.), the agricultural gods (**Telepinu**), the **Ištar**-goddesses, the war-gods (**Zababa**), the prominent local gods of the contracting parties, the underworld gods, **Primeval gods**, and finally all the numina of mountains, rivers, springs, heaven and earth.

Other important gods are only known from prayers or ritual texts. These include the **Mother-goddesses (*Mah*)**, **Mezulla**, **Halmasuit** and **Sarruma**.

Macqueen 1959, 171–88; Haas 1970; Gurney 1977; Lebrun 1980; Laroche, in Bonnefoy 1981, II, 235–9

Hittite myths

Like the Hittite gods, they were taken from a variety of sources, Hattian (**Telepinu** and **Illuyanka**), Hurrian (**Appu** and **Kumarbi**), Ugaritic (**Elqunirša**) and Babylonian (**Gilgameš**).

Humban – Elamite god

His name is probably connected with the word *huba*, 'to command'. During the second millennium BC it was replaced by the general appellative *DINGIR.GAL*, Elamite *napiriša*, 'great god'. He is first mentioned in an Akkadian treaty between Naram-Sin and Susa (23rd C BC), as the consort of the great Elamite goddess **Pinenkir**. During the second millennium BC he rose to the supreme rank and was worshipped in all Elam. His cult is even attested for the Achaemenian period, according to evidence from sacrificial lists.

Hinz, RLA IV (1975), 492

Hurrian gods

The Hurrians were a people speaking an agglutinative, probably northeast Caucasian language, who made significant contributions to the history and civilizations of the Ancient Near East. They probably settled in northern Mesopotamia some time in the third millennium BC and became an important political factor during the second and the beginning of the first millennium BC. They lived in northern Syria and Mesopotamia, and their influence can be traced to Ugarit, Assyria and the Hittite Empire. The original gods of the Hurrians, as far as can be discerned through external source-material, were the weather-god **Tešub**, the sun-god Šimegi, the moon-god Kusuh, the warrior-god Astabi, **Kumarbi** and the goddess **Šaušga** (equated with **Ištar**). The proximity to Mesopotamia resulted in the importation of Babylonian gods (**Anu, Ea, Enlil, Ningal, Ninurta** etc.), who were partly identified with native deities. In the fourteenth century BC, many Hurrian deities, myths and cults were introduced to Anatolia via Kizzuwatna and translated into Hittite.

Güterbock 1954, 383–94; von Schuler, WdM 1965, 176–7

I

Igigi – Akkadian collective of gods

The term (^{d}i-gi_4-gi_4-ne) has not yet been satisfactorily explained. In some bilingual Sumero-Akkadian texts the gods are also referred to as ^{d}nun-gal-e-ne, 'the great lords'. They do not appear before the Old Babylonian period and are only mentioned in literary texts. There is no indication of an actual cult, although the Igigi occasionally occur in personal names.

The origin and even the function of the Igigi in mythological texts is still unclear and so is their relationship with the **Anunnaki**. While the two terms were often used synonymously, the Igigi could also be contrasted with the Anunnaki – as, for instance, in Atra-hasis (see **Flood-myths**), where the Igigi are said to have been burdened with labour for the gods by the **Anunnaki**. After forty days they rebelled by burning their tools, which led to the creation of man to take over their work. A general distinction between chthonic Igigi and celestial Anunnaki may be discernible in some texts but was certainly not consistent.

Kienast 1965, 142–58; Soden 1966, 140–5; Kienast, RLA V 1976, 40–4

Illuyanka

A giant, dragon-like sea-monster which appears in a Hattian myth. The story formed the mythical introduction to the Hattian New Year rites which were celebrated at Nerik, the main cult-centre of the **Weather-god** Zaliyanu. The text (KBo III 7) contains two versions of the myth and it has recently been proposed (Gonnet) that the two successive accounts reflect the historical conflict between the Hittites (represented by the weather-god) and the Gašgaeans (Illuyanka).

The first tale begins with the defeat of the weather-god in a fight against Illuyanka. He asks the other deities for help. The goddess **Inara** prepares a banquet, filling many large vessels with various kinds of alcoholic drink. She then goes to enlist the help of a human being, called Hupašiya. He agrees to come, but only on condition that she first has sex with him. Inara does as he wishes and then takes the man to the banquet to which she had invited the dragon and all his children. The dragon family get so drunk that they are unable to leave. Hupašiya ties them securely with ropes and keeps them ready for the weather-god, who kills Illuyanka forthwith. Inara then takes the man 'far away' to live with her. However, she forbids him expressively to look out of the window, where he will perceive his wife and family. After twenty days he can resist no longer and opens the window. Filled with longing, he asks the returning goddess to let him go back home. The end of the story is only fragmentary; but it seems likely that the goddess kills Hupašiya for his disobedience. The myth also includes its own etiology by mentioning that Inara had given her house to the king for the celebration of the *purulliya* (New Year) festival.

The second story of Illuyanka and the weather-god also involves the collaboration of a human being. Again Illuyanka has managed to take away the power of the weather-god, this time by depriving him of his heart and his eyes. The vulnerable god then marries the daughter of a 'poor man' and she bears him a son, who in turn woos the daughter of Illuyanka. As a bride-prize he demands the stolen organs of his father. He restores them to his father and the weather-god is now able to take up the fight again. He not only kills his enemy but also his son, who is now part of his wife's clan and asks not to be spared.

Goetze, in Pritchard 1955, 124f; Haas 1977, 109ff; Beckman 1982, 11–25; Gonnet 1987, 88–100

Inanna/Innin/Ninni(n) – Sumerian goddess (*see figures 29, 42 and 43*)

The etymology of her name is doubtful; by the end of the third millennium BC it was taken to derive from ^{d}*nin.an.na*, 'Lady of Heaven' (in the Emesal-dialect, *gašan.an.na*). The cuneiform sign mùš, with which her name is usually written, goes back to an archaic pictograph representing a rolled-up reed-stalk . It is found among the earliest written records from Uruk. The god-list of Fara mentions Inanna behind **An** and **Enlil** and before **Enki**. Otherwise the sources of the pre-Sargonic period do not indicate a very widespread veneration of the goddess. She is invoked in only few personal names and does not appear to be a recipient of frequent offerings. There are no indications of Inanna's role either as a specific goddess of love or of war. Towards the middle of the third millennium BC, kings of the Kish-dynasties (Enannatum I, Lugalatarsi), as well as Lugalzaggesi of Uruk, mention Inanna in their royal inscriptions. The earliest literary texts dedicated to Inanna are usually taken to date from the period of Agade, when the daughter of king Sargon, Enheduanna, composed some lengthy hymns in praise of the goddess. (Since all the compositions ascribed to Enheduanna are only preserved on later Neo-Sumerian copies, the dating of the texts remains hypothetical.) It is likely that the tutelary deity of the dynasty was actually the Semitic goddess Eštar/**Ištar**, the bisexual deity of the Venus-star, who was made acceptable to the Sumerian population by a syncretism with the local Inanna. The hymns elaborate the goddess's complex personality and her bid for divine power may well reflect the political rise of the Sargonic rulers (Hallo, van Dijk). Her epithets in these texts are *nin.me.šar.ra*, 'Queen of all the *me*', a title which makes her the most influential of deities in the world of gods and humans. She is also *nu-(u₈).gig.an.na*, 'the hierodule of heaven' (and/or of **Anu**), a projection of her erotic functions to the cosmic scale. She is *munus.zi*, '*the* woman', *ù.sún.zi.an.na*, 'exalted Cow of Heaven', who provides life and sustenance. Inanna represented the force of sexual reproduction, 'who multiplies the people of all countries like sheep'. She is called the beloved wife of Ušumgalanna (**Dumuzi**) and in her martial aspect she is an *ur.sag*, a 'heroic champion', 'the destroyer of foreign lands, foremost in battle'.

During the Neo-Sumerian period, her cult was well established and several rulers, such as Eannatum and Ur-Ninurta, refer to themselves as 'beloved husbands of Ninnin'. Her main cult-centre was the É-anna at Uruk. Other important temples were at Nippur, Lagash, Shuruppak, Zabalam and Ur. Regular monthly festivals were celebrated in her honour. During the Isin-Larsa period her cult seems to have reached its climax; she was identified with **Ninisina**, the city-goddess of Isin, as well as many other female deities. Apart from several important mythical compositions (see below), a large number of hymns and liturgical songs dedicated to the goddess were compiled in this period. The astral character of Inanna as the planet **Venus** is an important subject of many of these texts. In a self-laudatory hymn (Römer), Inanna claims to have received special prerogatives from **Enlil**, 'who put the sky as a cap on my head, the earth as sandals on my feet' – poetic metaphor for her cosmic dominance. A special category are the songs written for the so-called **Sacred Marriage** rituals, in which the 'Queen of Heaven' symbolically united herself with the king, in order to renew life and fertility in the land.

The complexity of notions surrounding Inanna in Mesopotamian sources is well illustrated by her contradictory genealogy and her astral aspects. Her role vis-à-vis An is typically ambiguous. In Uruk, an old cult-centre of An as well as Inanna, she was known as the daughter of An. It is not clear whether the title *nu.gig.an.na*, 'hierodule of *AN*', refers to An, the god, and thereby implies an erotic relationship, or more generally to *AN* as the sky (see above). Enlil too, possibly in his role as leader of the pantheon, is called the father of Inanna/Ištar. (In a later tradition, Inanna/Ištar is also made the consort of either An or Enlil.) The Isin tradition, which emphasized her astral character, called Inanna the daughter of the moon-god **Nanna** and the twin-sister of sun-god **Utu**. In some literary compositions (see below), Inanna's mother is specified as **Ningal**.

The astronomical aspect of Inanna is somewhat ambiguous. According to the evidence of seasonal festivals during the Ur III period, Inanna was primarily associated with the moon (as the daughter of Nanna) and the phases of the moon were celebrated in her honour, while the heliacal settings of the planet Venus were marked by the festivals of **Nanaya** and **Anunnitum** (Sauren). The majority of the literary texts on the other hand (**Inanna's Descent**, **Inanna and Ebih**, hymns etc.) seem to emphasize the astral rather than the lunar interpretation of the goddess.

In the myths Inanna is described as restless and ambitious. She tries to extend the areas of her influence and power, to mediate between heaven and the underworld. She visits the *kur* to gain knowledge (see **Inanna and Utu**, and **Inanna and Šukalletuda**), which she transmits to 'her people'. Although immensely powerful, her access to authority is fundamentally circumscribed because of her femininity; and her attempts at transcending her position constituted an abuse, a *hybris* for which she is punished (Inanna's Descent). On the other hand, there may also be etiological motifs behind the narratives concerning her disappearances, considering her association with Venus, a planet subject to periodical invisibility.

Inanna's femininity is proverbial but also contradictory. While she no doubt incorporated various different local female numina, remnants of the old **Mother-goddess**, she does not behave like a mother. She remained primarily a goddess of sexual rather than conjugal love (see her epithet *nu.gig*). She represents the force of fertility rather than the process of birth itself. Only during the post-Sumerian period did Inanna become a deity capable of empathy with human misery, having herself been subjected to humiliation and suffering. There are a number of *balag* and **eršemma** liturgical texts, in which she laments the death of her lover (Dumuzi), the destruction of her cities and the cruel fate of her people. She intercedes humbly with the great gods (notably Enlil) to reverse it on behalf of herself, her city and mankind.

Hallo, van Dijk 1968; Römer 1969, 97–114; Sjöberg 1976, 161–253; Wilcke, RLA IV 1976, 74–87; Cohen 1981; Kramer 1987, 171–89; Bruschweiler, 1989

More than any other Mesopotamian deity she inspired poets and singers; some of the most beautiful hymns and laments were composed in her honour. There are also a number of mythological texts that have survived:

Inanna and Bilulu

is a badly mutilated text, which was found among the tablets of Nippur. Its Sumerian title is *edin.na ^d dumu.zi.mu*. It has been interpreted in very different ways, as belonging to a cycle of Dumuzi-texts centred around Babtibira (Kramer), as a 'nature-myth' (Jacobsen) or part of a liturgy for a Neo-Sumerian king who died in the desert (Cohen).

The beginning is very damaged, it seems to have the form of a lament. When the text becomes intelligible, Inanna is longing for her husband Dumuzi, who is out in the steppe with his flocks. On the pretext of doing an errand for her mother **Ningal**, she sets out to join him. A large gap follows. Then someone informs Inanna that Dumuzi has been killed. She bursts into song of tender praise for her husband, who 'stood guard over her sheep'. The scene then shifts to the farmstead (*edin.líl.lá*) of Bilulu, 'the old woman', where her son Girgirre is busy filling his pens and storing his grain, chatting with another man, called *SIR.RU*. Inanna thinks of revenge. She takes the road to Edinlilla and enters an inn, rightly expecting to find her victims there. She steps onto a seat and utters a curse which becomes immediately effective: 'Begone! I have killed you (...) and with you I destroy your name. May you become the waterskin (that men carry) in the desert!' Girgirre is turned into the wandering evil spirits of the desert and *SIR.RU* has to keep an eye on spilled flour. She forces them to present the libation of water and the offering of flour as gifts for (the spirit of) Dumuzi.

Jacobsen 1953, 160–87; Kramer 1953, 187; Jacobsen 1970, 52–71; Alster 1975; Cohen 1981, 72

Inanna and Ebih (*in.nin.me.huš.a*)

is a mythological fragment in a hymn-cycle to Inanna in which all exult the goddess. It is composed on similar lines as the songs by Enheduanna and may reflect the political events in the later part of Sargon's reign, although an astral interpretation which would account for the temporary disappearance of Venus 'behind the mountain' has also been proposed (Alster).

It tells how the goddess intends to defeat the 'rebellious' *kur* (mountain, country) Ebih, who refused to acknowledge her superiority. She ascends to Heaven to ask for An's approval, but he warns the goddess not to go there. However, she does not heed his advice and successfully repels Ebih, which she utterly destroys.

van Dijk, Hallo 1968, 3; Limet 1971, 11–28; Alster 1975, 106

Inanna and Enki

is a lengthy composition of doubtful date and origin (Ur III ?). It describes the rise of Inanna and her city Uruk to pre-eminence in Sumer by a trick of the goddess. She decides to visit Enki, who dwells in the **Apsu** in possession of the *me*. Enki has some premonition of her coming and prepares for her reception. He instructs his vizier Išum to provide them with plenty of food and drink, and when the goddess arrives they sit down together and feast. Under the influence of the wine and beer, Enki hands out the *me* one by one to Inanna. The goddess then counts them out, declaring at each item that 'he has given [it] to me'. When Enki (after a gap) asks Išum for the *me*, he is told that Inanna has already loaded them into her ship and departed. Enki sends Išum and some demons after her, instructing him to take away the ship with the *me* but Inanna, helped by **Ninšubur**, manages to repel them with magic spells. This is repeated several times at different locations and eventually the goddess lands in Uruk and unloads the *me*, enumerating them all once more. She then prepares a feast. The end is obscure, but by the intercession of a third god, Enki seems to become reconciled to Inanna.

Farber-Flügge 1973; Alster 1973, 20–34

Inanna and Šukalletuda

is a fragmentary myth which still awaits publication. Inanna leaves 'heaven and earth' to visit the mysterious *kur* (generally 'mountain, foreign country'; but for a new interpretation of this concept, see Bruschweiler 1987, passim) in order to learn how to distinguish right from wrong. When she emerges again, she lies down in a garden and falls asleep. Taking advantage of her exhaustion, Šukalletuda approaches the goddess and rapes her. By the time Inanna discovers what has happened, the man has hidden himself among his compatriots (the Sumerians). Since she cannot find him there, Inanna sends three plagues over the whole country. Eventually she goes to Enki in the **Apsu**, who seems to help her. When she emerges, she is dazzling like a rainbow and apparently effects the punishment of her attacker by turning him into a shepherd.

Kramer 1949, 399–405; Alster 1973, 30ff

Inanna and Utu

is a mythical incident in a Sumerian hymn (BM 23631), which explains how Inanna came to be the goddess of sexual love. The goddess asks her brother Utu to help her to go down to the *kur* (see above, Inanna and Šukalletuda), where various plants and trees are growing. She wants to eat them in order to know the secrets of sexuality of which she is as yet deprived: 'What concerns women, (namely) man, I do not know. What concerns women: love-making I do not know.' Utu seems to comply and Inanna tastes of the fruit (the same motif is also employed in **Enki and Ninhursag** and of course in Genesis I) which brings her knowledge.

Kramer 1985, 117–32

Inanna's Descent to the Underworld

Sumerian title: *an.gal.ta ki.gal.šè*, 'From the great Above to the great Below' ('Inanna set her mind' is the initial line of the composition). This long text (c. 410 lines preserved) incorporates two story-lines: first the account of Inanna's futile attempt to extend her dominion even into the domain of the underworld, which results in her death and the subsequent escape from the underworld, and second, the story of her husband Dumuzi, who is fated to die or at best spend half his life below the earth.

The text begins with Inanna's decision to turn towards the 'Great Below'. She temporarily abandons heaven and earth and her queenship over them, as well as her temples in Sumer. But she takes her *me* and dresses in all her regalia. She also makes arrangements for the eventual failure of her expedition by instructing her vizier **Ninšubur** on emergency measures should she not return. Ninšubur is to assume mourning and set up laments for her mistress in all her temples. She is to go to

Enlil to enlist his help and should that fail, to **Nanna**. In the last recourse she should go to **Enki**, who is wise and knows of 'life-giving' plants and water.

Inanna arrives at the palace Ganzir, the entrance to the netherworld, where she bangs against the gate, shouting to the guardian Neti to let her in. When he questions her on her motives for such an unprecedented request, she tells him her name and that she has come to attend the funeral of her brother-in-law **Gugalanna**. Neti leaves her by the gate and goes for further instructions from his mistress **Ereškigal**, the ruler of the underworld and Inanna's sister. He informs her of Inanna's arrival and describes her appearance and that she has all the *me*. Ereškigal is furious and tells Neti to lock all the seven gates of the underworld. He is then to let Inanna enter, but at each gate she will have to remove one item of her outfit. All this Neti executes as commanded, and when Inanna wants to know the reason for this decree, Neti simply replies that 'these are the ways of the underworld'. When the seventh gate is passed, Inanna is completely stripped, not only of her garments, but of all her powers which they symbolized. As soon as Ereškigal sets eyes on her sister, she rises from her throne in anger. A scuffle ensues in which Inanna desperately tries to seize the throne herself, hoping to obtain control over the underworld. But as she sits down, the seven **Anunnaki**, here functioning as the judges of the underworld, condemn her to death. As a corpse she is hung on a nail in the wall.

When after three days and three nights Inanna does not reappear, Ninšubur concludes that something terrible has happened and begins to carry out the instructions of her mistress. She puts on mourning, sets up laments in the deserted temples, and goes first to Enlil and then to Nanna. She implores them not to let her mistress be broken up and destroyed like a cult-image by an enemy. But both refuse help, saying that it was Inanna's excessive ambition which got her into trouble and she has only herself to blame. When Ninšubur comes to Enki, he takes pity on Inanna and from the dirt of his fingernails creates two beings, the *kur.gar.ra* and the *gala.tur.ra* (persons who formed part of Inanna's cult-personnel, maybe some sort of transvestites). Enki is confident that they will gain access to the underworld by some subterfuge, and he gives them the Plant and Water of Life. They will see a woman, Ereškigal, in pain (labour?) and they are to commiserate with her suffering, 'echoing her cries'. Flattered by their attention, she will offer them a reward – a good fate, a river to drink, a field of grain to eat – which they have to refuse, claiming instead the inert body of Inanna. Then they have only to sprinkle it with the life-giving water and the holy plant and

Inanna will rise. The *gala.tur.ra* and *kur.gar.ra* obey Enki's instructions and 'flitting about like flies', they slip through the cracks of the door-pivots into the underworld. They find Ereškigal writhing in agony, and in return for their sympathy receive the body of Inanna. They duly revive her and Ereškigal sends them away, but the Anunnaki seize Inanna and demand that she delivers a substitute for herself. Immediately a host of **galla**-demons, small and large, cling to her side. On her way out she pauses at each gate to pick up her garments and insignia. When Inanna emerges from the underworld, she is met by her faithful Ninšubur, who, dressed in rags, throws herself at Inanna's feet. The demons cry out to the goddess to go back to her city, as they will take Ninšubur, but Inanna will not allow it because '(Ninšubur) is the one who has brought me back to life, how could I turn her over to you'. It is obviously her choice and not the demons' who will be the substitute. They proceed to Umma, where **Šara** too is mourning. Again Inanna forbids the demons to seize 'her manicurist and hairdresser'. They go on to Babtibira, where Ulul is also in obvious distress and he is spared as well. Finally they reach Kullaba and there sits her husband **Dumuzi**, not at all in rags but 'in a magnificent garment on a magnificent throne'. When Inanna sees him, 'she looks at him with the look of death, she speaks to him with speech of anger, she shouts at him with the shout of guilt' and commands the demons to take him away. Dumuzi in turn 'lets out a wail, turns very pale and raises his hand to **Utu**', his brother-in-law, asking him to change him into a reptile to let him escape the demons. Utu complies, but the demons track him down. (The text has some twenty lines missing, they probably contained the further attempts at escape by Dumuzi, as described in **Dumuzi's Dream**.) The final portion contains a speech (probably by Inanna), where she proclaims that Dumuzi will spend half a year and his sister, **Geštinanna**, the other half in the underworld. The final doxology is 'sweet is the praise of Ereškigal the pure'.

Kramer 1951, 1–17; Falkenstein 1968, 96–110; Draffkorn-Kilmer 1971, 299–309; Sladek 1974; Buccellati 1982, 53–7

Inar(a)

Anatolian goddess, probably a **Hattian** manifestation of the **Mother-goddess**. She is already mentioned in the 19th C texts from Kanish. During the Old Hittite Kingdom she was the city-goddess of Hattusa. Her popularity waned after the fourteenth century BC, when a number of Hurrian deities were introduced to the national Hittite pantheon, as can be seen from the declining number of personal names formed with Inar(a).

Inar(a) appears in the myth of **Illuyanka**, where she helps to overcome the enemy of the **Weather-god**. From the thirteenth century on her name was often substituted by the generic *^dKAL*, the protective deities. ^dKAL is also associated with a deity represented by the stag (Luwian Kurunta).

Kammenhuber 1975, 68–88

Inšušinak – Elamite god

City-god of Susa, his Sumerian name *^dnin.šušin.ak* means 'the lord of Susa'. He is mentioned in royal inscriptions dating from the late third millennium BC, but not as a very high-ranking god. However, he seems to have been popular among the people, as one of his epithets, 'Father of the Weak', implies. During the Old Babylonian period he was generally called 'king of the gods', and when Elam became a great political power towards the end of the second millennium BC, he belonged to the triad of gods at the head of the Elamite pantheon, with **Humban** and **Kirisha**. Every Elamite ruler called himself 'the beloved servant of Inšušinak'. His cult flourished until the Achaemenian period.

According to first millennium BC burial tablets, which were discovered in Susa, Inšušinak speaks 'judgement' over the dead souls in the underworld and in legal documents too he is often invoked with the sun-god, as the one of the 'lords of light and darkness'.

Hinz 1972, 45–7; RLA V 1976, 117–18

Išhara/Ešhara (*see figure 10*)

Mesopotamian goddess of unknown origin. No etymology for her name has been found.

Išhara first appears in the pre-Sargonic texts from Ebla and then as a goddess of love in Old Akkadian potency-incantations (Biggs). During the Ur III period she had a temple in Drehem and from the Old Babylonian time onwards, there were sanctuaries in Sippar, Larsa and Harbidum. In Mari she seems to have been very popular and many women were called after her, but she is well attested in personal names in Babylonia generally up to the late Kassite period. Her main epithet was *bēlet rāme*, 'Lady of Love', which was also applied to **Ištar**. In the **Epic of Gilgameš** (Tablet II, col. V, 28) it says: 'For Išhara the bed is made' and in Atra-hasis (see **Flood-myths**) (I 301–304) she is called upon to bless the couple on the honeymoon.

Her astronomical embodiment is the constellation Scorpio and she is also called the mother of the **Sibittu** (the Seven Stars) (Seux, 343). Išhara was well known in Syria from the third millennium BC (Ebla!). She became a great goddess of the Hurrian population. She was worshipped with **Tešub** and **Simegi** at Alalakh, and also at Ugarit, Emar and Chagar Bazar. While she was considered to belong to the entourage of **Ištar**, she was also invoked to heal the sick (Lebrun).

Išhara was probably incorporated into the Hittite pantheon via the Hurrians and her main cult centre was Kizzuwatna. She is known as an oath-deity since the reign of king Arnuwanda. According to the existing texts, her healing properties were less often evoked than her power to harm and cause diseases. The family of king Muršiliš II was said to have been bewitched by calling upon Išhara, and in curses she was asked to punish the perjurers.

Biggs 1967; Frantz and Szabo, RLA V 1976, 177–8; Seux 1974; Ichiro 1979, 284f; Lebrun 1984, 41

Iškur

Sumerian **Weather-god**; usually written with the logogram *ᵈIM*. He is already mentioned in the Fara god-list. During the Sargonic period he was identified with the Semitic **Adad**, but continued to be worshipped as Iškur in southern Babylon. His cult-centre was Karkar and his temple, the É.karkara, is described in the Sumerian Temple Hymns (Sjöberg, Bergmann, No.27).

Iškur is either called the son of **Enlil** or **An**; he is the twin brother of **Enki**. He appears in several literary and mythological texts. One *eršemma* (Römer 1972) states that Iškur 'rides on a storm', is a 'roaring wind', the 'lord of plenty' (*bēl hegallim*). Another (Cohen, 51), calls him 'the great ox who is radiant, the lord who mounts the storm, who mounts a great lion, producing grain'. In **Enki and the World Order** (308–316), Enki puts Iškur, 'the canal-inspector of heaven and earth', in charge of 'rain and clouds, storms and lightning'. The title 'canal-inspector' (Sum. *gu.gal*) is an interesting example of the assimilation of a weather-god – usually at home in areas with a higher rainfall than southern Mesopotamia – to the irrigation-based economy of Sumer. As the canal-inspector of 'heaven and earth' he acts on a cosmic plane, manipulating the celestial sluices to produce rain on earth.

Vanel 1965; Cohen 1981, 51f; Römer 1982, 298–317

Ištanu see **Sun-goddess of Arinna**

Ištar/Eštar – Babylonian goddess (*see figures 3, 10, 14, 26, 29, 38, 42 and 43*)

Her name is probably connected with the West-Semitic *Attar/Attart* which is attested in text from Ugarit, the Old Testament, South Arabia and pre-Sargonic Mari. The term seems to have originally designated the planet **Venus** under its two aspects of morning star (male) and evening star (female) (see **Astar** and **Astart**). In the east, the two manifestations were combined in one deity, who nevertheless retained the characteristics of both genders; Ištar is a goddess of war as well as of sex and procreation.

The goddess first appears in personal names during the Sargonic period (Mari, Ebla etc.) and significantly, in both female and male names. The kings of Agade seem to have had a special affinity to Ištar, according to the second-millennium 'historic legends' which describe their deeds. It has been proposed, that in order to make their goddess more acceptable to the Sumerian population, the Sargonic kings should promote a syncretism with the **Inanna** (Hallo and van Dijk). Henceforth, the name of Ištar was almost always written as *ᵈINANNA*. But since so little is known about the original character of Inanna, it is impossible to discern a meaningful difference between the 'Semitic' Ištar and the 'Sumerian' Inanna. She is customarily referred to as Ištar in an Akkadian and Inanna in a Sumerian context.

From the Old Babylonian period onwards, many hymns written in Akkadian sing the praises of the goddess. One such composition, from the time of Ammiditana (c. 1683–1647 BC), dwells on the beauty and charm of Ištar, her 'honeysweet lips' and 'shining eyes'. She loves to help men and women, spreads happiness and joy. All the gods bend their knee to their lady; together with **Anu**, her husband, she reigns from her temple in Uruk (Falkenstein and Soden 1953, 235). (For the genealogy of Ištar, see **Inanna**.) Other texts also concern her position in the Babylonian pantheon. In the EXALTATION OF IŠTAR (Hruška), a text from the Kassite period, Anu also accepts her as his wife under the name of

Antum, and declares that as 'Ištar the Star' she will have the same rank as the Sun (**Šamaš**) and the Moon (**Sîn**). **Enlil** permits her to act as she pleases and assigns her a temple in Nippur. The probably contemporary GREAT HYMN TO THE QUEEN OF NIPPUR (Lambert) is a long theological exposé (some 300 lines). It first attempts to straighten out Ištar's genealogy by making her descend from Anu, Enlil and Sîn. It then goes on to praise her for her skills to 'speak holy judgement', to 'grant king-ship' and to 'become angry and then to relent', 'to punish then show compassion'. She is the fierce warrior, the 'queen of heaven'. All these are epithets that were customarily applied to Inanna, but she is also called the 'creatress of the human race' (identified with Aruru, the **Mother-goddess**) and the one 'who turns men into women and women into men'. An important part of the text is taken up with the names and titles of the goddess, which show off the erudition of the writer. Ištar emerges as a great deity, able to inspire reverence and love as well as fear. After all, she is not only a goddess of love, procreation, justice, mercy and compassion, but of war and battle, of conflict and lamentation. She persecutes her enemies and those 'who sin against her' with relentless fury, inflicting them with every evil and misfortune. A great number of prayers were therefore addressed to Ištar (Seux 1973, passim) in an effort to appease her angry heart, to influence the omens and to grant peace and protection to her subjects.

Apart from these expressions of individual piety and religious fervour, there are some mythological compositions of the post-Old Babylonian period which approach the goddess in a less unequivocal manner. The so-called AGUŠAYA-HYMN (Foster, Groneweg) probably records the institution of a particular festival. The ironic tone of the poem is remarkable. It opens with a praise of the warlike Ištar, who runs down her enemies like an 'on-rushing vehicle'. Greedy for battle, she appears 'bellowing like a wild bull'. Her clamour exasperates **Ea** who decides to put an end to her aggressive behaviour. With 'the dirt of his nails' (as in **Inanna's Descent**!) he creates Şaltu, 'powerful in form, monstrous in her proportion', in fact an exaggerated version of Ištar. He provokes Şaltu to a violent temper and tells her to rudely challenge Ištar to a fight. The goddess, confronted with this virago, is appalled and demands Ea to remove the appalling monster. Ea is happy to do so, as long as Ištar agrees to modify her own behaviour. According to Ea's plan the confrontation has the desired effect: she resolves to give up her incessant and undignified clamour for battle. Ea instigates a festival in which people could dance madly about the streets, commemorating the warlike aspect of Ištar-Agušaya.

Ištar's Descent (Sladek, 35ff)

is a condensed version of the Sumerian **Inanna's Descent** (138 lines against 410 lines of the latter), preserved on Neo-Assyrian tablets from Nineveh. Ištar decides to 'set her mind to the Land of No Return, the realm of **Ereškigal**' which is described at length as a gloomy place, bereft of light, 'where dust is their fare and clay their food'. She goes straight to the gates (without, as in the Sumerian version, taking the precaution of giving instructions to her vizier) and demands to be admitted, threatening to 'smash the door' and 'raise up the dead, eating the living'. The gate-keeper lets her in and, as in Inanna's Descent, she has to strip all her accoutrements of divinity at each of the seven gates. In the ensuing scuffle between the two sisters, Ereškigal curses her with sixty diseases pronounced by Namtar, her vizier. The effect of Ištar's death on earth is drastic: 'The bull springs not on the cow, the ass impregnates not the jenny, in the street the man impregnates not the maiden'. Inanna's vizier dons mourning and goes to **Ea**, who creates Asušunamir, a handsome, heterosexually impotent 'eunuch'. Having pleased Ereškigal by his presence, he is to demand the 'waterskin' hanging on the wall, a metaphor for Ištar's corpse. Ereškigal gets very angry at this request and curses Asušunamir, making him a social outcast. She then orders the **Anunnaki** to appear and has Ištar's body sprinkled with the Water of Life. At each gate the goddess puts on one of her regalia. The ending is confusing and seems to be a quotation from a ritual of Tammuz (**Dumuzi**).

The best known account of a vilification of Ištar occurs on the VI tablet of the **Gilgameš Epic**, when the hero violently rejects her offers of marriage and enumerates the unhappy fate of her previous lovers. He calls her fickle and unfaithful, a liar and quite without consequence, which she tries to disprove by demanding the Bull of Heaven from Anu. This ploy also fails, as **Enkidu** and Gilgameš kill the creature and Enkidu heaps insult on injury when he throws the 'thigh' (probably a euphemism for testicles) of the bull into her face. There are also some other, still very obscure Babylonian texts, known as 'Love Lyrics', which seem to be satirical descriptions of rivalry between Ištar and **Sarpanitum**, the wife of Marduk (Lambert, in Goedicke, Roberts 1975). The reason for this negative approach to Ištar, at least among some literary circles, is not known.

In the post-Old Babylonian liturgical texts written in Sumerian (mostly *eršemmas*) she appears mainly as a suffering goddess, who deprived of husband, son and possessions roams the desert and humbly pleads to the great gods to restore her good fortunes and those of her people.

According to other, non-theological documents, such royal inscriptions, legal texts, letters, and of course personal names, from Babylon and Assyria, Ištar remained unchallenged as Mesopotamia's foremost goddess, in her traditional double aspect of goddess of war and sexuality.

The dual personality of Ištar also found expression in the cult. She could be worshipped either in male guise (the 'bearded Ištar'), concentrating on her function as a warrior, or as a beautiful woman, in her capacity of goddess of love. It seems that by the first millennium BC, the male Ištar was associated with the north and the feminine Ištar with southern Mesopotamia. The cult of the 'voluptuous' Ištar (*ra'imat kuzbi u rišati*, 'who loves lewdness and exuberance', emphasized her connection with all forms of sexuality; her cult-personnel, especially at Uruk, not only included prostitutes of both sexes, but also transvestites and transsexuals. One of Ištar's faculties, often quoted in the texts, was the power to 'change masculinity into femininity', to confuse people's sexuality as well as promote its legitimate channels.

Tallqvist 1938, 330–8; van Driel 1969; Sladek 1974; Kramer, in Pritchard 1955, 52–7; Foster 1977, 79–84; Groneweg 1981, 127, 129; Lambert 1982, 173–218

There were numerous local manifestations of Ištar in northern Mesopotamia, Syria and Anatolia during the latter part of the second and the first millennium BC.

Ištar of Arbela

was often invoked by Neo-Assyrian monarchs to give advice through oracles before important political or military decisions. Her astronomical correlation may be Sirius, taken to be Venus during the latter's invisibility.

Lewy 1965, 274

Ištar Aššuritum, wife of **Aššur**, the national god of Assyria.

Ištar of Nineveh (*Ištar kakkabu*), 'Lady of the (Venus) Star'

The foundation of her temple goes back to the third millennium BC and was traditionally ascribed to Maništusu. She was also very popular among the Hurrian population (called Ištar-**Šaušga**) and is frequently mentioned in the Nuzi-texts. According to the Amarna correspondence, the Mitannian king once sent the statue of this Ištar to Egypt, in an attempt to cure the ailing pharaoh Amenophis III. The northern Ištar was introduced to Anatolia by the Assyrian merchants early in the second millennium BC and occupied an important place in the later Hittite pantheon, probably merged with other female deities, but identified by the logogram *IŠTAR*.

Vieyra 1957, 83–102; Danmanville 1962

Išum – Babylonian god

The origin of his name is doubtful. He was identified with the Sumerian god **Hendursanga**, probably already in the third millennium BC. Išum was a very popular god, judging from the large number of theophoric names from the Ur III period onwards, but he never became a 'great' god with a national cult. In the mythological texts Išum has a somewhat more ambiguous nature than Hendursanga, who is mainly a benevolent, merciful deity. He is the *sukallu* ('lieutenant') of **An** and sometimes called 'the devourer of people and country'. In the **Erra-Epic** he forms a foil to the impulsive plague-god and advocates moderation, but shows remarkable prowess when his force is directed against the enemies of the country. Unlike his master, he is able to discriminate between a 'just' and an unjustified war. In a late Neo-Assyrian text called 'The Underworld Vision of an Assyrian Crown-prince' he pleads with **Nergal** on behalf of the victim, and thereby brings about his release. Like **Ea**, Išum is credited with superior intelligence and successfully employs psychological manipulation to achieve his goals.

Edzard and Wilcke 1976, 142f

Itur-Mer – Babylonian god

His name is formed with that of another deity, a Babylonian hypostasis of the **Weather-God** Mer, and means 'Mer has returned' (Sumer. *mer/wer* means 'rain, rainstorm'). The god is known mainly from Mari, where he was the eponymous patron deity.

Ichiro 1979

J

Journeys of gods

In Mesopotamia (as also in Egypt) gods could pay visits to other gods outside their domain, journeying mainly by boat along the numerous canals and river-arms. This custom is not only documented by literary texts describing the mythical antecedent to these visits (see **Inanna and Enki**, **Nanna-Suen's Journey to Nippur**; the Return of **Ninurta** to Nippur), hymns and liturgical songs, but also in the prosaic lists of sacrifices which form part of the 'accounts' of the temples. In these the divine journeys are referred to in formulaic expressions. They furnish evidence where the literary material is lacking. During the Ur III period, **Inanna** went from Uruk to Eridu, **Ningirsu** from Lagaš to Eridu as well as to Uruk, **Enki** to **Enlil** in Nippur, etc. The timing of the expeditions varied, but mainly coincided with major festivals (such as the *akîtu* or New Year festival) in half-yearly intervals. Some journeys were veritable tours of Sumer; the one undertaken by Inanna and **Dumuzi** lasted several months and involved many cities and sanctuaries. It is possible that various events known from mythological texts are connected wtih these ritual journeys, but it is impossible to decide whether the ritual inspired the journey or vice versa.

Edzard, WdM, 1965, 75–7; Sauren 1969, 214–36

K

^d**KAL** see **Inar(a)** and **Protective deities**

Kamoš/Kamiš – Ancient Semitic god.

The etymology of his name is unclear. During the second millennium BC, he was widely worshipped in Syria, notably in Ebla and Karkamish. During the first millennium BC he appears as the national god of the Moabites on the stela of Mesha. Solomon is said to have introduced his cult to Jerusalem (1 Kings 11, 7.33). Since the Greek tradition identifies him with Ares, it is likely that he was a warrior-god.

van Ziyl 1960, 197–202; Pomponio 1978, 237

Kamrušepa

Hittite name for a Luwian goddess which was also known as Kataḫ-zip/wuri. She was an important deity of magic and healing, and as such she was often invoked in purification rites. In the same capacity she officiates in the myth of **Telepinu**, where she treats the god for his bad temper with various rituals and spells.

Frantz-Szabo, RLA V 1976, 351–2

Keret

The hero of an eponymous fragmentary Ugaritic text (*lkrt*; KTU 1 14, 15, 16), which was written by the scribe **Elimelek**. The following synopsis follows the translation by de Moor.

Keret, the king of Khubur, is deeply unhappy. Not only has he lost all his male relatives, but none of the seven wives he married in succession lived long enough to give him children. The god **El** appears to Keret in a dream. He gives him detailed instructions on how to overcome his problems. First the king has to ascend a high tower and offer a bull to El. Then he has to prepare for a long military campaign against the neighbouring kingdom of Udum. The besieged king will offer him rich tribute, gold, chariots, slaves and other treasure, but Keret is to reject everything, and demand instead his daughter Hariya in marriage. Keret does exactly as bidden. Having raised a formidable army, which even includes the newly married men, he ventures to Udum. On the way, he stops at the shrine of the goddess **Aštart**. He promises to give her threefold the weight of his wife in gold and twice in silver if his mission should be successful. Once in Udum, all goes according to plan and he wins the beautiful bride. All the gods come to the wedding and bless the couple. El declares that Hariya will bear eight sons and eight daughters, but that the youngest daughter, Tatmanat, 'the Eighth', will be 'his first born' (his heir). Hariya indeed gives birth to sixteen children and all is well until Aštart remembers the vow, which has apparently never been honoured. She raises her voice and cries: 'Woe, two vows you have broken, I too will break my obligations'. [gap] She announces that Keret will become ill and advises him to make arrangements for his funeral. He is to give instructions to his wife to prepare the sacrificial banquets and lead the mourning. [gap] Aštart's commands are being obeyed, and people are assembled to weep over Keret, who is 'only a finger's breadth away from death'. The king taunts them with sarcastic words and eventually the guests depart and only his children remain to lament their sick father, 'prowling like puppies through the house'. Keret demands that his youngest daughter is sent for, 'whose passion is strongest', that she may weep for him and offer sacrifices to her personal god on her father's behalf. When she hears of Keret's dangerous illness, she immediately begins her wailing and laments. [gap] As the result of the king's ill health, the vegetation suffers from drought. Attempts are made to call down the rains by magic rituals. [gap] Somebody, probably **Baal**, convenes a divine assembly to deal with the problem of Keret's affliction and its consequences. [gap] Aštart states her case and the gods are asked who among them is able to expel the illness. As they all remain silent, El himself declares that he 'will perform magic (and) create a female being able to cast out the disease'. He fills his palm with clay and creates a winged woman, whom he names Šatiqtu, 'she-who-causes-to-pass'. He gives her a flower and puts a 'charm on her lips'. [gap] Šatiqtu flies into the town and cures Keret, she washes him clean of his sweat and restores his appetite. Immediately he calls out to his wife to prepare him a fat lamb and after two days, he is able to resume his throne. His son

Yassub, however, who had pondered the effects of his father's illness on the performance of kingship, enters the royal hall and challenges Keret to abdicate in his favour. The king has only scorn for his son and curses him, asking **Horon** to smash his skull. Here the text breaks off, but there is at least another tablet missing. The eventual outcome is unknown, but according to several hints in the preserved text, Keret loses all his children but the youngest daughter.

Ginsberg 1946; Gray 1964; Astour 1973, 29–39; Gibson 1978; Loewenstamm 1979, 505ff; de Moor 1987, 191–223

Ki – Sumerian goddess

The name means 'earth, land'. There is as yet no evidence that this was a 'real' deity, who had a cult under this name. It may well be more of a theological concept, a counterpart to **An**, as it only occurs in lists of divine names in a cosmogonic context. As there were several different traditions concerning the origin of the created world, Ki has different connotations. It is impossible to decide at which point and where these concepts changed. One tradition, preserved in an early version of the list An=*Anum* (text TRS 10), states that the goddess **Nammu** was the mother of Heaven and Earth (*ama-ù.tu.an.ki*), who in turn gave birth to the first generation of gods, such as **Enlil**. A late survivor of the same idea is contained in the ***Enuma eliš*** where the primeval pair **Apsu** and Tiamat engendered Lahmu and Lahamu, who in turn produced Anšar and Kišar. The later version of TRS 10 traces the genealogy of Enlil back through fifteen male-female pairs, including the couple En.ki and Nin.ki, to be interpreted in this context as Lord and Lady Earth. While **Enki** is one of the great Sumerian gods, Nin.ki seems to be an artificially constructed counterpart for the purpose of the list. The introduction to **Gilgameš, Enkidu and the Netherworld**, states that 'Enlil carried off the earth'. Kramer (1976) concluded 'that theologians unhappy with a female deity as the ruler of so important a cosmic entity as earth, had taken her power away from her and transferred it to a male deity'.

Kramer 1976, 14

Kiriša/Kiririša – Elamite goddess

Her name (*kiri.riša*) means 'great goddess'. She was originally a local goddess of Liyan (S.E. Iran) and in the course of the second millennium BC merged with the great mother-goddess, **Pin(en)kir**, at least since the

18th C BC. Hinz argued that Kiriša was a 'taboo-name' for the latter goddess which eventually developed to a separate divine personality.

Hinz 1972, 42–4; RLA V 1976–80, 605–6

Kothar/Kothar-and-Hasis

West Semitic god; his name (Ug. *ktr.w.hss*) could be translated as 'Skilful-and-Wise'. He is the craftsman of the gods, equated by Sunchiaton with Hephaistos and by the Egyptians with Ptah. He appears in the Ugaritic myths as a blacksmith and silversmith, an architect and a maker of weapons. In the **Baal-Myths** he fashions the palace for Baal, the presents for Ašera (**Aštart**) and the weapons Baal uses to defeat Yam. He also made the bow given to **Aqhat**. He is said to live in a distant place; either called *kptr* (Crete?) or *hkpt* (Egypt?). Outside the mythological text this god is little known.

Pope, WdM 1965, 295f

Kotharat

Canaanite goddesses, usually 'seven' in number, whose name, like that of Kothar, is derived from *ktr*, 'to be skilful'. They appear in the myth of **Yarik and Nikkal**, where they are compared to swallows, who sweep down with their potions. They are also called 'daughters of the New Moon' (*bnt hll snnt*), an allusion to their connection with childbirth and fertility. In Ugarit the term signified by extension professional singers, who were called at important occasions such as birth, marriage and death.

Lökkegaard 1956, 53–64; Margulis 1972, 52–61

Kubaba (*see figure 19*)

Anatolian goddess, maybe of Syrian or North Mesopotamian origin. She first appears as a major deity of Karkamish (as in Hittite or Luwian inscriptions). During the Neo-Hittite empire, her cult spread outwards throughout Syria and Anatolia. She does not feature in any known mythological texts. Kubaba is the ancient prototype for the Hellenistic deity Kybebe, a mother-goddess with an ecstatic cult.

Laroche 1960, 113–28; Hawkins 1981, 147–75

Kumarbi

Hurrian god, son of **Anu** and father of the **Weather-god**. The Hurrians identified him with **Enlil**, the Ugaritians with **El**. One of his cult-centres was Urkiš on the Habur in Syria. He may have been an agricultural (grain) deity. Several myths and fragments of myth have developed around Kumarbi. The best known concern dynastic difficulties between subsequent generations. The first, also known as KINGSHIP IN HEAVEN, is a Hittite version of a Hurrian myth. It describes the first generations of divine beings who fight for hegemony. Alalu is being deposed by Anu, his son and 'cup-bearer', who in his turn is attacked by his son Kumarbi. When Anu tries to escape, Ullikummi bites off his genitals. Anu tells him that he will now become pregnant with the weather-god, the Tigris and Tašmišu, which prompts Kumarbi to spit out the semen. Some of it falls to the ground and impregnates the earth with two children. The text is fragmentary from here on, but it seems that Kumarbi does become pregnant and has problems giving birth to the weather-god. But he manages, and in the end Anu and the weather-god overthrow Kumarbi, and the weather-god takes over the kingship.

The MYTH OF ULLIKUMMI may be a sequel. Kumarbi plots to overthrow the storm-god. He impregnates a great rock and it bears a stone monster called Ullikummi. Kumarbi installs him on the right shoulder of the giant Upelluri, in a distant place, where he may grow up unseen by the weather-god. Enlil suspects Ullikummi but does not betray him, although he divines Kumarbi's plan. The sun-god is the first to notice Ullikummi, who has already grown alarmingly in fifteen days. He informs the weather-god, who takes several other gods to go and inspect the monster. **Ištar** tries to entice him with her charms (see **Hedammu**), but as Ullikummi is still unable to see or hear, this plan falters. The weather-god now decides to use all his forces; he orders his bulls, the storm and lightning-bolts to be fetched. Eventually all the gods, including the war-god Aštabi, are fighting against Ullikummi, but he has grown so big that they are unable to harm him. The weather-god decides to consult **Ea**, who has not joined in the fighting. Ea goes to find Upelluri and inquires after Ullikummi. The giant answers that he has not noticed anything except some pain in his right shoulder. Ea then asks the **Primeval gods** to lend them the cutting-tool, which was originally used to sever the earth from the sky. He manages to cut Ullikummi off Upelluri, which immediately reduces his power. The gods are encouraged by Ea's news and renew their attack, in spite of Ullikummi's continued threats to take over the heavenly kingship. The end of the myth is not preserved but probably contained the final victory of the weather-god.

Güterbock 1946; 1951, 135–61; Otten 1950; von Schuler, WdM 1965, 185, 204–6; Hawkins 1981, 16f

L

Labbu

A monstrous creature with leonine and serpent features. The actual reading of its name (written as *KAL.bu*) is still uncertain. The slaying of this creature is described in a myth which is only partially known from Neo-Assyrian tablets. People as well as the gods are afraid of the monster, which had apparently been created by **Enlil** to decimate the noisy human race (excessive noise, Akk. *rigmu*, is also the reason for sending other plagues and the deluge. See **Flood-myths**). Labbu is 'fifty double-hours long' and has a voracious appetite, snatching the birds out of the sky and eating people and animals on land (see also the myth of **Hedammu**). The gods implore **Tišpak** to fight Labbu on their behalf and at first he raises objections. The text is broken but when it becomes legible again the battle is in full swing. The victorious god, probably Tišpak, although the name is not preserved, kills Labbu after holding 'the seal of his life' before its eyes.

Heidel 1942, 141–3; Lambert, in Hecker, Sommerfeld 1986, 55f

Lahar and Ašnan/ Cattle and Grain

Sumerian myth in the form of a 'disputation'.

An introduction *in illo tempore* describes how **An** created the **Anunnaki** in the 'mountains of heaven and earth'. But because the world was as yet not fully organized, because neither **Ašnan**, the grain goddess, nor Lahar, the cattle goddess, nor Uttu, the goddess of vegetation, had as yet been born, the Anunnaki had to eat grass with their mouth like sheep and drink water from a ditch. In the *du₆kù*, 'the pure place', 'the creation-place of the gods', Lahar and Ašnan are created. They are now able to produce more food, notably milk, but the Anunnaki are still not sated. 'For the sake of their pure sheepfolds, the good, man was given breath' and **Enki** and Enlil decide to send the goddess to the earth. 'For

Lahar they set up the sheepfold, plants and herbs in abundance they present her. For Ašnan they establish a house, plough and yoke they present her.' They thus introduce agriculture and animal husbandry and the people are able to supply the gods with abundant sustenance. The text continues in a manner that is characteristic for the genre of disputations; the two goddesses begin to quarrel, each extolling the advantages of her gifts and denigrating the achievements of the other. Finally, Enki and Enlil intervene and Ašnan is declared the winner.

Falkenstein 1948, 165; Kramer 1963, 220–2

Lahmu/ Lahamu/(Sum. Lahama)

Mesopotamian gods; the etymology of their name is unexplained. It is a collective title for groups of divine beings (see **Anunnaki** and **Igigi**) in some Sumerian and Babylonian mythological texts. The Sumerian texts relate them to the god **Enki**; they seem to belong to the sea or the **Apsu** and count fifty (so for example in **Enki and the World Order**, where the fifty Lahama 'of the sea' do homage to Enki). In **Inanna and Enki** the god sends them to pursue Inanna. Another text describes them as composite, half-fish, half-anthropomorphic creatures. In the Babylonian **Enuma eliš** they appear as a pair, Lahmu and Lahamu, and their watery nature is implied by the fact that they are the offspring of Apsu and Tiamat.

The same term also seems to stand for the protective spirits of the gate-posts, which guarded the entrances to buildings, during the Ur III and Old Babylonian period.

Edzard, WdM 1965; 93–4; Lambert 1985, 189–202

Lama, Lamma, Lamassu (*see figure 26*)

Sumerian protective minor deity or demon, with a predominantly intercessary role. She is well known from the Lagash pantheon since the Early Dynastic period. Her cult was most popular during the Old Babylonian period; inscriptions tell us that one or more Lamas resided in the major temples. She may also be represented on cylinder seals, introducing the worshipper to the presence of a great god (Spycket). After this time Lamassu became a term for protective spirits generally. In Assyria, the giant winged bulls or lions with human heads, which flanked the gateways of temples and palaces, were known as Šedu and Lamassu.

The concept of this deity also spread to Syria. The Hurrians probably introduced her to Anatolia. In the Hittite texts $^dKAL = {^dLAMA} = annaris$ formed a group of many different gods and goddesses and it is difficult to assign them all a primarily protective function.

Spycket 1960, 73–84; Foxvog, Heimpel et al, RLA VI 1980–83, 446–89

Lamaštu

A Babylonian female demon; a daughter of **Anu**. She is mentioned in many rituals and incantations. One such text offers a vivid description of her appearance and activity; she is a terrible goddess, 'like a leopard, her feet are like those of **Anzu**, her hands are dirty, her face that of a lion; she comes out of the marshes, her hair in disorder, her breasts uncovered, she follows the cattle and the sheep, her hands in flesh and blood. Like a serpent she glides in through the windows, leaves the house, "Bring me your children to suckle, I shall be their nurse" (is her call)' (Thureau-Dangin). She represented the danger of infant and children's mortality; many charms and masks have been excavated in the ancient towns which used to hang by doorways in the hope of keeping her at bay.

Thureau-Dangin 1921, 13ff; Farber, in RLA VI 1980–83, 439; Black, Green forthcoming

Lelwani/Leluwani

Anatolian chthonic deity, in the Hittite texts written as $^dEREŠ.KI.GAL$. During the Old Hittite kingdom the underworld deity was male, as his titles were 'lord' or 'king'. Under the influence of the Hurrians, Lelwani became female and was identified with **Allani** and the Mesopotamian **Ereškigal**. As such she became an important goddess and was often invoked by queen Puduhepa. Later, Lelwani seemed to acquire solar aspects, maybe because of a further process of assimilation to the Hattian **Sun-goddess of Arinna**, who in turn assumed chthonic characteristics.

Otten 1950, 119–36; Lebrun 1980, 59; von Schuler, RLA VI 1980–83; 595–8

Lugalbanda – Deified Sumerian king and hero

He is mentioned in the King-list as the third king of the First Dynasty of Uruk, the son of Enmerkar. He also appears in the Fara god-lists as the husband of **Ninsun**. As a god he was worshipped during the Old Babylonian period in Nippur and Uruk. In **Gilgameš and Huwawa** he is called the husband of the goddess **Ninsun** and the father of **Gilgameš**.

He is the hero of two Sumerian compositions which are known from tablets found at Nippur, Kish, Uruk and Nineveh, going back to Ur III and Old Babylonian editions. For the proposal that the texts formed one coherent whole, see Falkowitz.

Lugalbanda and Hurrum/Lugalbanda I

The introduction consists of a brief reference to the separation of heaven and earth and the subsequent organization of the civilized world, specifically the irrigation-based, barley-producing Sumer. **Enmerkar** is the lord of Uruk-Kullaba. As described in other myths (**Enmerkar and Enšukeš-dana**, **Enmerkar and the Lord of Aratta**), his main rival is Aratta, a faraway city to the east of Mesopotamia. In this story, Enmerkar is again leading his troops across the mountains to set siege to Aratta. Lugalbanda is with them. On the way, he suddenly becomes 'paralysed'. His comrades are obliged to leave him behind. They hand him his weapons, leave some provisions and promise to collect him or his body, should he have died by then, on their way home. Left by himself, Lugalbanda prays to the astral gods, **Utu**, **Inanna** and Su'en (see **Nanna**). As a result, good demons chase the sickness away and he is able to get up. They also help him to find the Plant of Life and the Water of Life which he consumes. His energy is now fully restored and joyfully he runs across the mountain slopes to get himself something to eat with the food his companions have left him. He discovers that he has no fire to cook it with, but after some experimenting he manages to produce a spark with two stones. He lights a small fire and bakes some bread in the ashes, which he eats with date-syrup. Then he catches a brown wild bull and some mountain goats. He falls asleep and in his dream the dream-god advises him what to do next. He is to kill the captured animals and to offer the hearts to the sun-god and the blood to the serpents of the steppe. When Lugalbanda awakes, he does as bidden, and furthermore prepares a splendid feast of the roast meats and his own provisions, to which he invites the great gods (**An**, **Enlil** and **Ninhursag**). He erects a separate altar for the astral deities, Su'en, Inanna and Utu. One by one they manifest themselves as evening falls and the moon appears. Then the morning star shines brightly and finally the sun rises. The demons of the night are overcome. The final passages of the text are not preserved.

Alster 1976, 15; Wilcke, RLA VI 1980–83, 121–5; Hallo 1984, 165–80

Lugalbanda and Anzu/Lugalbanda and Enmerkar/Lugalbanda II

Lugalbanda finds himself alone in the wild mountains of Zabu while his companions are on their way to Aratta. He decides to seek out the fabulous **Anzu**-bird, that he may show him the right way. Anzu's nest is on the 'eagle tree on top of Inanna's carneol mountain'. When Lugalbanda discovers this nest, in which the young birds are sitting, he shows them due respect by setting aside some of the sacrifice to feed the fledglings and he also decorates them with kohl and white feathers (a well-known ritual act which was usually performed on cult statues). Meanwhile, the old bird had been herding bulls for the eaglets' supper. When he arrives at his nest, the young birds show no signs of appetite, which greatly worries Anzu. But when he discovers that they had been fed and decorated, he bursts into a song of self-praise, enumerates the great powers he received from **Enlil** and finally promises to decide a favourable fate for the benefactor. Lugalbanda, who had hidden himself at the bird's arrival, now approaches and prostrates himself before Anzu. The bird in turn pronounces his fate. Among other more obscure blessings, Lugalbanda is to have unfailing arrows, prowess in battle like **Ninurta**, abundance of milk and fat. Lugalbanda, however, wishes for the 'speed of sunlight, the power of storms', to go where he pleases and not to cause a quarrel by his arrival. In return he promises Anzu to dedicate a wooden statue to him. The bird grants these requests and commands Lugalbanda not to tell anyone of his new capacities or how he acquired them. Then he flies up to look for the troops of Uruk (apparently led by **Enmerkar**) and tells Lugalbanda to join them. His comrades are greatly surprised to find their lost friend suddenly in their midst and feed him 'like a young bird'. The army swiftly marches to Aratta and they begin to besiege the city. However, the inhabitants defend themselves successfully and the Urukians spend a year in vain trying to overcome their resistance. Someone will have to go back to Uruk to plead with the city goddess **Inanna**. Lugalbanda volunteers to go alone and receives a detailed message from Enmerkar. He is to remind Inanna that the goddess herself had organized the wet lands and the dry lands of Uruk, that she had chosen Enmerkar to be its *en*, build her temples and fight off the encroaching nomads. But now she has turned away from her subject and his rulership is in jeopardy. She obviously prefers the Lord of Aratta and has stopped loving Enmerkar. Lugalbanda departs and arrives in an instant at Inanna's temple. The goddess receives him gracefully and he delivers the message. In response Inanna describes a ritual to Lugalbanda which will rejuvenate his troops. She also reminds Enmerkar not only to seize the precious metals and minerals for which Aratta is famous but to bring the craftsmen and their tools as well. The poem then ends with a doxology in praise of Lugalbanda.

Wilcke 1969; Kramer 1971, 363–78; Wilcke, RLA VI (1980–83), 126–30; Falkowitz in Sasson 1984, 103–14

Luwian gods

The Luwians were a people of S.W. Anatolia who also spoke an Indo-European language. During the Hittite Empire their gods were incorporated into the Hittite pantheon. They include a **Weather-god** called Tarhunta, the moon-god Arma, as well as Sanda (written as *MARDUK*) and Yarri, who were both gods of pestilence. The goddess of healing and magic, **Kamrušepa**, appears in the myth of **Telepinu**.

M

Malik – Semitic god

His name means 'king'. He was apparently an important deity in Ebla where many people were called after him. However, he appears only rarely in official cult texts or lists of sacrifices. Maybe he was not even a god in his own right, but a synonym or epithet of another deity such as **El**.

Lebrun 1984, 38

Mamitu – Akkadian goddess

The name derives from Akk.*māmītum*, 'oath', and she seems to have originally been a personification of the oath, who pursues and punishes the perjurer. Later she acquired chthonic aspects and was considered to be the wife of **Nergal** or **Erra**. In the **Gilgameš Epic** (Tablet 10,6) she is called 'creatress of destiny', who with the **Anunnaki** 'allots life and death'.

The short version of the name is Mami or Mame, which is easily confused with **Mamma**.

Edzard, WdM 1965, 95

Mamma/Mama/Mami – Akkadian goddess

The name is the baby-word for 'mother'. Her most common epithets are *ummi*, 'mother', or *asû*, 'midwife'. Mamma occurs frequently in Mesopotamian female personal names since the Pre-Sargonic period, but never in Sumerian names.

Roberts 1972, 43f; Krebernik, RLA VII 1989, 330

Marduk – Babylonian god (*see figures 8, 10 and 37*)

His name was usually written logographically as ^{d}*amar.UD*, more rarely as ^{d}*MES*, ^{d}*ŠÀ.ZU* or ^{d}*ŠÙ*. Syllabic versions from various periods allow the phonetic reading of Marduk. While the most common logogram, ^{d}*amar.UD*, may be read either as a genitive construction, 'the Young Bull of the Sun', or an apposition, meaning something like 'the son, the sun', it is not certain that Marduk was a Sumerian name. Like the etymology of his city Babylon, it may belong to a proto-Sumerian, non-Semitic linguistic stratum which is as yet unknown. The very obscurity of the divine name provoked numerous attempts at etymological speculation among the scholars of ancient Mesopotamia, which is reflected in god-lists and the ***Enuma eliš*** (Bottéro). Isolated examples of the mention of Marduk exist since the Old Sumerian period, as for instance in a god-list from Abu Salabikh. His rise to national importance, however, was directly linked with the political success of the First Dynasty of Babylon, and specifically its most famous king, Hammurabi. His elevation to one of the great gods of Hammurabi's empire found expression in the prologue to his 'law-code' (I, 1–15): 'When the exalted **Anu**, king of the **Anunnaki** and Ellil (**Enlil**), lord of heaven and earth, ... allotted the divine lordship (*ellilutu*) of the multitude of the people unto Marduk, the first-born son of **Ea**, he magnified him amongst the **Igigi** ...' There is little evidence outside the royal inscriptions of the Old Babylonian Dynasty that the cult of Marduk reached much beyond the sanctuary of Babylon. There are also very few religious texts from this period which concern the god. His growing popularity among the people, however, seems to be proved by the fact, that even at the beginning of his 'career' he appears in a significant list of personal names (Lambert 1984). The popular success of Marduk is one of the most interesting religious developments of the second millennium BC, as it cannot be reduced to political or theological promotion alone. At an age when personal piety was an important element of worship, Marduk was seen as an approachable deity, who cares for human beings and their sufferings. Together with the sun-god **Šamaš** and the other 'friendly' god, **Ea**, he was one of the triad of the most important gods of incantations, who avert evil influences. Although there was no genealogical relationship between Šamaš and Marduk, there was much the two deities had in common, especially the aspects of justice, impartiality and compassion. Ea was considered the father of Marduk (see above, in the prologue).

During the Kassite period, the cult of Marduk gradually spread beyond central Mesopotamia. The great god-list An=*anum*, which probably dates from this period, attributes the sacred number fifty to Marduk, which had hitherto been accorded to **Enlil**. By the time of the Babylonian 'restoration', the second Dynasty of Isin, Marduk was officially acknowledged as the 'lord of the gods'. The most comprehensive text arguing for this pre-eminence, the *Enuma eliš*, was probably composed at this period. Marduk was also introduced to Assyria, where he was honoured as one of the great gods in official inscriptions, without quite reaching the popularity of his son **Nabû**. In the Neo-Babylonian period Marduk, the national god, the chief of the pantheon and the 'father of mankind', had no rival. His main sanctuary, the temple É-sagil and the ziggurat, É-temenanki, formed the pivot of the universe; their wealth and splendour was still proverbial when Herodotus visited the city several hundred years after its destruction.

The nature of Marduk became increasingly complex as he gradually absorbed the functions and characteristics of many other gods. This is well documented by the great number of hymns and prayers (Seux 1973, passim), of theological works dedicated to Marduk, as well as numerous references in private and official documents, personal names etc. (For the range of official epithets, see Tallqvist 1938, 362–72). As the son of Ea, Marduk was a god of wisdom, healing, the magic arts, and to some extent, irrigation and fertility. The connection with magic was further strengthened by his identification with the Sumerian incantation-god **Asarluhi**. The *Enuma eliš* celebrates the glory of Marduk by enumerating his fifty names and functions. It provided a mythological justification for his superior position in the pantheon, as the deliverer from the forces of primeval chaos and the organizer of the known universe. In these multiple capacities he virtually replaced Anu, Ellil and some of the energetic young warrior gods who traditionally battled against demonic powers (e.g. **Ninurta**). For his relationship with Šamaš, see above. In the **Erra-Epic** he is the guarantee of peace and prosperity; war and rebellion are the direct consequence of his absence; not a new theological explanation for the existence of evil, but dramatically expressed to suit the historical events of the Neo-Babylonian period.

Marduk's wife was **Sarpanitum**, his son Nabû, and **Ištar** became his sister. Numerous other minor gods were employed in his 'court'.

The emblematic animal of Marduk is the Mušhuššu, a composite snake and dragon, his symbol the *marru* a hoe-shaped implement.

van Dijk 1966, 61f; Edzard, WdM 1965, 96–7; Lambert 1975, 193–4; Bottéro 1977, 5–18; Sommerfeld 1982; RLA VII 1989, 360–70; Lambert 1984, 1–9

Martu see **Amurru**

me

Sumerian word, probably derived from the verb 'to be'. No adequate translation has yet been proposed. The Akkadian translation *parşu*, 'regulation, rule', also only partially conveys the Sumerian range of connotations. In modern editions of Sumerian texts, *me* is usually left untranslated, but it has been rendered among others, as 'divine force' (Kramer), 'divine decree' (Landsberger), 'modus operandi', 'norm' (Jacobsen) and 'prescriptions' (Rosengarten).

The gods are said to possess *me*, the more the better. Divine epithets take this fact into account: **Inanna**, for example, is called the 'Queen of all the *me*'. It seems that **An** and **Enlil** are the only gods who bestow but do not receive *me* from others. They can also give it to cities, temples, kings and countries. The transfer of *me* is the subject of many Sumerian compositions, such as **Enki and the World Order**, and most notably **Inanna and Enki**, where a list of over a hundred *me* is enumerated several times. They include kingship, priestly offices, ritual implements, crafts and music, as well as intercourse, prostitution, old age, heroism, strength, justice, flattery, the descending and ascending from the netherworld (Inanna's specific *me*?), peace and war. Other *me* are perjury, rebellious cities, hard work, silence, intelligence, the scribal arts and a great variety of ritual implements, the significance of which is poorly understood. The list is not composed along any discernible structure and is probably only meant as a sample of the 'totality' of possible *me*. There are a great number of *me*, as expressed by the collective numeralia 7, 50 and 3,000. The possession of the totality of the *me* (*me.nig.nam.ma*) entails not only absolute power but also absolute responsibility towards their realization or implementation in the world. The *me* are not immune to destruction, or at least to temporary disappearance. In the lamentations and prayers, the loss of *me* results in all manners of calamities, natural as well as political, and the concept here furnishes a theology able to explain misfortune and catastrophes in an otherwise ideally created world. Rosengarten has stressed the proto-platonic aspect of the *me*. She described them as pre-ordained matrices of an ideal society which become immanent and fully realized in the civilized world.

Landsberger 1926, 369; Oberhuber 1963; Jacobsen 1970, 359, n.20; Farber-Flügge 1973; Alster 1975, 20–34; Rosengarten 1977

Melqart – West Semitic god

His name means 'king of the city'. In the Phoenician period he was the main deity of Tyre and later of its colony Carthage, which was called after the god. He is first mentioned in a treaty between Esarhaddon of Assyria and Baal of Tyre. The Greeks and Romans identified him with Heracles and he was shown with a lion-skin.

Röllig, WdM 1965, 297

Meslamta'ea – Sumerian god

His name derives from his temple called Meslam at Kutha and means something like 'The One who emerges from Meslam'. He is already mentioned in the Fara texts as an underworld deity. By the Ur III period he became identified with **Nergal**.

Mezulla – Anatolian goddess

Daughter of the **Weather-god** and the **Sun-goddess of Arinna**. She is often invoked in Hittite texts together with her mother, as an intermediary between mankind and the great gods.

Lebrun 1980, 46

Milkom – West Semitic god

The name is probably derived from the word *mlk*, 'king'.

During the first millennium BC he was known as the national deity of Ammon and mentioned several times in the Old Testament ('the abomination of the Ammonites'), since Solomo instituted his cult in Juda (1 Kings, 11, 5, 7, 33).

Röllig, WdM 1965, 299

Moon-gods

Anatolian: usually written ^{d}XXX (= 30; the traditional number for the moon) or $^{d}EN.ZU$. The Luwian moon-god was called Arma, the Hurrian Kušuh, and the proto-Hattian Kašku. A fragmentary **myth** (Kammenhuber) tells how Kašku falls from the sky in a storm. Fortunately **Kamrušepa**, the goddess of healing and magic, helps him with an incantation to withstand the raging of the **weather-god** and get back to heaven.

Laroche 1955, 13ff; Kammenhuber 1955, 130ff
Sumerian: see **Nanna**; **Akkadian**: see **Suen/Sin**; **West Semitic**: see **Nikkal** and **Yarih**.

Mot – West Semitic god

The etymology of his name derives from Semitic *mwt, 'to die'; Akkad. *mutum*, 'death'. He is the deification of death; to die is to be 'eaten by Mot'. He is mainly known from the mythological texts of Ugarit, as the great adversary of **Baal**. His epithets are *bn ilm mt*, 'Mot (is) a son of the gods' and *ydd il gzr*, 'beloved of El', which prove that he is part of the divine order. His realm in the myths is 'the innermost part of the earth', a land of 'decay, filth, spittle and slime'. He can appear as a serpent, but the richness of metaphors typical of Ugaritic poetry also evokes other images. Most characteristic is his enormous appetite: 'the appetite of the whale in the sea (...) Lo, verdure is the subsistence of my life, my appetite is for clay and verdure, of all (that) dies do I eat' (Margalit, 14). Baal is overcome by Mot but rises again, and likewise Mot is overcome by **Anat** and then reassembles himself at a later date. It has been proposed that while one of Baal's aspects is the greening of the vegetation following the winter rains, Mot stands for the barren hard-baked earth of the dry summer, but probably also for the ripening of the corn. Both gods succeed one another in the agricultural year; one can never completely triumph over the other.

Pope, WdM 1965, 390–402; Watson 1971; Loewenstamm 1972; Margalit 1980; Stolz, in Assmann, Burkert, Stolz 1982

Mother-goddess/Great Goddess (*see figure 21*)

The earliest manifestations of religious activities, only known from artefacts of prehistoric sites, seem to be connected with the worship of a female deity.

Countless figurines of the goddess are known from the European stone age and from the 7th and 6th millennia in Anatolia (Çatal Hüyük, Hacilar). Most of these sculptures emphasize the physical attributes of female fertility – large hips, swollen bellies and pendulous breasts. Figures of nude women continued to appear in all later periods and in all areas of the Near East, from Egypt to Iran. On the whole, however, post-Neolithic figures underline sexual characteristics rather than those of pregnancy. The universal cult of the mother-goddess seems to have declined when urban civilizations evolved, with the profound change of social conditions and a complex as well as patriarchially structured pantheon. There are indications, however, that as a 'popular religion' it survived many official local and national cults – see for instance in Egypt, the re-emergence of the Hathor/Isis cult in times of political instability (Rundle Clark, 29, 87). But since the literate circles of the city-states had little interest in the 'folk-religions' of their time, the textual sources do not yield much information on this subject.

In **Anatolia**, probably the ancient epicentre of the mother-goddess, she remained the most powerful divine figure throughout the different historical periods. In the Neolithic levels of Çatal Hüyük she appeared primarily in connection with fertility, shown in the process of giving birth, suckling, and in a sexual embrace. Her images were found in grain bins. But the association with death and the underworld is also evident in the curious painted 'shrines' of the city, where the symbols of the goddess (modelled breasts incorporated into the wall) were found next to funerary scenes (vultures swooping down on headless corpses). The goddess was also shown with felines, leopards or lions, and these animals remained attached to her throughout history. Her male partner and/or son was represented by the bull. In historical times, she was worshipped in Hatti as **Wurunšemu**, 'earth' or **Inara**, the protective deity of the land. The Hurrians called her simply 'the Lady' (Allani), the Hittites **Hannahanna**, 'grandmother' or **Hebat**. It is likely that many of the local goddesses, whose names were simply written with the logo-gram for **Ištar**, were manifestations of the mother-goddess.

In **Mesopotamia**, cheap and mass-produced clay figurines of nude females with wide hips and clearly defined pudenda were discovered in practically all archaeological levels. This may be evidence for the contin-uing veneration of the goddess. It is interesting that the majority of Sumerian divine names are male and that there does not seem to be a genuine Sumerian name for the mother-goddess. Instead we have a variety of appellatives, the oldest of which are **Ninhursaga**, 'Lady of the mountain', **Ninmah**, 'Exalted Lady', and **Damgalnunna**, 'great wife of the lord'. Their cult-centres were in Tell Obeid, Adab and Kesh. Lambert (p. 126) speculated whether 'decline of Kesh is to blame for the mother-goddess's wavering position in the Babylonian top-group of gods'. Several male gods have names composed with the feminine *nin*, origin-ally 'Lady', such as **Ninurta**, **Ningirsu**, **Ningišzida** etc., which may go back to female deities, although, or maybe because, their masculine qualities (warrior gods!) are usually emphasized. It has been proposed (Kienast), that the original agricultural population of Sumer worshipped a female goddess, each community their own, which were in due time replaced by male gods, either by 'marriage' (as **Enki** and Damgalnunna at Eridu, one of the oldest Sumerian religious sites) or by suppression. This situation is sometimes reflected in mythological texts or god-lists (see **Cosmogonies**), where the mother-goddess was usually listed on third or fourth place behind **An**, **Enlil** (and **Enki**), but never comes first. In the great god-list An=^{d}*Anum* the identity of different mother-goddesses (Ninhursaga, Ninmah, Nintu, Ninmenna, Aruru, Dingirmah, Mamma, Bēlet-ilî) merged almost completely, and by the time of the Isin-Larsa period she almost disappeared from the lists. In mythological texts, the mother-goddess is involved in the creation of mankind (**Enki and Ninmah**, Atra-hasis (see **Flood-myths**), **Epic of Gilgameš**). There are also numerous, if almost subliminal references in other myths and religious texts which underline her essential role as the sustainer of animal and human life. During the Old Babylonian period, many formerly independent mother-goddesses became wives of gods, and assumed an increasingly mediating and interceding function. 'Feminine' qualities, such as compassion, forgiveness and humility were ascribed to these goddesses and even **Ištar**, the most independent of Mesopotamian goddesses, is addressed as a merciful mother-goddess in the first millennium BC, maybe under Hurrian influence.

In **Ugarit and Syria**, the mother-goddess (see **Aštart**) has a relatively inferior role compared to the **Weather-god** as far as the mythological texts are concerned. The archaeological evidence of the ubiquitous nude goddess and the evidence of the personal and geographical names, however, seems to point to a similar popularity as elsewhere in the Near East.

Helck 1971; Urbin-Choffray 1983, 380–1; Kienast 1985, 106–16; Lambert 1986, 125–30

Mountain-gods

In Anatolia mountains, as well as rivers and springs, were worshipped as divine powers. On another level of religious experience, the cloud-wreathed mountains were considered as the abodes of the gods, especially of the **Mother-goddess** and the **Weather-god**. The latter connection was very widespread in Asia Minor, Syria and Greece (see also **Baal** and his mountains and the role of Olympos in Greece). Hittite iconography

121

shows the weather-god standing on two mountains, but there is also a hieroglyph denoting 'mountain-god'. A 'female mountain' was apparently Zashapuna in Central Anatolia. Several Hittite kings were named after divine mountains: Tuthalia, Arnuwanda and Ammuna. There is also a fragmentary myth about the mountain-god **Pišaysa**. He perceives the (sleeping?) goddess **Ištar** and rapes her. When the goddess awakes, he humbly bows down before her and begs her to spare his life. In order to appease her, he prophesies that the weather-god will overcome his enemy, the sea (Otten).

von Schuler, WdM 1965, 160; van Buren 1943, 76–84; Otten 1953, 27ff

N

Nabû – Babylonian god (*see figures 10 and 37*)

His name could be written syllabically ^{d}*na-bi-um* or logographically ^{d}*AK* or ^{d}*PA*. The etymology is disputed; it could derive from *nb'*, 'to call, announce', meaning something like 'He who has Called', or it could be from *ne/abu*, 'shining, brilliant' (Dhorme), or from a quite different, unknown old-Syrian root (Pomponio).

The god was originally a West Semitic deity; he is mentioned among the Ebla gods. By the beginning of the second millennium BC the Amorites had introduced him to Mesopotamia, probably at the same time as **Marduk**. The two gods continued to have close connections throughout their history (well into the Persian period and beyond). While Marduk became the city-god of Babylon, Nabû resided in nearby Borsippa in his temple É-zida. He was first called the 'scribe and minister of Marduk', and when the latter was assimilated into the official pantheon as the son of **Ea**, Nabû in turn became known as the son of Marduk from his wife **Şarpanitum**. He was also accorded the office of patron of the scribes, taking over from the Sumerian goddess **Nisaba**. A fair number of beautifully written tablets were deposited in this sanctuary as ex-voto offerings, but so far no literary text extolling the deeds and functions of the god have been found. Nabû was also worshipped in Assyria; Shalmaneser I built the first Nabû sanctuary in Assur (13th C BC), and others followed in Nineveh, Kalah and Khorsabad. Following the expansion of the Assyrian empire from Sargon II onwards, he became one of the great gods of the realm and was frequently invoked in royal inscriptions. His popularity among the Assyrian people is also well documented by numerous private names, letters and prayers (for the latter see Seux 1976, passim). In this respect he may have substituted his father Marduk, who as the national god of the Babylonians, was not as acceptable to the Assyrians as his son. Being the patron of the scribal arts, he also represented the cultural traditions of the South, which were greatly admired. After the downfall of Assyria, Nabû rose to a high rank in the Neo-Babylonian pantheon, first in his capacity as Marduk's son and then in his own right. His cult in fact endured well into the Parthian period.

With his elevation to the ranks of the great gods, Nabû became a cosmic deity, entrusted with the Tablets of Destiny, 'pronouncing the Fate' of mankind. The texts equate him with **Ninurta**. He was also sometimes mentioned as a god of water and the fertility of fields, maybe through his descent from **Ea**; he also shares the epitheton of 'god of wisdom'.

Pomponio 1978

Nahhunte/Nahundi – Elamite god

His name *nan-hunde* means 'creator of the day'. Not much is known about this deity except that he was the sun-god and as such the supreme judge of men.

Hinz 1972, 47f

Nammu – Sumerian goddess

Her name is usually written with the sign *engur* which was also used to write **Apsu**. In ancient times she personified the Apsu as the source of water and hence fertility in lower Mesopotamia. She may well have been worshipped in Eridu before **Enki**, who took over most of her prerogatives and functions. Significantly he was called the son of Nammu. In spite of her decline following the superiority of Enki, during the Neo-Sumerian period, at least at Ur, she was still considered important enough to have statues commissioned in her honour and she also features in the name of the famous king Urnammu.

In mythology, Nammu appears as the primeval **Mother-goddess** in **Enki and Ninmah** who 'has given birth to the great gods'. She has the idea of creating mankind as a help for the gods and it is she who goes to wake her son Enki, asleep in the Apsu, that he may set the process going.

Nana – Sumerian goddess

She appears in women's names since the Old Akkadian period. During the Ur III period she had temples in Drehem and Umma, and in the Old

Babylonian period also at Uruk. For king Rimsin of Larsa she was the tutelary deity and in an inscription he praises her as 'the child, over-flowing with the strength of life, of the great **An**'. In a date formula of this time she is mentioned with An and **Inanna** as part of the Uruk triad. She seems to have affinities with Inanna and **Baba** as a goddess of fertility.

Wohlstein 1976; Ichiro 1979, 371–2

Nanaya – Sumerian goddess, known since the Ur III period

Like **Inanna** she is called the daughter of **An** and the sister of **Utu**, and she also seems to have been venerated as the planet **Venus**. She was, however, a deity in her own right, since in the offering-lists of Uruk she is mentioned alongside Inanna. In a bilingual Sumero-Akkadian hymn (Reiner), the goddess describes herself as having 'heavy breasts in Dadumu' and 'a beard in Babylon' – both references to the two genders that Ištar could be worshipped in – but she declares: 'yet I am still Nanaya'. She does not feature in any mythological texts, but is often invoked in love-incantations of a later date, where she is called *ᵈNa-na-a bel et kuzbu*, 'Nanaya, lady of sexual attractiveness' (Biggs). It is not always possible to differentiate Nanaya from **Nana**.

Biggs 1967; Edzard, WdM 1965, 108; Reiner 1974, 221–6

Nanna(r) – Sumerian moon-god

His name was usually written *ᵈŠEŠ.KI* probably because of his connec-tion with the city of Ur (Sum. *ŠEŠ.AB.KI*); an alternative spelling was *ᵈ30*, the symbolic number of the moon.

Nanna is already mentioned in the Old Sumerian god-list from Fara. He seems to have been worshipped at Ur since at least the middle of the second millennium BC. His temple there was the É-kišnugal, praised in the Sumerian Temple Hymn No. 8 (Sjöberg, Bergmann). The office of high-priestess at Ur was customarily filled by a royal princess, her enthronement was an event of national importance and duly recorded in year-names. References and theophoric names composed with Nanna are particularly frequent from the Ur III period. At this time many other sanctuaries and shrines were built or restored for him, notably the famous ziggurat at Ur by Urnammu.

Nanna is the son of **Ninlil** and the 'first-born son' of **Enlil**. He confers with his father in deciding the Fates. His wife is **Ningal**, and various

125

poetical compositions describe their courtship and the rapturous consummation of their love (Jacobsen, 124f). A result of their union is **Utu**, the sun-god. In Sumerian thought, night gives birth to day; the time of darkness has a creative potential which finds expression in Nanna's fertility aspects (see below). The Sun in contrast, was not directly associated with the source of life.

Nanna's epithets are *ašimbabbar*, 'the luminous', an allusion to the bright light of the moon; *amar*, 'calf', also *amar.ban.da.^{d}en.lil.a*, 'young calf of Enlil', *má.gur$_8$*, 'boat'. Both references are allusions to the crescent shape of the young moon, either recalling horns or the slender reed-boats of the marshes.

The moon-god in many cultures has associations with fertility; probably inspired by the menstrual cycle. In Sumer he was closely linked with the fertility of animals, especially cattle (the shape of the crescent moon is likened to horns). One hymn (ISET 1, 96–97 Ni 2781) declares '(you) make the breed bull and the good bull mount (the cow) for you, he makes the good seed flow for you. Top-grade milk and fat he is increasing.' Another composition, NANNA'S JOURNEY TO NIPPUR (Kramer), extends the connection with fertility to include all aspects of Sumerian agriculture. It begins with a description of Nippur, which is ready built, rich in animal and plant life but devoid of people. Nanna decides to visit his father's city by boat. He loads it with trees, plants and animals. On the way he stops several times and is greeted by the local gods. Eventually he reaches Nippur, where he enumerates all his presents to the gate-keeper. The delighted Enlil prepares a feast and they sit down together. Finally Nanna comes to the point and asks for favours in return: 'In the river give me overflow, in the field give me much grain, in the swampland give me grass(?) and reeds (...) in the palm-grove and vineyard give me honey and wine, in the palace give me long life.' When Enlil grants all these wishes, he returns to Ur. This myth is probably connected with a yearly ritual **Journey** between Ur and Nippur, which may have entailed a ritual exchange of dairy and agricultural products.

During the new moon, Nanna spends his 'days of sleep' in the **Underworld**, where he decides the fates of the dead.

Nanna was also called Su'en (later contracted to **Sîn**). In some texts, Su'en referred to the crescent, Nanna to the full moon and Ašimbabbar to the young waxing moon, but this was not consistently adhered to. The various phases of the lunar cycle were celebrated in regular festivals. Purification rituals for the moon were also performed at the New Year. Special care had to be taken during the invisibility of the planet, especially during eclipses. In a mythological introduction to a ritual (Jacobsen, 123), this event is said to have been the work of demonic forces who had attacked Nanna and subdued his children, Inanna and **Iškur**. Eventually he is saved and restored by the intervention of **Marduk**.

Kramer 1944, 47–9; Sjöberg 1960; Jacobsen 1976, 121–7; Hall 1986, 152–66

Nanše – Sumerian goddess

Her name is written with a composite sign for 'house' and 'fish' ⊵🏶. Like **Nammu** she is associated with water, although specifically with rivers and canals, quite a few of which were named after her. In **Enki and the World Order** (417–420) she is called 'the fishery inspector of the "sea"; fishes, good things, sweet things, she presents to her father **Enlil** in Nippur'. Nanše was an important goddess in the Old and Neo-Sumerian period and appeared frequently in personal names (e.g. Urnanše), offering lists and royal inscriptions. She had several sanctuaries in Lagaš. Gudea calls her the daughter of **Enki**, the sister of **Ningirsu** and **Nisaba**, as well as *nin.kur.kur.ra*, 'the Lady of the Lands', who helps Ningirsu to overcome Gudea's enemies in battle. At this period she became also known as the 'female diviner of the gods' and Gudea consulted her oracles on several occasions. In the same capacity she is invoked in the incantation series 'Evil Demons' (*utukki lemnuti*).

Jean 1931, 49–53

Nergal/Nerigal – Babylonian god

His name, written *dGÌR.UNU.GAL* or *dU.GAR*, does not seem to be originally Sumerian; Babylonian theologians constructed a derivation from *nè.eri.gal*, 'lord of the underworld'. Lambert (in Alster 1980, 60f) has suggested that it should not be considered as the name of a distinct divine personality, but rather as a generic term of an **Underworld** deity, of which several were worshipped in Mesopotamia (see **Ereškigal**, **Ninazu**, **Girra**, **Erra** and especially **Meslamta'ea**).

Nergal as a divine name is only known since the Old Akkadian period and features almost exclusively in Akkadian inscriptions of the time. He seems to have been promoted by the Sargonic kings together with his cult-centre Kutha, which is mentioned in the Sumerian Temple Hymns (Sjöberg, Bergmann, No. 36). By the Old Babylonian period he seems to have assimilated several rival Sumerian chthonic gods (Ninazu,

127

Meslamta'ea) and in the course of the second millennium BC, he had temples throughout the country. His name appears frequently in personal names, greeting formulae and cylinder-seals of the Middle and Neo-Babylonian period. Numerous prayers and hymns were addressed to the god, in attempts to avert his dangerous influence (Seux 1976, passim). In Assyria Nergal was particularly worshipped by Sargon II and his descendants.

Nergal is the subject of numerous literary compositions. A number of these refer to Nergal as an astral deity, who finds himself in the under-world against his inclinations. His elevation to the rulership of the underworld for instance, is described in the myth NERGAL AND EREŠKIGAL (see Ereškigal). He is initially sent there by the heavenly gods as an atonement for having failed to observe the divine laws concerning the dealings between heaven and the netherworld. When he trespasses against another taboo of the underworld, that of sexual intercourse, he is doomed to stay for ever. In an esoteric text from the Kassite period, Nergal's sojourn in the underworld is associated with the dark winter months; as the blazing sun he descends to the netherworld and remains there for 160 days (Langdon). But he was also called $nūr^d nergal$, 'Nergal' (god of) light' and became associated with the planet Mars ($^{mul}SAL.BAY.a.nu$). In this capacity he resides in heaven as well as in the netherworld and is 'clothed in frightful splendour' (labiš namurrat), reflecting the intermittent and awe-inspiring luminescence of the star.

The hymns speak of Nergal as a warrior, a god of pestilence and disease, but also of fertility and vegetation.

Langdon 1919, 330ff; Weiher 1971; Lambert 1973, 355–63; Steinkeller 1987, 161–8

Nikkal see Ningal

Ninazu – Sumerian god

His name means 'Lord healer'. Ninazu appears in cuneiform literature under several, sometimes quite contradictory, aspects. His is a typical case of different traditions being fused and confused around a single divine name in the course of time.

Ninazu is known since the Old Sumerian period as the city god of Eshnunna, residing in the temple É-sikil. In a hymn to this temple (Sjö-berg, Bergmann, No. 34), he is described as a warrior, an ur-sag 'cham-pion' Ninazu, destroying the cities of the 'rebellious lands', and as the son of **Enlil** and **Ninlil**. During Akkadian times he was replaced at

Eshnunna by **Tišpak**. The same collection of temple hymns also associates Ninazu with the city Enegi (No. 14). This place is described as the 'Kutha of Sumer' – Kutha (Gudua in Sumerian) is often used as a synonym for the **Underworld**. In this chthonic capacity Ninazu is the son of **Ereškigal** and the 'Great Lord' (**Nergal?**). The myth **Enlil and Ninlil**, while confirming their parenthood as in hymn 34, seems to furnish an explanation for Ninazu's ties with the underworld. Together with two other gods he was engendered to serve as a substitute for **Enlil**, who was apparently decreed to go there himself. In the same text, however, Ninazu is called *lugal.eš.ganá.gíd.da*, 'lord who stretches the measuring line over the fields', a long version of his more common epithet *lugal.é.gid.da* which has something to do with the re-establishment of field boundaries after flooding. This makes him an agrarian deity. The same function is described in another myth, NINAZU AND NINMADU or THE CREATION OF GRAIN. In the beginning, so the story tells, people ate grass like sheep, they knew neither grain nor beans. **An** and Enlil now let grain appear in the *kur*, here a primordial countryside, and then Enlil locks the *kur* and bars its entrance. Ninazu suggests to his brother Ninmada that they fetch the grain to Sumer and they appeal to the sun-god **Utu** for help. The composition ends there, but the success of their expedition can be taken for granted in accordance with the usual pattern of such texts (see **Inanna and Utu**, **Lahar and Ašnan**) (Bruschweiler, 54ff).

In the Ur III period, Ninazu was connected with **Nanna(r)**, the god of Ur, as well as with **Enki**, in a Shulgi-hymn (Klein, 156f). In the post-Ur III period Ninazu seems to have been venerated primarily as a healing deity; he was invoked in purification rituals and is called the father of **Ningišzida**. The 'Weidner' god-list, on the other hand, still calls him the *bēl erṣeti*, the 'lord of the underworld'.

Sjöberg-Bergmann 1969, 27–8; 42–3; Edzard 1965, WdM, 110; Lambert, in Alster 1980, 61f; Klein 1981; Bruschweiler 1987, 55

Ningal – Sumerian goddess; her name means 'Great Lady'

Ningal as the wife of the moon-god **Nanna** was worshipped with her husband at Ur, especially during the Ur III period. The kings of this dynasty built her a temple, É-karzida, and dedicated statues and stelae to her. Maybe in an analogy to the **Dumuzi-Inanna Sacred Marriage** texts, the poets of Ur wrote songs which describe the courtship of the young couple. Like Dumuzi, Nanna brings dairy products to the house of his prospective mother-in-law, Ningikuga, 'the lady of the pure reed', who lives in the marshes with her daughter. Ningal promises to marry him once he has brought fertility and abundance to the whole country, and to live with him in his sanctuary at Ur (Jacobsen, 124f). As the lady of this city it is Ningal's sad fate to lament its downfall and destruction in the famous 'Lamentation over the Destruction of Ur'. In vain she tries to move the great gods **An** and **Enlil** to alter their decision; her city and her people are irrevocably doomed (Jacobsen, 87–91).

Ningal as the mother of Inanna also features in the Sumerian 'love-lyrics'. Inanna tries to deceive her mother by pretending that she will be going out with a girl-friend, when instead she will be with her lover (Kramer, in ANET 1969, 639–40).

Ningal was also a goddess of dream interpretation.

In the second millennium BC, if not earlier, she was introduced to Syria, probably via Harran, the ancient centre of moon-worship (see **Sîn**). In Ugarit she was known as **Nikkal**. She appears in a hymn which praises her marriage to the moon-god **Yarih**.

Edzard, Pope, WdM 1965, 111, 302; Jacobsen 1973

Ningirin – Sumerian goddess

Her name, which was written as *dNin.A.HA.KUD.DU*, means 'lady of Incantations'. She appears already in the Fara texts. In the Sumerian Temple Hymn collection, she is associated with a sanctuary in Murum (Sjöberg, Bergmann, No. 19). The temple is said to 'recite conjurations of heaven and earth'. In later periods too, she is mainly mentioned in incantation texts.

Ningirsu – Sumerian god

His name means 'lord of Girsu', a city belonging to the district of Lagash. Ningirsu was an ancient local god; he first appears in the Fara god-list and was worshipped by all the kings of Lagash. Typically, Eannatum and Uruinimgina call the boundaries of their territory the 'limits of Ningirsu' and any destruction of their land was a sin against its god. With Uruin-imgina's political success, the god became more widely known in Sumer. Ningirsu as a city-god is not only a warrior, who calls the ruler to defend his boundaries, but is also in charge of the fertility of his 'beloved fields'. Numerous artefacts, such as mace-heads, statues, vases etc. have been dedicated to Ningirsu; several canals and waterways bore his name. There were of course many festivals in his honour and he is well represented among the gods chosen for personal names. His temple was the famous É-ninnu, the reconstruction of which during the Neo-Sumerian period was described by Gudea. The god appeared to Gudea in a dream, he was terrifyingly large, with wings and a 'head like a god', his lower body ending in a storm and flanked by lions (Falkenstein, Soden, 137–82).

Numerous goddesses surround Ningirsu in the Lagash pantheon: his wife **Baba**, his sisters **Nisaba** and **Nanše** and his mother Gatumdug (his father is **Anu**. His emblem or *alter ego* was the lion-headed eagle **Anzu/**Imdugud.

The personality of Ningirsu was close to that of **Ninurta** who replaced Ningirsu in Akkadian texts of the Old Babylonian period (cf. the myth of Anzu). They are often mentioned together in god-lists.

Jean 1931, 71–81; Falkenstein, Soden 1953

Ningišzida – Sumerian god (*see figure 24*)

The meaning of his name *ⁿnin.giš.zid.da*, 'Lord of the good tree', is obscure (although Jacobsen 1973, 7, reads it as: 'the power of the tree to draw sustenance through its roots').

He was an **Underworld** deity; the Sumerian Temple-Hymn (Sjöberg, Bergmann, No. 15) describes his 'house' in Gišbanda as 'a dark cellar, (an) awe-inspiring place'; maybe it had a subterrranean sanctuary. Ningišzida himself is 'the prince who stretches out his pure hand to heaven, with luxuriant and abundant hair (flowing down his) back'. In the Neo-Sumerian period, Gudea introduced him into the Lagash pantheon as his personal god, whom he loved 'above all others'. He was also worshipped in Shuruppak, Ur, Umma, Larsa, Nippur and Uruk.

Ningišzida's chthonian aspects are confirmed by the god-list An=*Anum*. His emblem was the horned serpent and Gilgameš sees him officiating in the underworld (**Gilgameš, Enkidu and the Netherworld**). He was sometimes identified with **Damu**, the dying god, and was mourned by his sisters. As a (temporarily) absent god in the company of Dumuzi, he was found by **Adapa** at **An**'s gate in heaven. This close connection with Dumuzi and fertility is further underlined by the fact that his wife was **Geštinanna**, Dumuzi's sister. His astronomical correlate was Hydra.

van Buren 1934, 166–71; Roux 1961, 22–4

Ninhursanga/Ninhursag (*see figure 25*)

Sumerian goddess: 'The Lady of the *hursag*' (the stony desert ground; Jacobsen 1970, 118). The myth *Lugal.e* (see **Ninurta**) explains how she was given this title by her son Ninurta after he had defeated his enemies and heaped up the rocks of the *hursag*.

Ninhursag is one of the many appellatives of the ancient **Mother-goddess**. It is first mentioned in the Fara god-list. Her epithets include 'mother of the gods' and 'mother of all children'. She had temples at Kesh, Lagash and Tell Obeid. The Kesh sanctuary is the subject of an Old Sumerian hymn (Sjöberg, Bergmann, 157ff). It was the centre of the goddess's cult from the Early Dynastic period to the Old Babylonian Dynasty; after this time it lost its importance in favour of the nearby Adab. Many Mesopotamian kings (from the Old Sumerian period to Nebukadzrezzar I) called themselves 'beloved of Ninhursag' and claim to have built temples and chapels for her. Eannatum, Entemena and Uruinimgina say in their inscriptions that they had been suckled by the goddess.

In the literary texts, Ninhursag is the female creative counterpart to Enki in **Enki and Ninhursag**. She is associated with several male gods apart from Enki; as the mother of Ninurta she was **Enlil's** wife, in another tradition she was Enlil's sister and the wife of **Šulpa'e**, 'the lord of the wild beasts'. Several songs describe her particular function as the lady of the *hursag*, the uncultivated hills. She mourns the capture of wild creatures, especially the donkeys, but she is also a mother to the herd animals.

Jacobsen 1973, 104–6

Ninisina/Nin'insina – Sumerian goddess

As her name 'Lady of Isin' implies, she was the tutelary goddess of this city. Her temple was the É-galmah, 'the great temple', described in a Temple Hymn (Sjöberg, Bergmann, No. 30); the goddess is called the *ama nu.gig*, the 'mother hierodule', 'whose word fills the heaven'. When Isin became the capital of Sumer and Akkad during the reign of Ishbi'erra and Lipit-Ištar, she was promoted to the rank of a 'great goddess' and assumed some of the functions of **Inanna**, including her military aspects. In fact, in **Enki and the World Order** (402f) Inanna complains that Ninisina had usurped her position as the 'hierodule of An' and had taken her '*šuba*-stone jewellery'.

Ninisina was the daughter of **An** and the earth-deity Uraš; her husband is **Pabilsag**, although **Damu** and Gunura, who are known other-wise as her offspring, are also mentioned as consorts in some Ur III texts.

As a healing goddess, her most common epithet is *a.zu.gal.kalam.ma*, 'the great healer/doctor of the land', and as such she is addressed in various hymns and 'letters'; the manner of her treatment was the uttering of the right incantation. She was also a midwife. Towards the end of the Old Babylonian period she became identified with the Semitic goddess **Gula**. In a well-known *eršemma* (Cohen, No. 171) she is in great distress, seemingly wandering in the **Arali**, her temple in ruins. She cries out to **Enlil** who shows her the Tablets of Destiny which have an entry for her misfortune. Another appeal by her mother is also in vain, since she exclaims that her child is dead. Another composition (ibid, No. 159) ends on a more optimistic note, and Ninisina joyfully returns to her temple.

Römer 1969, 279–305; Cohen 1981

Ninlil – Sumerian goddess

Her name, 'Lady Air', is an honorific title to complement **Enlil**. Her orig-inal name was Sud. The myth **Enlil and Sud** describes how the new title was conferred upon the young goddess on her wedding-day.

As the wife of Enlil she was known in Nippur since the Old Sumerian period. Many votive offerings were brought to her, particularly during the time of the Third Dynasty of Ur.

The above-mentioned myth also explains her background and func-tion. Sud's mother was Ninšebargunu, the goddess of Ereš, an ancient agricultural deity and her father was Haia, god of the stores. Ninlil is explicitly identified with the grain-goddess **Ašnan** as well as **Nintu**, the birth-goddess. Her sons were **Ninurta** and **Nanna** and she appears in hymns and other texts in praise of these gods. Most texts however, concentrate on her relationship with Enlil. While in **Enlil and Ninlil** she is concerned to legitimize their union, many compositions stress the high degree of influence and power of the goddess. The two deities act in unison, administering the *Me*, which they were said to have brought forth together; conferring the highest privileges upon the goddess **Inanna** (SRT 36), and decreeing the 'fates' of gods and men. During the Old Babylonian period, various hymns and prayers were written in which the supplicant addresses Ninlil in an attempt to influence her husband. In Assyria, Ninlil became the wife of the national god **Aššur**.

Edzard, WdM 1965, 113

Ninmah – Sumerian goddess

Her name 'Great Lady' is another example of an appellative designation for the **Mother-goddess**. **Ninlil** as well as **Ninhursag** were called Ninmah in certain contexts (see **Enlil and Sud** and **Ninurta**, *Lugal.e*).

Uruinimgina of Lagash mentions Ninmah in his diatribe against his enemy, the city of Umma. She is also known from Adab where she had a temple, the É-mah. In the myth **Enki and Ninmah**, she is the mother-goddess who challenges Enki to a contest of creativity which the god wins.

Ninsianna – Sumerian goddess

A personification of the planet **Venus**; '*ša nu-ur-šu ša-me-e u KI ma-lu-ú*', 'whose light fills heaven and earth', as an Akkadian text says. She was identified with **Ištar** (as in the great bilingual hymn of Iddin-Dagan; Römer, IV).

Kraus 1971, 30–1; Römer 1965

Ninšubur – Sumerian god/goddess; 'Lady/Lord of the East'

The sex of this deity varies. In the Old Sumerian time he is known as the tutelary deity of Uruinimgina of Lagash; several personal names with Ninšubur are also preserved from the Neo-Sumerian period. According to the Sumerian temple hymns (Sjöberg, Bergmann, No. 18) she had a temple in Akkil.

In mythological texts, Ninšubur is the *sukkal* 'vizier' of either **An** or **Inanna**. The earliest reference to this function is from an Early Dynastic votive offering. In the service of the male god he is male; in the service of the goddess, most prominently in **Inanna's Descent**, female. The function of *sukkal* is a combination of different offices, herald and messenger, minister with executive powers in the absence of the master. In the **Sacred Marriage** texts of Isin, Ninšubur leads the bridegroom to his beloved. In this context she is 'the holy handmaid of E-anna (Jacobsen, 41).

Bergmann, ZA 56; Jacobsen 1973

Ninsun – Sumerian goddess

Her name means 'Lady of the wild cows'. She had a sanctuary in Kullab, a district of Uruk and belonged to the herding-circle around **Dumuzi**; she is in fact his mother and therefore the mother-in-law of **Inanna**. **Gilgameš** was also said to be a son of Ninsun's and in the epic she interprets his dreams. In the Neo-Sumerian period, several kings claimed to have been the 'children' of goddesses, such as Gudea of Lagash, as well as Urnammu and Shulgi of Ur.

Nintu/Nintur – Sumerian goddess

Her name means 'Lady who gives Birth'; the archaic form of the cuneiform sign TU𒆳 depicts a reed-shelter, the sort that may have been used as lambing sheds. In the god-list An=A-num she is identified with the Akkadian Šassurum (=$šag_4$-$tùr$), 'Lady Womb'. She is one of the ancient **Mother-goddesses**, already present in the Fara-list. Her epithet is $ama\ dumu\ dumu.ne$, 'mother of all little ones'. From the Neo-Sumerian period onwards, she was often identified with **Ninhursag**, but at least at Ur she received offerings in her own name. In a mythological context she is mentioned in the Sumerian **Flood-myth** and also appears in **Enki and the World Order** (395), where she is called 'the umbilical cord-cutter', the 'midwife of the land'.

Jacobsen 1973, 274–98

Ninurta – Sumerian god

His name 'Lord Earth' probably derives from the old vegetation-god Uraš (Jacobsen 1973, 127, suggested 'Lord Plough').

He is well known since the Old Sumerian period and closely resembles the Lagashite god **Ningirsu** with whom he was eventually identified. Ninurta instead of Ningirsu features in the Akkadian versions of some myths (as the one of **Anzu** from the Old Babylonian period). In Nippur he was worshipped in the temple E-šumeša. In this city (and in Lagash) he was called the firstborn son of **Enlil**, in preference over **Nanna**, who was also accorded this title. After the Old Babylonian period, Ninurta's popularity waned since **Marduk** assumed some of his characteristics (for the precedent of Ninurta's role in fighting Anzu for the *Enuma eliš*, see Lambert, in Hecker, Sommerfeld, 55–60). In Assyria, however, since late Middle Assyrian times, he was much promoted as a fearsome warrior.

As his name implies, Ninurta was originally an agricultural and rain deity. The so-called 'Farmer's Almanac', a compilation of the annual tasks related to the growing of barley, was called the 'Instructions of

Ninurta'. He was called the 'farmer of Enlil' and praised as the 'life-giving semen', the source of fertility and abundance throughout the land: 'you fill the canal, let grow the barley, you fill the pond with carp, let reed and grass grow in the cranebrake, you fill the forest with game, let the tamarisk(?) grow in the steppe, you fill the orchard and garden with honey and wine, cause long life to sprout in the palace' (Falkenstein, Soden, 59f). For some reason Ninurta changed from an agrarian god to the archetypical 'young god' or 'god of wrath'. Several compositions, mainly from the Neo-Sumerian and Ur III period emphasize this warlike character of the 'champion' (*ur.sag*) Ninurta: 'eternal warrior, greatly respected, with a broad chest, the strength of a lion (...) stepping into battle (...) the heroic warrior, the right arm of Enlil' (Sjöberg 1976). Some of his power derives from the violent floods of springtime; in the Atra-hasis myth he is the one who opens the dikes (see **Flood-myths**). A long and complex bilingual composition is called LUGAL UD ME.LAM.BI NIR.GÁL, 'king, storm whose splendour is overwhelming' (also known as *lugal.e*). The text manages to reconcile both the fertility and the martial aspects of the god. The myth describes the time when irrigation was as yet unknown in Sumer and consequently there was no agriculture to feed the population. After his victory over the demon, Ninurta makes a stone wall, a gigantic dike to keep the waters of the Tigris from flowing eastwards. The result of this labour are fruit-filled fields and orchards and the kings and gods rejoice. When his mother **Ninlil** is impatient to congratulate her son in person and travels to the hills to find him, he presents her with a vast range he had accumulated over his enemy's remains. First, however, he provides the barren stones with vegetation and wildlife and calls it the *hursag*; Ninlil herself from now on becomes **Ninhursag**. Finally Ninurta decides the fates of the stones, the former soldiers of Asag. Some are rewarded for having behaved decently and are given some posts in his administration, others are punished by curses; an interesting etiological analysis of the properties of certain minerals (van Dijk 1983). A similar, also bilingual composition is THE RETURN OF NINURTA TO NIPPUR (or Sum. **an-gim dim.ma**, 'created like An'). It begins with a long description of Ninurta's character and achievements, especially on the battlefield. He is returning to Nippur in his chariot which is decorated all over with awe-inspiring trophies, surrounded by a large and terrifying retinue. The momentum of his cavalcade threatens the well-being of the country and **Nusku**, Enlil's vizier, tries to persuade the young god to slow down and to dim his fearsome radiance. He also points out that Enlil will reward him highly upon his return but that he finds his present style of progress objectionable.

Ninurta does put away his whip and mace, but drives the rest of the trophies to Nippur. The gods are greatly impressed and even frightened at the display of booty and his mother, Ninlil, greets him affectionately. The text ends in a speech of self-glorification by Ninurta, in which he also refers to his battle with the stones described in *lugal.e* (Cooper). Ninurta's one fault seems to have been arrogance. This is alluded to in the RETURN TO NIPPUR, and another mythological fragment tells of an accident in the retrieval of the Tablets of Destiny (see Anzu-myth). The eaglet (*amar-anzu*) addresses Ninurta and complains that because the god had attacked him, he dropped the Tablets of Destiny into the **Apsu**. This implies their loss to Ninurta who is crestfallen. The eaglet accompanies him to the dwelling of **Enki** in the Apsu, who receives them in a friendly fashion but does not offer to give back the Tablets. When Ninurta refuses to leave without them and even attacks the vizier, Enki fashions a giant turtle out of the Apsu-clay which attacks the divine hero, biting his toes. Ninurta starts to defend himself and Enki quickly digs out a pit into which both the god and his tormentor fall. Only the pleas of Ninurta's mother Ninmena (**Ninlil**) persuade Enki to set him free, by reminding him that he owes her a favour (Kramer).

Falkenstein, Soden 1953, 59f; van Dijk 1962, 19–32; Sjöberg 1976, 411–26; Cooper 1978; van Dijk 1983; Kramer 1984, 231–7

Nisaba/Nidaba – Sumerian goddess

Her name was written with the cuneiform sign *NAGA* which was used as a determinative for different kinds of grain; her iconographic symbol was an ear of corn. The pronunciation Ni-is-sa-bi is attested from the earliest written documents, meaning *Ninsaba, 'The Lady of Sab(a)' (Lambert, 64). She is first mentioned in the Fara-lists as the Lady of Eresh (see the Temple Hymn, Sjöberg, Bergmann, No. 42). She was also worshipped at Umma; Lugalzagesi calls her 'his mother'. Under his reign and that of the following Akkadian dynasty, her cult proliferated in other Sumerian towns. According to Gudea she was the sister of **Ningirsu** and **Nanše** and as such part of the Lagash pantheon. Gudea is also the first reference to Nisaba's aspect as the patroness of scribes; she holds the 'pure stylus'; the laws of the land are known as the 'laws of Nisaba' and 'she knows the numbers'. She was very popular during the first half of the second millennium BC, maybe as long as the Babylonian scribal 'schools', the *é.dub.bas*, flourished. Numerous hymns were composed in her honour which describe the totality of her functions: 'O Lady coloured like the stars of heaven, holding the lapis lazuli tablet, born in the great sheep-fold by the divine Earth (...) born in wisdom by the Great Mountain (Enlil), honest woman, chief scribe of Heaven, record-keeper of Enlil, all knowing sage of the gods' she makes vegetation grow, establishes ritual ablutions and appoints the high priest, (Hallo). Another hymn by the Isin king Ishbi-Erra dwells on her maternal qualities: '(...) you place the good semen in the womb, you enlarge the foetus in the womb, in order that the mother may love her son ...' (Reisman, 1, 49f). With the growing popularity of **Nabû** during the Kassite and Neo-Babylonian period, Nisaba lost her importance and had to be content with being his wife.

In the Hittite sources, a variety of grain gods were written with the logogram ᵈ**Nisaba**, such as **Telepinu**, Halki and the Hurrian **Kumarbi**.

van Dijk 1953; Hallo 1969, 123–34; Reisman 1976, 357–65; Lambert, in Hecker, Sommerfeld 1986, 55–60

Nungal – Sumerian goddess

Her name literally means 'great prince'. Nungal is not documented before the Neo-Sumerian period, when she appeared in the Nippur pantheon as the 'daughter-in-law of **Enlil**', the daughter of **An** and **Ereškigal** and the wife of a god called Birtum. During the Old Babylonian period a number of hymns and prayers were addressed to the goddess, which depict her as a chthonic deity who 'pursues the wicked', but with overtones of a **Mother-goddess**. Her epithets include *agrig zi.ᵈen.lil.la*, 'true stewardess of Enlil', and *ša ṣibitte ša maṣṣarte ša habalata*, 'goddess of imprisonment, detention, of the ropes', probably an allusion to her underworld aspect which was important in magic.

Sjöberg 1973, 19–46

Nusku – Sumerian god

Also known under the same name by the Babylonians. As one of **Enlil**'s sons, he was worshipped in Nippur in the temple É-sušihušria. In the mythological texts he is usually described as a high official in Enlil's service (see for instance in Atra-hasis – **Flood-myths**). In his own right he was a god of light and fire. As such he was often mentioned in magical incantations where he is asked to burn the evil witches and sorcerers (Seux). During the Neo-Assyrian period he was known as the son of the moon-god **Sîn** and had his main cult-centre in Syrian Harran like his father. His symbol is the lamp.

Edzard, WdM 1965, 116; Seux 1976, 318, 340, 373, 377, 388

P

Pabilsag – Sumerian god

He is well attested as the god of Larag, but little is known about his personality. In later texts he merged with **Ninurta** in his warrior-aspect. In astronomical texts he stands for the constellation of Sagittarius.

Pick-axe myth

The invention of the pick-axe or hoe (Sum. ^{giš}al) as one of the most important tools in horticulture and building, is the subject of a Sumerian, etiological composition. In the beginning, **Enlil** separated heaven and earth. Then he created or invented the pick-axe and tried it out. As he breaks up the crust of the earth, the first people shoot up like young plants. The gods immediately consign mankind to its task of wielding the instrument for their benefit. A **Mother-goddess** (**Damkina** or Ninmenna), gives birth to the first royal couple and thereby institutes kingship.

Jacobsen 1949, 134–7

Pinenkir/Pinkir – Elamite goddess

As a **Mother-goddess**, she was the highest deity of the Elamite pantheon during the third millennium BC. During the second millennium she was generally referred to as **Kiriša**. At the same time the god **Humban** replaced her as chief deity. Only in the Neo-Elamite period (7th C BC) did the goddess regain some of her previous importance.

Hinz 1972, 42

Pirwa – Anatolian deity

His name is connected with the Hittite $^{na4}peru$, 'rock'. He is an ancient

140

god of Kanesh, and inhabitants during the time of the Assyrian merchant colonies bore his name. He may have affinities with the open-air rock-sanctuaries much favoured by the Hittites as burial places for important persons. The original sex of the deity is difficult to determine, but in some texts it is female (appellative 'queen'; or **Istar**). During the latter part of the second millennium BC and later, Pirwa had connections with horses.

Lebrun, in Donceel, Lebrun 1984, 145

Primeval gods

In Hittite mythology they are called *siuneš karuiles* and are sometimes named as Nara, Napsara, Minki, Ammunki, Tuhusi, Ammizadu etc. They were sometimes equated by the Hittite scribes with the Babylonian **Anunnaki**, but they also represent an earlier generation of gods who had retired or were banished by the younger gods now in charge. These gods were often invoked in treaties to guarantee sworn oaths. In the myth of Ullikummi (cf. **Kumarbi**) they look after the implement which was used to sever the earth from the sky.

von Schuler, WdM 1965, 167; Laroche 1984

Protective deities

In Hittite texts they were summarily written as *ᵈKAL*. As such they formed one of the functional categories of the official Hittite pantheon which included many different gods and goddesses of the various ethnic and linguistic communities of Anatolia. The most important of the old gods was probably Innara, the Hittite-Luwian protective god, not to be confused with the stag god *ᵈKAL*. In addition to the distinct divine personalities there were a host of lesser divine beings or demons, rather like the Roman 'genii'. They protected temples, gateways, hearths and herds.

Q

The Queen of Neša and her Children

Anatolian myth; probably of Hattian origin, translated into Hittite.

One year, the queen of Nesha (Kanesh), whose name is not mentioned, gave birth to thirty sons. She is worried, however, about this extraordinary number of offspring and decides not to make it public. She puts her babies in reed-baskets caulked with excrement and puts them into the river. Miraculously preserved, they reach the seashore and there the gods take pity on the children and raise them. After some years, the queen experiences a multiple birth again. This time she produces thirty daughters and keeps them. The boys decide to go back to the place of their origin and find their mother who does not recognize them and gives her daughters in marriage to her sons. The youngest brothers warn them against committing the crime of incest, but the siblings marry. The text on the reverse of the tablets establishes some connection with the town Zalpa. Maybe the myth furnishes a reason for the destruction of this city by the Hittites.

Otten 1973, 6ff; Ünal, in Hecker, Sommerfeld 1986, 129–36

R

Rephaim

Ugaritic *rp'm*, translated as 'Saviours', are mentioned in some tablets found at the city of Ugarit as well as in the Old Testament. There is as yet no general agreement whether the term was consistently applied to one meaning. Some interpret them as chthonic deities and others as the spirits of dead kings and heroes (Spronk). As such they are invoked in an Ugaritic incantation (de Moor 187).

Caquot-Sznycer 1981, 19; Spronk 1986, 145ff; de Moor 1987

Rešep

West Semitic god; his name is connected with *ršp*, 'fire'. He is an ancient god and already appears in the Ebla pantheon. In Ugarit, although he hardly figures in the myths, he was popular enough to receive regular offerings and feature prominently in the personal names. He was identified with the Babylonian chthonic god **Nergal**. The Egyptians adopted him too; as a plague god he was invoked to fight against the forces of evil. The Phoenicians left several carvings of this god in Cyprus, Anatolia and Syria.

Pope, Röllig, WdM 1965, 305

Rivers, deified

Rivers as the source of water are the basis of fertility in arid climates (cf. the Nile, the Ganges, Bramaputhra etc.). From a very early age they were considered sacred. In the Ebla texts the local rivers were written with the divine determinative (*dBa-li-ha*, *dBa-ru=du-ma-du'*, Euphrates). In Babylonian texts *dID* = *nâru* was the deified river as such; the term was applied to any waterway. This god determined the guilt or innocence of individuals accused of having committed certain crimes for which there were no witnesses by means of the river ordeal (cf. Code of Hammurabi, 2, 132, 133). Several myths explain the origin of the Tigris and Euphrates, which were created by the gods (see **Enki and the World Order**, *Enuma eliš*). In Anatolia, rivers and sources were normally connected with goddesses.

S

Sacred Marriage

In anthropological literature this term has been applied to a great variety of ritual practices which celebrate the sexual act as the prerequisite for the flourishing of all life in the community (Frazer, James). The notion that sexuality is of divine origin (a *Me* in Sumerian) is well documented in the Ancient Near East. In **Ištar's Descent**, the death of the goddess entails the disappearance of intercourse, which severely endangers the continuity of life. Nuptials between gods and goddesses seem to have been periodically celebrated in Mesopotamia from the Early Dynastic period onwards. The iconography of early cylinder seals, vases and other artefacts which depict festive occasions and the bringing of gifts to a female personality, might refer to such celebrations (van Buren, Moortgat).

Apart from the probably widespread idea of a 'holy marriage' between gods and goddesses, there is a special case of the union between a goddess and the king. It is this aspect of 'Sacred Marriage' that has been most commented upon and most hotly debated. Some scholars assume that such a rite is of great antiquity and probably originated in the Old Sumerian period in Uruk (Kramer, Jacobsen). However, almost all relevant texts date from the Ur III and Isin-Larsa period, a time when kings were elevated to divine status. In the well-known epic compositions **Enmerkar and the Lord of Aratta** and **Enmerkar and Enšuhkešdana** the heroes, who are kings of Uruk, compete for the favour of the goddess **Inanna**. In addition there are passionate love-songs which are also in some way connected with Inanna and her cult, some of which mention **Dumuzi** as her partner.

A special group of texts which are characteristic of the Ur III/Isin-Larsa period are the so-called royal hymns, highly crafted poetical compositions which praise the king and his universal responsibility for the well-being of the country. The text Shulgi X (see Klein 1981) describes a ritual in which the king assumes the personality of Dumuzi, the husband of Inanna, and visits the goddess in the bridal chamber. After the consummation of the rite the goddess pronounces the 'good fate' for the king and country. In Isin, the ceremonies differ in detail and the goddess is **Ninisina** (Römer 1965). In view of the fact that these kings regarded themselves as gods rather than mortals, their eligibility as divine bridegrooms seems to be more important than their representation of mankind which is so often emphasized.

Jacobsen (1973) has drawn attention to the erotic compositions concerning the moon-god **Nanna** and his wife **Ningal**. He concluded that there may have been Sacred Marriage ceremonies at Ur as well, with the high priestess (Sum.*entum*) representing Ningal in the symbolic rite.

After the establishment of the Amorite dynasty in Babylon, the concept of kingship changed and the only well-known reference to the Sacred Marriage rite after this date is satirical in tone, uttered by Gilgameš in the 6th tablet of the **Gilgameš Epic**.

D. van Buren 1944, 1ff; Moortgat 1949; Frazer 1964; James 1965; Römer 1965; Kramer 1969; Kramer 1970, 135–41; Jacobsen 1973, 125f; Jacobsen, in Goedicke, Roberts 1975, 65–97; Renger, RLA IV, 251–69; Klein 1981

Šahr and Šalim

Ugaritic deities, *šhr w slm*, probably 'Dawn' and 'Dusk', also known by their epithet as *ilm n'mm wjsmm*, 'Gracious and Merciful Gods'. Not much is known about them; they occur in some offering texts and personal names as well as in a ritual text with mythological passages, usually called the Birth of the Gracious Gods or just SS (KTU 1, 23). Although the text is well preserved it is difficult to understand, as it is not always obvious when the ritual is described or the story told. **El** is the prominent figure. He sees two women (or goddesses?) whom he desires and after performing some rites(?) involving roast birds, the women are asked whether they want him as a father or a husband. They choose the latter and he has intercourse with both. They each give birth to a god, Šahr and Šalim respectively. When El hears the news, he orders offerings for **Šapaš** and the stars, The Gracious Gods, however, have an enormous appetite, their mouths reach from the earth to the sky. They devour everything in their way, birds and fishes. El sends them into the desert where they hunt for food for many years until they find the 'guardian of the sown land', maybe an oasis. They plead with him to let them in and he allows them to enter, offering wine to the gods. The end is not preserved.

Pope, WdM 288; Gibson 1978, 29f; de Moor, 116–28

Šakan/Šakkan

Sumerian god; in Akkadian texts the Emesal variant **Šumuqan** is used. The etymology is doubtful, but the name seems to denote some four-legged animal. He is an ancient god, known since the Early Dynastic period (Ebla, Mari). In **Enki and the World Order** (348–356) he is described as 'the hero who is the crown of the high plain, who is the lord of the plain, the lion of the high plain, the strong one, the lofty hand of **Enlil**' who has been put in charge of *an.edin*, the high plain, a 'good place complete with grass, herbs and abundance', teeming with cattle and the 'wild rams of the pasture'.

In the **Death of Gilgameš**, **Enkidu** sees him in the Underworld. Maybe like **Dumuzi**, who is also associated with the *edin*, he is absent during the hot months of the summer.

Albright 1926, 181–3; Lambert 1986, 152–8

ᵈSAL.LUGAL

In Hittite god-lists this Sumerogram which means 'divine queen' stands for the many different female deities who were worshipped in the major towns.

Šamaš (*see figures 3, 10, 26 and 40*)

Babylonian sun-god; *šmš* is the common Semitic root for 'sun'. The name of this god first appears in Akkadian personal names from the pre-Sargonic period, although in the majority of cases it was written logographically as *ᵈUTU*. Some of these names (e.g. *Ummī-Šamaš* – 'My mother is Šamaš') seem to suggest that the Sun was originally a female deity, as it was for the Canaanites and the Arabs later (Roberts). It may have been the influence of the Sumerian sun-god **Utu** which turned Šamaš into the male deity depicted on seals and stelae. Unlike the Sumerian god, however, who did not achieve a very prominent position in the pantheon, the Akkadian Šamaš, as a god of justice, was a deity of cosmic and national importance, 'the lord of heaven and earth'. But in the existing god-lists he was never awarded the supreme rank. His main cult centre was Sippar, a major town during the second and first millennia BC. The extent of Šamaš's popularity can be gauged from many personal names, cylinder seals and the considerable number of hymns and prayers in his honour. Some of these hymns, with their skilful poetic structure imitating the movement of the planet, are the best exponent of the solar theology devised by the Babylonians. A bilingual hymn celebrates the all-encompassing vigilance and mercy of the sun-god. His rising in the morning renews all life; as he ascends into high heaven, he surveys living beings wherever they may be, from the highest to the humblest. He crosses all seas and sees all countries; in his universal knowledge he understands all languages. Throughout his journey he is the companion of travellers. At the zenith he reveals himself as the god of justice who destroys the wicked and rewards the just. He looks after the interests of the socially deprived and no secret is hidden from him. He is also praised for giving omens and for regulating the seasons (Lambert, Castellino). Another composition describes the activities of the sun-god at night. After opening the western door of heaven he passes through the interior of heaven (the underworld), where he judges the dead. Then he has his evening meal and sleeps in his chamber. In the morning he opens the eastern door of heaven and his journey begins again (Heimpel). A large number of incantations also address Šamaš personally. He is asked to make the omen favourable, to banish all evil influences and grant happiness and long life (Seux).

Šamaš is also a warrior, especially in Neo-Assyrian texts, and he is called the 'lord of heaven and earth and all human beings' (Tallqvist).

In the mythological texts, Šamaš does not often play a very prominent role. In the myth of **Etana** he watches over the treaty between the eagle and the serpent and he is also the personal god of Etana. He is also the god closest to **Gilgameš** in the **Gilgameš Epic**, and not only when the king takes to roaming the wilderness. Although Gilgameš is the king of Uruk, the city of **Inanna** and **An**, he owes no allegiance to either, relying entirely on the sun-god to see him through his troubles. His direct approach through prayer and the god's answer by dreams was characteristic of this age of personal piety and the rise of solar theology (Liagre-Böhl).

Tallqvist 1938, 457f; Lambert 1960, 121–38; Roberts 1972, 51f; Alster 1974; Castellino 1976, 71–4; Seux 1976, passim; Liagre-Böhl, in Oberhuber 1977, 37–276; Heimpel 1986, 127–51

Šapaš

Ugaritic sun-goddess; her name is related to *šmš*, 'sun'. As for the pre-Islamic Arabs and the Hurrians, the sun-deity in Ugarit was female. She is mentioned in offering lists, which implies a certain importance for her cult. She also features in some of the mythological texts from Ugarit. Her epithet is *nrt ilm*, 'torch of the gods'. Her perpetual journeying through the sky makes her the messenger of **El**. Like other solar deities she can see all that happens on earth, which is why **Anat** asks her to find the body of the dead **Baal**. In **Baal and Mot** she is said to traverse the underworld at night, hence her influence over Mot. The final doxology of that composition praises her as being pre-eminent over the shades in the underworld.

There is no evidence that a strong solar theology, with the element of justice, as in second millennium BC Mesopotamia (and Egypt!), ever developed in Ugarit.

In Ebla, the sun-deity could be written as *dZI.KIR* and *dUTU*, but it has been assumed that it stood for something like Sipiš (cf. a king named Ibbi-Sipiš) (Lebrun).

Caquot 1959, 90–101; Lebrun 1984, 36

Šara – Sumerian god

He is well known as the city-god of Umma, at least during the Neo-Sumerian period. His temple É-mah is praised in a Sumerian temple hymn (Sjöberg, Bergmann, No. 25). He received regular offerings and a number of people are known to have borne his name (Jean). In mythological texts he appears but rarely, usually in association with **Inanna** (**Lugalbanda and Hurrum, Inanna's Descent**).

Jean 1931, 94f; Sjöberg, Bergmann 1967, 34 111f

Şarpanitum – Babylonian goddess

Her name means 'the one from Zarpa', although Babylonian theologians preferred to read it as *Zêr-banitu*, 'who creates the seed'.

During the late second and the first millennium BC she was worshipped as the wife of **Marduk** and shared his main temple in Babylon. In this capacity she assumed many functions of other goddesses, such as creation, protection of the country, intercession for the faithful, giver of progeny etc.

Seux 1976, 329

Šarruma – Anatolian god

His name is often written as *^dLUGAL-ma*. He appears in the imperial Hittite pantheon since Shuppiluliuma I, but only reached a prominent position as the tutelary god of king Tuthalia IV. As such he is represented on a rock-relief at Yazilikaya, putting his arms around the king. The Hittite theologians call him the son of **Tešup** and **Hebat**, 'the strong bull-calf'. He was linked to Hebat in various festivals and rituals, mainly in Kizzuwatna. It is interesting that most people bearing his name seem to have been foreigners living in Syrian towns such as Aleppo or Ugarit. Šarruma is often thought to have been a Hurrian god as he is so strongly associated with Hebat. However, he does not feature in any of the Hurrian myths and is not mentioned in the cult of Hurrian influenced areas. It has therefore been suggested (Laroche) that he was one of the ancient Anatolian **Mountain-gods**, appearing in the guise of a holy bull-calf, to be eventually associated with another old Anatolian divinity, the **Weather-god**, as his young son.

Laroche 1963, 277–303

Šaušga – Anatolian goddess of Hurrian origin

Her name is usually written as *^dIŠTAR LÍL* ('Ištar of the Field') in Hittite inscriptions. She is the Hurrian equivalent of **Ištar of Nineveh**. The centre of her cult was south Anatolia and northern Syria, especially Samuha. She was very popular with the Hittites during the time between the Old Kingdom and the Empire (first half of the second millennium BC) and king Hattushili III made her his tutelary goddess. Like Ištar, Šaušga has a bisexual character. She can appear dressed like a man and armed as a warrior. In her female form she is the goddess of love. Accordingly, she appears on the Yazilikaya reliefs twice, once as a warrior among the male gods and then again as a woman with the goddesses. A hymn describes the contradictory sides of the androgynous deity. She is said to promote harmony as well as dispute in the family, inspire conjugal love as well as hatred; her character is fundamentally unpredictable (Güterbock). Šaušga is traditionally accompanied by two servant 'hierodules', the music goddesses Ninatta and Kulitta. It seems that during the Hellenistic period her cult experienced a revival by association with Aphrodite.

Haas 1979, 397–401; Lebrun 1980, 49f; Wegner 1981; Güterbock, in Sasson 1984, 155–64

Šeri and Hurri – Anatolian divine bulls

Their names are of Hurrian origin and mean 'Day and Night'. In the Hittite imperial pantheon they are the bulls of the great **Weather-god** and pull his chariot. They were said to graze on destroyed cities. Iconographically they are the trabants of the weather-god; he stands on them on the reliefs and seal-designs. They were invoked in treaties and oaths, but also in prayers, where they were asked to intercede with their master as well as with other deities.

von Schuler, WdM 1965, 195f

Seven Sages

In Mesopotamian mythology the process of civilization had to be gradually implemented by various deities (see **Lahar and Ašnan**, **Ninazu and Ninmadu**, **Inanna and Utu** etc.). In another tradition, the task of teaching mankind the achievements of culture was ascribed to Seven Sages (Akk. *apkallu*). References to these Sages are found in several myths. In the **Erra-Epic**, **Marduk** asks 'Where are the Seven Sages of the **Apsu**, the pure *purādu* fish, who just as their lord **Ea**, have been endowed with sublime wisdom?' A bilingual ritual from Nineveh (Reiner) begins with a mythological introduction, referring to the Seven Sages. They are called 'the seven *apkallu* grown in the river, who ensure the correct functioning of the plan of heaven and earth, Nunpiriggaldim, the *apkallu* of **Enmerkar**, who brought down **Ištar** from heaven to É-anna, Piriggalnungal, from Kish, who angered **Adad** ... so that he let no vegetation be in the country for three years, Piriggalabzu, from Eridu, who angered Ea [...], LU-name is only ⅔ *apkallu*, he drove the *ušumgallu*-dragon from É-ninkarnunna, the temple of Ištar of Shulgi ...' (the names of the other three Sages are lost). The gist of the story is that all these Sages angered the gods and were therefore banned to the Apsu. **Berossus** also reports that before the flood, fish-like monsters were sent by Ea to teach mankind. The names of the Sages vary in the different texts; some also include **Adapa** (whom Berossus calls Oannes).

Reiner 1961, 1–11

Sibittu

Babylonian group of demons, called 'the Seven' (Sumerian *imina.bi.*). There are two groups of Sibittu, good and evil ones. The texts mainly refer to the second category. According to the **Erra** epic, they are the offspring of **Anu** and the Earth. He declares the fate (and function) of each; the first is to cause fury, the second fire, the third to brandish arms etc. Erra is their leader and it is the Seven who instigate his revolt. Otherwise they are mentioned in various incantations, such as *utukki lemnuti.* Their astronomical correlates are the Pleiades.

Edzard, WdM 1965, 124

Siduri – Babylonian goddess

The name means something like 'She is my wall/protection'. She is first to be found in Old Akkadian inscriptions. By the Middle Babylonian period she seems to have been assimilated to **Ištar**. In the Late Babylonian version of the **Gilgameš Epic** (tablet 10) she is called *sābitum*, 'ale-wife', who lives at the edge of the world. She advises the weary hero to live for the day and enjoy pleasure while it lasts, since the gods have allotted death to mankind as their fate. In other versions of the myth it is Ištar who gives this advice.

Sin; Su'en – Babylonian moon-god (*see figures 3, 10 and 37*)

The name is the result of a contraction of Sum. *en.zu,* 'lord of wisdom' – Su'en. The personality of Sîn in the Akkadian sources corresponds generally with that of **Nanna(r)**. He was seen as a horned bull (*qarnū*), a 'fruit that grows by itself' (*enbu ša ina ramānišu ibbanu*) (a reference to the old belief that the moon generates itself after each waning), the one 'who promotes abundance to the crops' (*nadin hegalli ana mašrē*), who regulates time, is wise, decides the Fates and is merciful. Sîn was an important oracle god and also a healer, even a 'midwife'. A Middle Assyrian medical text describes a fragment of a myth in which Sîn is assisting a cow to give birth to her calf; the following text asks the god to help the human mothers in throes of childbirth as well (Lambert, van Dijk). Apart from the Old Sumerian cult-centre at Ur, Sîn was worshipped in Harran, in the temple É-hulhul. In most god-lists, the group Sîn, **Šamaš**, **Adad** and **Ištar** follow after the three great gods, **Anu**, **Enlil** and **Ea**, with the **Mother-goddess** sometimes following after Ea. In spite of his high rank, the cult of Sîn was not considered to be of national importance, except during the reign of Nabonidus, whose family was particularly devoted to the god of Harran. It is well known that this preference was not shared by the Babylonian establishment. Among the astral deities, the moon-god was considered to be the most gentle and reliable, intimately connected with the fertility and fruitfulness of man and beast. He was therefore always a popular god, as the many occurrences in personal names, private documents and seal inscriptions prove. Many prayers were addressed to Sîn (Seux), asking him for favourable omens, but he hardly plays any role in Babylonian mythology.

Edzard, WdM 1965, 101f; Lambert 1969, 28ff; van Dijk 1975, 52ff; Seux 1976, passim

Šukalletuda see Inanna and Šukalletuda

Šulpa'e – Sumerian god

His name means something like 'radiantly appearing youth'. He is already well attested in the Fara tablets. According to the Nippur tradition he was the husband of **Ninhursag**, the brother-in-law of **Enlil**. Like Ninhursag, he was associated with the wild animals of the steppe, but there are also martial as well as demonic aspects to this complex divine personality. He is well represented in the onomasticon of the Neo-Sumerian period. From the Old Babylonian period onwards he was identified with the planet Jupiter and his wife was the Akkadian equivalent of the **Mother-goddess**, **Bēlet-Ilî**.

Falkenstein 1963, 33ff; Edzard, WdM 1965, 128

Sumerian mythology

is mainly known from texts that were written down during the Ur III and Old Babylonian periods. However, there are some compositions whose origin can with certainty be traced to the beginnings of Sumerian literary activity, represented by the tablet finds of Abu Ṣalabikh, some 700 years earlier (e.g. **Enlil and Ninhursag**). It is generally assumed that the majority of mythological texts go back to earlier periods, but the history and manner of transmission are unknown. The editing process of the Ur III scribes and the extent to which it transformed or merely preserved existing narratives is therefore a matter of speculation. The understanding of the texts themselves is problematic. Translations remain literal and tentative, since the poetic structure of Sumerian, with its possible references to oral techniques, as well as the very meaning of some of the most widely used words and phrases, are still debated.

An analysis of the texts found in the Nippur library (M. Lambert) seems to suggest that the great religious centres such as Nippur, Uruk and Eridu developed independent cycles of myth, featuring their gods or goddesses as the main protagonists – **Enki and the World Order**, **Enki and Ninmah**, **Enki and Eridu**; **Inanna and Enki**, **Inanna and Ebih**, **Descent of Inanna**, as well as **Enmerkar**, **Lugalbanda** and **Gilgameš** – Uruk; **Enlil and Ninlil**, and the **Ninurta** myths – Nippur, **Dumuzi** – Babtibira(?). As such they would appear to have been the product of a conscious literary effort. On the other hand it has been shown (Alster) that in terms of poetical structure, most genres of Sumerian literature have a close affinity to oral traditions and 'popular' religious practices. The connection between mythological texts and the cult is also still a subject of debate. Although a number of compositions end in a doxology which 'praises' the main deity in the same terms as a hymn, this does not necessarily imply that they all originated from temple rituals. The historical argument poses similar problems. Although some texts refer to a political situation or a historical personality at a given point of time, in the myth such facts become the raw material for an exposition that ultimately goes beyond actuality.

In spite of the many different theoretical responses of modern Sumerologists, the texts have a remarkable intellectual homogeneity which is characterized by the concept of the *Me* and the 'Fate'. Each mythical protagonist, hero, god or goddess, fulfils some essential role in the realization of divine order in the universe or the world. He or she contributes to the totality of eternally decreed phenomena which constitute the universe which includes Sumerian civilization. The emphasis is on the ultimately harmonious order of the world, in which life and death are cyclically balanced.

Kramer 1944; M. Lambert 1961, 177–96; Kirk 1970; Alster 1972; Hallo 1974, 181–203; Sauren, in Ries et al. (eds) 1978, 110ff; Bruschweiler 1987, 187–90

Sumuqan see Šakkan

Sun-goddess of Arinna – Anatolian deity

In the Hittite inscriptions she usually appears as $^{d}UTU^{URU}Arinna$ after her main cult centre Arinna; she could also just be referred to as the 'one of Arinna', rather like the 'Ninivite' for **Ištar**. Her Hattian name was Wurunšemu, but as this appears only in later texts it is not clear whether this is her original name. As the Sun-goddess of Arinna she is first mentioned in the annals of Hattushili I, who calls himself her 'beloved', and reports that she led him into battle. She then became a national deity of the Hittite empire, usually in conjunction with the **Weather-god**. After the 14th C BC she became increasingly identified with the Hurrian goddess **Hebat**.

The worship of the sun in Anatolia seems to go back to the prehistoric period as the solar discs from Alaça Hüyük testify. Nor was it limited to a single deity. We know also of a male Hattian sun-god called **Eštan** (the Hattian word for 'sun') and its corresponding version in Luwian Tiwat, Palaic Tivaz and Hurrian Šimegi. The Indo-Europeans brought their own god Siu. It seems that as a result of these different traditions, the sun had two major aspects in the Hittite mythology, in many ways analogous to the dual nature of the Venus-star for Semitic peoples. They differentiated between the 'sun of heaven' (*nepišaš ᵈUTU*) and the 'sun of the earth' (*taknaš ᵈUTU*). The latter refers to the nightly sojourn of the sun in the underworld (for the same notion see **Nahhunte**, **Šamaš**, **Šapaš**, **Utu**). As such she is also a chthonic goddess with strong magic connections, much invoked in rituals. The sun of heaven on the other hand is thought to be masculine and has many of the traits of other solar deities, such as justice, valour, omniscience etc.

von Schuler, WdM 1965, 196–200; Lebrun 1980, 48f

T

Tammuz see **Dumuzi**

Tašmetum – Babylonian goddess

Her name, which derives from Akkadian *šamû*, means something like 'the granting (of requests)'. She was wife of **Nabû** and was worshipped with him in Borsippa. With Nabû she is often invoked in Late Babylonian and Late Assyrian prayers and ritual texts, as a merciful mediator, protector from evil and goddess of love and potency. Astronomically she was identified with Capricorn.

Seux 1976, 351, 334

Telepinu – Anatolian god, probably of Hattian origin

According to some Hittite god-lists, his main cult centres were Tawinya, Durmitta and Hanhana, all on the central Anatolian plateau. He also appears in descriptions of rituals and festivals. Although he was called the son of the **Weather-god**, he was primarily an agricultural deity. In one text (VBoT 58, 29ff) the weather-god sends for Telepinu who 'cultivates, ploughs, irrigates and hardens the grain' (Laroche 127). He is part of the ^{d}KAL, the **protective gods** of all living beings; among them he forms a subdivision with his *kaluti*, or group of related gods, which includes the god Suwaliyat, as well as Miyantanzipa and Halki ('grain'), two ancient vegetation goddesses.

The MYTH OF TELEPINU is preserved as part of a ritual intended to soothe the anger of the gods in a time of national emergency. At least three different versions exist, which implies that the text was in continuous use from the Old Hittite to the Empire Period. The beginning is lost but it is clear that Telepinu has disappeared. This has dire consequences for the whole country. The fires go out in the hearths, gods and men feel stifled, the ewes and cows neglect their young, grain fails to ripen, animals and men no longer copulate; the springs and pastures are dry. The sun-god sends envoys to the eagle and then also to the weather-god, that they might look for Telepinu, but their search is in vain. Finally, **Hannahanna**, the mother-goddess, sends out a bee. The bee finds the god asleep and wakes him with his sting. Telepinu is furious and in his anger he brings down yet more calamities which frighten even the gods. The divine magician **Kamrušepa**, however, knows how to calm the god. With magic formulae and special rites she purifies him from his bad temper and restores his good qualities and goodwill towards mankind. Telepinu returns home and revives the fertility in the country. Furthermore, he gives the whole wealth of the earth to the Hittite king (Goetze, Kellerman).

Another, fragmentary myth, THE SUN-GOD, THE COW AND THE FISHER-MAN, tells how Telepinu woos his future wife, Hatepinu, the daughter of the Sea. At the same time he manages to free the sun-god whom the Sea had imprisoned by paying him a compensation (Hoffner).

von Schuler, WdM 1965, 201f; Goetze, in Pritchard 1950, 126–8; Hoffner, in Morrison, Owen 1981, 189–94; Laroche 1984, 127–33; Kellerman 1986, 115–23

Tešup – Hurrian god

The etymology of his name is uncertain (maybe from *tašbi*, 'to strike'?). He was much worshipped in all areas which came into cultural contact with the Hurrians during the second half of the second millennium BC. He is much in evidence in the onomasticon of places like Nuzi, Chagar Bazar, Mari, Ugarit, Aleppo, Karkamish, Alalakh and Boğazköy. As a **Weather-god** he was assimilated to the various local manifestations of this type of deity. Tešup features in the role of the hero in the myth of **Kumarbi**, where he confirms his authority over the other gods by successfully defeating the stone-giant Ullikummi. His epitheton 'king of heaven' expresses his superior position in the divine hierarchy. Tešub's wife was **Hebat**, his sister **Šaušga** and his son **Sarruma**. They all became important deities in the Hittite imperial pantheon after the 14th C BC.

Laroche, in Bonnefoy 1981, vol. II, 486

U

Ugaritic mythology

Our present knowledge of Ugaritic mythology is based on a number of tablets found in and around the temple of **Baal** in Ugarit (Ras Shamra). They were written in a West Semitic dialect in the cuneiform version of the Canaanite 'alphabet' between c. 1425 and 1350 BC. Although the tablets were deciphered and published soon after their discovery by the French scholars Virroleaud and Dhorme in the 1930s, the texts still pose serious problems, enhanced by the fragmentary state of preservation of many tablets. The interpretation of many key-passages is often a matter of debate. Therefore extant translations differ from each other quite considerably.

The majority of myths concern Baal; after all they were found in the archives of his temple. Other important sanctuaries may have had their own collections of mythological texts. We know for instance from the sacrificial lists that **Dagan** and **Astarte** were much worshipped in Ugarit but neither plays a major role in the Baal-cycle. There are some fragments which concern **El** and omit to mention Baal.

In the material available now, the range and content of Ugaritic mythology is local, reflecting the needs and circumstances of a mid-second millennium BC Syrian coastal town. The continuous conflict between the weather-god Baal and the forces of Drought and Death (**Mot**) as well as the stormy waters (**Yam**), offers a paradigm for hope in a precarious existence, forever at the mercy of unreliable weather conditions, the foreign policy of major political powers and the instability of local city-states surrounded by nomad populations. In the light of these considerations it is not surprising that the mythic situation reflects a constant struggle; Baal never decisively beats Mot or Yam, nor achieves absolute supremacy.

There are many different interpretations of Ugaritic myths; some scholars maintain they were primarily used in seasonal rites enacted at periodic intervals (Gaster, de Moor), others see historical events such as the rise of the Sea-peoples behind them, while some can discern a complexity of mythical paradigms relevant to a whole range of human psychology (Hillers, Margalit).

Gaster 1950; Hillers 1973, Margalit 1980; Caquot, Sznycer 1980; de Moor 1987

Ullikummi see **Kumarbi**

Underworld

(a) In **Mesopotamia** the underworld was known by various euphemisms, such as in Sumerian *kur*, 'mountainous country', or 'abroad', *ki-gal*, 'the great place', *edin*, 'the steppe', **arali**, *kur.nu.gi₄*, = 'land of no return', which have their equivalents in Akkadian. Underworld and heaven were linked and complementary and there was a balance between the living and the dead which must not be upset (cf. the proverbial threat 'to break down the gates of the underworld' in **Inanna's Descent** or the **Gilgameš Epic** – see also **Nergal and Ereškigal** on the relations between the gods of either sphere). Little is known about the topography of the place; it has seven gates, one 'descends' or, according to the tenth tablet of the Gilgameš Epic, crosses the River of Death to reach it. The souls of all human beings have to go to the underworld after their death; there is no notion of a heaven or Elysium in either the Egyptian or the Greek sense. The conditions are dismal and described in some detail in **Gilgameš, Enkidu and the Netherworld** and **The Descent of Ištar** (4–11): The abode of Ereškigal is a 'dark house … wherein the entrants are bereft of light, where dust is their fare and clay their food … (where) they are clothed like birds, with wings for garments, (and where) over door and bolt is spread dust'. However, according to the solar theology, the sun-god **Utu**, or Akkadian **Šamaš**, travels through the underworld at night, bringing some cheer with his light. The sun-hymns also mention that he brings sustenance and drink, and judges the dead. The Gilgameš account reports that there is a hierarchy in the underworld; one who had many sons is better off than one with none and the worst fate awaits the unhappy mortal who was not buried in accordance with the funerary practices; he is doomed to become an *eṭimmu*, an errant spirit. The organization of the underworld reflects Mesopotamian institutions. There is a monarch in overall command (first **Ereškigal**, later **Nergal**). They are surrounded by various officials, the **Anunnaki** of the Underworld, who confirm the death sentence and have the name of the deceased entered on a register. Namtar is the *sukkal*, 'vizier', **Ningišzida** the commissionaire, Nedu the great porter. In addition there are a number of other chthonian deities who are associated with the underworld in god-lists and other texts, such as the Old Gods (**Lahmu** and **Lahamu**), Alala-Belili, etc., **Ninazu**, **Meslamta'ea**, **Ištaran** of Dēr and others. Once someone has entered and the death sentence has been pronounced, he has to stay for ever. This rule also applies to gods, as the myth of the Descent of Inanna explains. Although she is revived through the agency of the god **Ea**, the rules of the underworld state that she has to find a substitute to take her place. The same thought is probably also expressed in **Enlil and Ninlil**. During the Neo-Assyrian period there was a great interest in matters related to death and the underworld. A text usually called 'The underworld vision of an Assyrian Crown-Prince' (Soden) is a typical example. It contains detailed descriptions of the horrific demons and guardians in the realm of death.

Soden 1936, 1–39; Kramer 1960; Alster (ed.) 1980; Afanasieva 1981, 161–9; Hutter 1985

(b) **Anatolia** The name for the underworld in Hittite is *dankuis dagan-zipas*, 'dark earth', and in Hurrian *turi*, 'the deep'. The location is under the earth and many of the waterways which dry up during the summer are said to be in the underworld. Sources and springs are the natural entrances and some of them were associated with certain disappearing gods and their rituals. There was also the notion of a 'meadow', somewhere in the 'west' (cf. the Greek asphodel?). All human beings lead a shadowy existence after death and need regular food-offerings to stop them from haunting the living. The fate of evil-doers was worse than that of others, they had to eat excrement. The dead Hittite kings became deified and it was thought that they became 'farmers' and cattle-breeders; this may be the reason why they were given agricultural implements in their burials. The gods of the underworld were called *taknas siunes*, 'the gods of the earth', as opposed to the *siunes kattares*, 'the upper gods' (of heaven). The ancient gods dwell there and it is the realm of the chthonic goddesses: the Hattian Wurunšemu, the Hurrian **Allani** as well as the *taknas ^{d}UTU*, 'the Sun-goddess of the Earth'. It seems that the infernal goddesses have direct connections with the fertility of the earth and are often invoked for this purpose in incantations and rituals. In this respect we also find that the only important male deity, **Kumarbi**, the old Hurrian grain-god, is thought to reside in the underworld.

Haas 1976, 197–212; Lebrun 1980, 57ff

(c) **Syria** The **Baal-Myths** of Ugarit contain numerous accounts of the underworld, the domain of **Mot**, whose very name means 'death'. He says that his appetite for living beings is insatiable; he is also in need of fresh water (as are the dead) and this may be one of the reasons why he wants to get hold of Baal, who personifies among other things, rainfall. It is not clear to what extent Mot was regarded as a god outside the myths as there is no evidence for his cult. Archaeological evidence has shown that the graves, at least those of the royal family, were connected with libation rooms; funerary rites involving water were therefore an established practice.

(d) **Iran** The same kind of libation installations were discovered in Elamite cemeteries. Otherwise there are a few texts which pertain to notions about the underworld. There are prayers in which the departed asks to be received well; he prostrates himself before the god **Inšušinak** who will pronounce his fate and who weighs his soul. All mortals have to undergo judgement, poor and powerful alike. He is also asked to provide the dead with water.

Hinz 1972, 65ff

Utu – Sumerian god (*see figure 43*)

His name means 'sun' and its pictographic sign appears in the earliest written cuneiform records. Several Old Sumerian kings speak of Utu as their king and Lugalzaggesi declares that he was called by Utu 'the supreme minister of **Sîn**'. His main sanctuary was at Larsa, where his temple was called the É-babbar, 'the shining house'. In the Neo-Sumerian period, Gudea speaks of him as the son of **Nanna**, the moon-god – echoing the notion that the day was born of the night. During this period the cult of Utu spread to other Sumerian cities such as Sippar and Eridu, where he had well-endowed sanctuaries. Utu, or his epitheton *babbar*, 'shining, brilliant', often occur in personal names. His character is described in **Enki and the World Order** (11, 374–379): 'The valiant Utu, the bull who stands secure, who proudly displays his power, the father of the great city, the place where the sun rises, the great herald of holy **An** the judge, the decision-maker of the gods, who wears a lapislazuli beard, who comes from the holy heaven (...), Utu, the son born of

161

Ningal, Enki placed in charge of the entire universe.' In mythological texts, Utu appears as a helper for those in trouble and grave danger, as in **Inanna's Descent**, when he allows **Dumuzi** to escape from the underworld demons, if only temporarily. Likewise in **Lugalbanda and Hurrum**, Utu was identified with the Akkadian **Šamaš** probably as early as the pre-Sargonic period.

Jean 1931, 59ff

V

Venus

The planet Venus is one of the great luminaries of the sky, appearing as the first star in the evening, and the last at dawn, when its brilliance alone illuminates the heavens. One or the other of these manifestations could be singled out for special reverence. It seems that the Sumerians preferred the evening star, which was usually endowed with female qualities. Two goddesses were worshipped as Venus: **Inanna** (see the myths which may describe the journey of the planet from the western horizon to the eastern morning sky in the inferior conjunction; **Inanna's Descent**; **Inanna and Ebih**), and **Ninisina** (especially during the Ur III period). The Semites originally preferred the morning star, which had male characteristics (see **Astar**). Under Sumerian influence they added a female manifestation; during the third millennium BC, **Astar** as well as Inanna were worshipped at Ebla and Mari. Eventually one deity emerged which had a 'split personality', consisting of the female evening star and the male morning star. The Babylonian **Ištar** is the prime example. In the first millennium documents the development is clearly expressed; the martial morning star became the well-known bearded Ištar of Babylon (the northern part of the country), while the feminine Ištar was the love-goddess of the South. The Aramean Venus goddess **Nanaya**, who became a very important deity in the first millennium BC, also had male and female characteristics.

Heimpel 1982, 9–22

W

Weather-god

Weather and storm gods were widely worshipped in the northern and mountainous regions of the Ancient Near East which depended on annual rainfall for the fertility of the crops. From a purely cosmic and agrarian deity, the weather-god turned into the supreme power in a hierarchically structured pantheon during the political expansion of the Mitanni and Hittites. There were many local manifestations of the weather-god and we know him under various different names (see **Adad**, **Baal**, **Dagan**, **Ištaran**, **Tešup**, **Tišpak**). His main attribute and symbol is the bull, and he is equipped with bolts of lightning. His consort is usually one of the ancient **Mother-goddesses** and judging from the combination of bull and seated females in Neolithic art, this association may go back to the beginnings of agriculture, or at least to the 7th millennium BC Anatolian settlements.

The Hittites wrote the various weather-gods with the logogram *ᵈIM*. The Hittite name of the weather-god was Tarhunda. It may ultimately go back to one original pan-Anatolian deity who was worshipped in different cult-centres. A number of such sanctuaries were connected with springs or underground waterways. The WEATHER-GOD OF THE SKY was the principal god of the capital Hattusas. Often identified with him was the WEATHER-GOD OF HATTI the national god. The weather-god of Nerik, the ancient Hattian sanctuary, was TARU. He was considered to be the son of the weather-god of the Sky and the **Sun-goddess of Arinna**, although sometimes **Lelwani**, the underworld goddess, is mentioned as his mother. He was the personal god of King Hattusili III. Like **Telepinu** he sometimes gets very angry and disappears through a cave or a spring in the underworld. Various rituals exist which try to bring him back.

The most important festival in honour of the weather-god was the *purulli* festival in spring (cf. **Illuyanka**).

von Schuler, WdM 1965, 209–13; Haas 1970; Macqueen 1980, 179–87; Deighton 1982; Gonnet 1987, 89–100

Weeping goddesses

are a particular topic in Sumerian lamentations and *eršemma* compositions. There are apparently no male weeping deities. The goddesses
recount the cause of their grief, bewail their fate and often appeal to
Enlil as the god responsible for their misery. It is thought that such
laments formed part of rituals, such as the 'Lifting of the Hands' or the
'Soothing of the Heart' which aimed at reconciling angry gods. Some
were recited at the re-dedication of renovated temples. There are a
number of laments by city-goddesses over their destroyed cities (for
instance the famous text 'Lamentation over the Destruction of Ur',
spoken by the goddess **Ninlil**, or a similar text concerning Eridu and its
goddess **Damgalnunna**, the wife of Nippur's chief god Enlil).

There is a second category of lamentation texts, and they involve dead
or disappearing gods, uttered by their wives, mothers or sisters. Most of
them concern **Dumuzi**, and his wife **Inanna** is a favourite protagonist,
although there are also laments for him by his sister **Geštinanna**.
Nergal's mother laments over her son, and so do the sisters of **Damu**. A
generic appellative for the weeping goddesses seems to be LISIN.

Cohen 1981; Kramer 1982, 133ff

Wurunkatte

Anatolian god, usually written as *ᵈZABABA*, a warrior god of the Hittite
imperial pantheon.

Wurunšemu see Sun-goddess of Arinna

Y

Yam – Ugaritic god, (*jm*)

His epitheta *zbl jm*, 'lord sea' and *ṯpṭ nhr*, 'prince river', make it clear that the Ugaritians did not differentiate between sweet waters and the sea. Unlike **Mot** he did have a place in the cult and received regular offerings. He was no doubt an important god for a seafaring nation and his personality seems to reflect the two very different seasons, the calm summer when maritime expeditions are feasible and the stormy winter, when the winds are too adverse.

Yam features in the **Baal-Myths** as one of the young god's enemies. He challenges Baal to a fight and is finally defeated by the magic weapons brought by **Kothar-and-Hasis**.

Pope, WdM 1965, 289

Yarik and Nikkal – Ugaritic moon-deities

Nikkal is the local variant of the Sumerian **Ningal** and Yarik is a West Semitic moon-god. A fragmentary myth describes how Nikkal is wed to Yarik by her father Hrhb, the 'king of the summer-fruit'. The **Kotharat** are called to bless the girl and bestow on her a son. The marriage ceremony is described in some detail and the text might have been used for the celebration of human weddings.

Hermann 1968; de Moor, 141ff

Z

Zababa – Sumerian and Akkadian god (*see figure 10*)

The etymology of his name is uncertain. He is attested in the Old Sumerian period and features in pre-Sargonic personal names. He was the city of god of Kish, a warrior, and later identified with **Ningirsu** and **Ninurta**. **Inanna** in her martial aspect was said to be his wife, and other texts mention **Baba**. In Hittite inscriptions the Sumerogram *ᵈZABABA* can stand for local war-gods, such as the Hattian **Wurunkatte**, the Hurrian Aštabi, Hešui and Nubadig and the Hittite–Luwian Hašamili, Iyarri and Zappana.

GLOSSARY

Abu Salabikh Site of an ancient Sumerian city in the vicinity of Nippur on the old course of the Euphrates. It was occupied until the middle of the third millennium BC. The archives have yielded a number of archaic literary texts (c. 2500 BC).

Akkad (Agade) A city in northern Babylonia which has as yet not been found. It was the capital of the 'empire' founded by Sargon (c. 2334–2279). By the Ur III period it was also the name of the northern district as opposed to the southern, which was called Sumer.

Akkadian Originally the language of Akkad – in distinction to Sumerian. In modern usage it stands for the various dialects of ancient Eastern Semitic, in which the documents of Babylon and Assyria were written. Old Akkadian refers to the texts written during the Sargonic Period (c. 24th–22nd C BC).

Alalakh Modern Tell Atchana in southern Turkey (near Antakya). It was an important town during the mid-second millennium BC. A large archive, with cuneiform tablets written mainly in Akkadian, contained mainly administrative material plus some scholastic texts.

Amarna City in middle Egypt, the ancient Akhetaten, capital of Amenophis IV, called Akhenaten (c. 1369–1353 BC). Numerous cuneiform tablets, found in the ancient state archives, constituted the diplomatic correspondence with the rulers of Babylonia, Assyria, Mitanni, Syria and the Hittites. In this context, the term Amarna period also includes the reign of the pharaoh's predecessor, Amenophis III (c. 1398–1361 BC), since the archives contain letters addressed to this king.

Amorites Akkadian *amurru* (Sumerian *mar.tu*) was rather widely used to designate the various Semitic tribes living to the west of Mesopotamia. Because of their nomadic or semi-nomadic life-style, these people were considered to be barbarians 'who know not grain, who build no houses' and who were given to raiding the towns and villages of Babylon and Sumer. Following the collapse of the Ur III 'empire', the Amorites penetrated deeper into the agricultural and urban areas, formed cohesive political units and eventually one of their leaders,

Hammurabi (c. 1794–1750 BC), initiated the Amorite or First Babylonian Dynasty.

Assur Modern Qalat Sherqat, the old capital of Assyria, on the Tigris, until 883 BC.

Assyria The hilly area of northern Mesopotamia (the Jezirah) was called Assyria after its capital Assur. During the second and first millennia BC, the term also applied to the political configurations of the Middle and Neo-Assyrian empires which came to an end in 612 BC.

Babtibira An ancient city in Sumer which according to the Sumerian King-list had political importance in the antediluvial time, when Dumuzi, 'the shepherd reigned for 36,000 years'.

Babylon The ancient and famous metropolis on the Euphrates first became an important city when Hammurabi made it his capital in the 18th C BC. It was much enlarged during the reigns of Nebukadrezzar II and his descendants in the mid-first millennium BC, and destroyed by Alexander the Great. The name was also applied to the country from the Old Babylonian period, superseding the old names of Sumer and Akkad, in distinction to Assyria.

Boğazköy Modern name for the site of the Hittite capital Hattusa, c. 300 km west of Ankara. The large archive of cuneiform tablets, written in Hittite as well as Akkadian and other Anatolian languages, contained most of the extant mythological literature of ancient Anatolia.

Borsippa A city near Babylon, known from the Ur III to the Seleucid period. It seems to have been politically dependent on Babylon and never formed the seat of a government. Of importance are the considerable amounts of legal and literary tablets that originate from the city.

Canaanites Semitic inhabitants of the westernmost parts of the Near East, along the Mediterranean coast (an area now covered by modern Lebanon, West Syria and Israel). Their civilization was strongly influenced by Egypt, which controlled the coastal areas of the country through most of the second millennium BC.

Çatal Hüyük Site of a neolilithic town in Anatolia (south of Konya). Extensive urban installations, houses, granaries and 'shrines' have been discovered, as well as successive layers of wall-paintings and small sculptures (c. 6500–5650 BC).

Chagar Bazar Syrian town in the Habur valley with an archive dating to the time of Shamshi-Adad I of Assyria (c. 1831–1781 BC).

Dêr City in the East Tigris region which was inhabited from Old Sumerian until Seleucid times.

Dunnu City in central Mesopotamia, between Isin and Larsa; important during the Old Babylonian period.

Eanatum Sumerian king; ruler (*ensi*) of Lagash, grandson of Urnanshe (25th century BC). He made a successful bid for the supremacy of Sumer and called himself 'king of Kish'. On his most famous monument, the Stele of Vultures (Louvre), his god Ningirsu has caught all the king's enemies in a big net.

Ebla Ancient Syrian city, excavated at the mound of Tell Mardikh in the late 1960s. The site was occupied from about 3500 BC and destroyed in 1600 BC. The most important period for Ebla corresponds to the archaeological level IIB (between 2400 and 2250 BC) when it was the capital of a powerful Syrian kingdom. Ebla maintained political as well as cultural relations with Sumer, and its system of cuneiform writing was borrowed from Mesopotamia. The language is an ancient West Semitic dialect ('Eblaite').

Elam The country to the East of Sumer (in modern south-west Iran) had strong cultural links with Mesopotamia throughout its history. There were frequent invasions of each other's territories and Elam exercised political hegemony over Babylonia for several periods in the second and the beginning of the first millennium BC. The Elamite language, which does not belong to any known group, was written in cuneiform; no mythological texts as such have yet been discovered.

emesal Sumerian 'woman's tongue' – a 'dialect' of written Sumerian used for direct speeches of goddesses, and for certain liturgical texts, such as *eršemmas*.

Enheduanna Daughter of Sargon of Agade (c. 2334–2279 BC). She was the high priestess of the moon-god Nanna at Ur. The princess was also famous for her literary efforts; she is quoted in several colophons as the composer of a collection of Temple Hymns as well as a number of eulogies in honour of Inanna-Ištar, some of which may in fact date from much later periods.

Eridu Ancient city in southern Sumer (modern Abu Shahrein) on the old coast of the Persian sea. It was the city of the god Enki. According to the Sumerian king-list, Eridu was the first dynasty in the land and archaeological excavations have confirmed the great antiquity of the site and its main sanctuary. As a major religious centre, Eridu remained an important city throughout Mesopotamian history.

Eshnunna (modern Tell Asmar) Capital of a small kingdom in the East Tigris area which flourished during the Old Babylonian period.

Fara Modern name for the site of the ancient city of Shuruppak, near Nippur on the old course of the Euphrates. The archives, which are roughly contemporary with those of Abu Ṣalabikh, have yielded important Old Sumerian texts and notably the earlist extant lists of gods (c. 2500 BC).

Gudea Ruler (*ensi*) of Lagash in the Neo-Sumerian period (c. 2199–2180 BC). Lagash under his reign was powerful and prosperous. Gudea devoted much effort to public building works (temples, quays), encouraged the arts (some twenty statues of him graced the temple courts – many of them are now in the Louvre) and composed a number of elaborate literary and religious texts.

Harran A city in northern Mesopotamia (now Syria) near the Euphrates. It was an ancient centre for the worship of the Semitic moon-god Sîn.

Hatti Term used to describe the indigenous population of Anatolia prior to the invasion of the Hittites (18th C BC). Since the Indo-European Hittites took over the term to refer to themselves, the culture and language of the Hatti is usually referred to as Proto-Hattian to avoid confusion.

Hattusa see Boğazköy.

Hittites Indo-Europeans who settled in Anatolia in the 18th C BC and soon developed an independent kingdom around their capital Hattusa. In the middle of the second millennium BC, after King Tuthalia II, the Hittites built an empire which controlled all of Anatolia, Upper Mesopotamia and successfully challenged Egyptian supremacy in Syria and Palestine. It was eventually destroyed in the 12th C BC.

Hurrians entered Upper Mesopotamia from the north-east some time before the mid-third millennium BC. Hurrian names are attested since the Sargonic period. Their language, which does not belong to any known group, was written in cuneiform. By Old Babylonian times, Hurrians had spread right across northern Mesopotamia, from Shusara in the east to Alalakh in the west. Eventually they also invaded Anatolia, especially Cilicia which the Hittites called Kizzuwatna. Around 1500 BC, they established the kingdom of Mitanni, ruled by an Indo-European aristocracy. It became one of the most powerful political configurations of its time, stretching from the Mediterranean to the east of the Tigris, with a capital in (the yet still undiscovered) Washukanni. The Hurrians absorbed many Babylonian cultural traits, which they transmitted throughout the Near East. In religious and literary terms, their impact is most clearly discernible on the Hittites. The official pantheon of the Hittites is a syncretistic mixture of Hurrian, Hittite and proto-Hattian elements.

Isin (modern Bahriyat) Ancient Sumerian town. Following the breakdown of the Ur III empire, the dynasty of Isin, founded by Ishbi-Erra, dominated Sumer and Akkad (c. 2017–1924 BC). After the reign of Lipit-Ishtar, Isin was conquered by Rimsin of Larsa. The ensuing period was characterized by a continuous fight for supremacy between the two states and the growing importance of Amorite tribes. It was brought to an end by the rise of Hammurabi (1794). Although the population of southern Mesopotamia at this time consisted of large numbers of Akkadians, Sumerian remained the official language and Sumerian cultural and religious practices continued as under the Ur III period. A large number of royal hymns to various deities were composed.

The Second Dynasty of Isin (c. 1158–1050 BC), also known as the Fourth Dynasty of Babylon, brought to an end the long rule of Kassite kings in Babylonia (1158). Their most important ruler was Nebukadrezzar I. This period is of great interest in the realm of literature and religion, as it heralds a new consciousness of Babylonian cultural traditions and especially the elevation of Marduk to the supreme rank in the pantheon.

Karkamish (modern Djerablus) Ancient city in North Syria, near Aleppo. It was occupied from Neolithic to Hellenistic times. During the second millennium BC it was at first the capital of an independent kingdom, then it was taken by the Hittites and later incorporated into the Mitanni empire. A considerable portion of the population were Hurrians.

Kassites The Kassites were a tribal people who settled in the Middle Euphrates region in the early second millennium BC; their language does not belong to any known group. Kassite petty kings first established themselves in Middle Mesopotamia and eventually ruled Babylonia for almost half a millennium (c. 1740–1158 BC). It was a relatively peaceful time and the Kassite rulers were much concerned with keeping Babylonian traditions alive. Many works of Akkadian literature and science were edited and collected and some compositions created. During the Amarna period, Kassite kings corresponded regularly with Egyptian pharaohs.

King-list There are several such lists which record a sequence of dynasties. The nature of the list is strictly one-dimensional and not synchronistic. The best known version of the Sumerian king-list was compiled during the Isin-Larsa period. It begins with the seven antediluvian kings, then followed the flood, after which 'kingship came down from heaven' again. There is a schematic change of hegemony over Sumer from north to south and vice versa, down to the end of the Isin dynasty. Following a similar pattern, there are also Babylonian king-lists, which concentrate on the dynasties of Babylon, and Assyrian ones. They were compiled in the first millennium BC.

Kish Sumerian town (modern Tell el Oheimir) near Babylon. Kish was an important town, the seat of several dynasties, during the third millennium BC. The title 'King of Kish' implied the hegemony over Sumer and Akkad. In the second millennium BC, the neighbouring Babylon all but eclipsed Kish's status.

Kizzuwatna An area in Southern Anatolia, roughly equivalent to classical Cilicia. During the second millennium BC it had a large Hurrian population. Although initially an independent kingdom, it became increasingly dominated by the Hittites. Kizzuwatna as a 'land of magic' became proverbial; it had a great number of different cults and famous sanctuaries.

Lagash Sumerian city-state (half way between the Tigris and Euphrates), incorporating, among others, the sites of Tello (ancient Girsu) and Tell al-Hibba (ancient Uruku). Excavations have unearthed a vast number of artefacts and inscriptions from these sites. Because of the wealth of textual material we are unusually well informed about the political fortunes and cultural institutions of this Sumerian state. Lagash played a very prominent role in the third millennium BC and was the seat of dominant dynasties during the Early Dynastic and the Neo-Sumerian period. Among its outstanding rulers are Eannatum, Entemena, Uruinimgina and Gudea.

Larsa Southern Babylonian city (modern Senkereh). After the collapse of the Ur III empire, the small kingdom of Larsa, ruled by kings with foreign names, destroyed the city of Ur and took over much of its prosperous trade. It contended with Isin for supremacy over the country, until it achieved a final phase of glory under Rimsin (1822–1763 BC) which lasted until the conquest by Hammurabi of Babylon. Larsa was an ancient cult-centre of the sun-god Utu.

Mari Ancient Mesopotamian city in the middle Euphrates region (now Tell Hariri in Syria). It was inhabited since the Old Sumerian period, blossomed under the native and Assyrian rulers in the Isin-Larsa time and was finally destroyed by Hammurabi in c. 1759 BC. The extensive archives of Mari mainly date from the beginning of the second millennium BC, but numerous inscribed votive offerings from the pre-Sargonic period have been found.

Nineveh Ancient Assyrian town on the Tigris (near Mossul in modern Iraq), occupied since the fifth millennium BC. The famous temple of the goddess Ištar was traditionally associated with Manishtusu, a successor of Sargon of Agade. Nineveh became the capital of the Assyrian empire under Sennacherib (8th century BC) and again under Ashubanipal (7th C BC). The latter king was responsible for the extensive collection of cuneiform documents, which were found on the mound of Kuyunjik. Many mythological and other literary texts were discovered in this 'library'. In many cases they are copies of older texts from Babylonian archives.

Nippur Ancient Sumerian city in central Babylonia (modern Nuffar). It was occupied for more than three thousand years, well into the Parthian period. The city was never the seat of a ruling dynasty, but for most of the third and the first half of the second millennium BC it commanded a high political status as the seat of the god Enlil, 'who conferred kingship'. Nippur was also a famous intellectual centre; vast numbers of cuneiform tablets were discovered and in fact, most literary texts in Sumerian come from this site.

Nuzi (modern Yorgan Tepe in Iraq, east of the Tigris, near Kirkuk). The cuneiform documents of this city date mainly from the middle of the second millennium BC. The Hurrian influence of its population is clearly attested in the surviving legal and administrative texts.

Personal names As naming was tantamount to creating, the name of a person was more than a means of identification. It was the source of his personality and vitality – to have one's name destroyed threatened total annihilation for ever. Most ancient names therefore take the form of an evocation of divine forces, which spell out a commitment to a particular deity and the hope to be under his or her special protection (e.g. Ištar-is-my-beloved; Adad-has-granted-an-heir; My-protection-is-Marduk, etc.). The vast numbers of administrative and legal documents, especially from Mesopotamia, contain many thousands of personal names. The names of the gods and goddesses quoted in the personal names are the only source for the study of popular religious attitudes and reveal much about the true extent of popularity of an official cult.

Sargon of Agade (c. 2334–2279 BC) Founder of the Sargonic dynasty, who established the first extensive Mesopotamian empire, which reached 'from the Upper to the Lower Sea'. His long reign, the obscure circumstances of his early career and the extraordinary success of his ambition, eventually made Sargon into a legendary figure.

Sippar Ancient city in northern Babylonia (modern Abu Habba), in continuous occupation from the third to the first millennium BC. It was the seat of the sun-god Šamaš. The numerous tablets date mainly from the Old and Neo-Babylonian periods.

Susa Ancient city in the Susiana (on the Ulai river in south-west Iran). The site was occupied for more than 5,000 years. In the third and second millennia BC it was the capital of Elam. The texts found at Susa not only comprise almost all extant Elamite sources, but a lot of Sumerian and Old Babylonian material too.

Temple Hymns Temples were the subject of many Sumerian literary compositions. The oldest collection of such hymns is associated with Enheduanna, daughter of Sargon of Agade.

Ugarit Modern Ras Shamra, on the Mediterranean south Syrian coast. During the middle of the second millennium BC, Ugarit was a civilization which made use of the medium of clay to write an 'alphabetic' version of cuneiform. The language (Ugaritic) is a western Semitic dialect. The temple archives of this site included a number of mythological and ritual compositions.

Umma Sumerian city-state, near Lagash, its arch-enemy.

Ur Modern Tell Muqqayir, in southern Iraq (originally by the ancient coast of the Arabian sea); ancient Sumerian city which spans the whole of Mesopotamian history. Ur was the city of the moon-god; it was also the seat of several dynasties and one of the most important Mesopotamian sites, and a large number of Sumerian and Babylonian texts have been found there, dating from all levels of the city's occupation.

Ur III The third Dynasty of Ur (c. 2113–2004) built the second great empire in Mesopotamia (following that of the Sargonic period).

Uuinimgina (formerly Urukagina) Sumerian ruler of Lagaš (c. 25th century BC), best known for his social reforms.

Uruk (modern Warka, South Iraq) Ancient Mesopotamian city, continuously occupied from the fourth to the middle of the first millennium BC, associated with the gods Anu and Inanna. Documents from Uruk range from the earliest archaic texts to those of the Seleucid period. The city was the seat of several important dynasties during the Old Sumerian period. In later times it was mainly renowned as a religious centre and a seat of learning.

Yazilikaya Near Boğazköy, the Hittite capital Hattusas. A rock-sanctuary with the carved images of the Hittite gods and goddesses (14th C BC).

Ziggurat Mesopotamian sanctuaries in the form of a step pyramid; probably with a chapel at the top.

BIBLIOGRAPHY

Afanasieva, V. (1974) 'Mündlich überlieferte Dichtung ('Oral Poetry') und schriftliche Literatur in Mesopotamien', *Acta Antiqua* 22, 121–35

Afanasieva, V. (1980) 'Vom Gleichgewicht der Toten und Lebenden', *Zeitschrift für Assyriologie* 70

Aisleitner, J. (1939) 'Die Anat-texte aus Ras Shamra', *Zeitschrift der alttestamentarischen Wissenschaft* 57

Aistleitner, J. (1959) *Die mythologischen und kultischen Texte aus Ras Schamra* (Budapest)

Albright, B. (1936) 'The Canaanite God Haurôn' (Hôrôn), *American Journal of Semitic Languages* 53

Albright, W.F. (1926) 'The Babylonian Gazelle-God Arwium-Sumukan', *Archiv für Orientforschung* 3

Albright, W.F. (1941) 'Anat and the Dragon' *Bulletin of the American Schools of Oriental Research* 84

Alster, B. (1972) *Dumuzi's Dream* (Mesopotamia 1) (Copenhagen)

Alster, B. (1973) 'An Aspect of "Enmerkar and the Lord of Aratta"', *Revue d'Assyriologie* 67

Alster, B. (1973) 'On the Interpretation of the Sumerian Myth "Inanna and Enki"', *Zeitschrift für Assyriologie* 64

Alster, B. (1974) 'The Paradigmatic Character of Mesopotamian Heroes', *Revue d'Assyriologie* 68

Alster, B. (1975) *Studies in Sumerian Proverbs* (Mesopotamia 3) (Copenhagen)

Alster, B. (1976) 'Early Patterns in Mesopotamian Literature', in *Kramer Anniversary Volume* (Alter Orient und Altes Testament 25) (Neukirchen-Vluyn)

Alster, B. (ed.) (1980) *Death in Mesopotamia*, 26ième Rencontre Assyriologique Internationale (Mesopotamia 8) (Copenhagen)

Alster, B. (1985) 'Geštinanna as Singer and the Chorus of Uruk and Zabalam: UET6ii/22' *Journal of Cuneiform Studies* 37/2

Assmann, J., Burkert, W., Stolz F. (1982) *Funktionen und Leistungen des Mythos* (Freiburg/Göttingen)

Astour, M.C. (1973) 'A North-Mesopotamian Locale of the Keret-Epic?', *Ugarit Forschungen* 5

Attinger, P. (1985) 'Enki and Ninhursaga', *Zeitschrift für Assyriologie* 74

Beckman, G. (1982) 'The Anatolian Myth of Illuyanka', *Journal of the Ancient Near Eastern Societies* 14

Beckman, G. (1983) *Hittite Birth Rituals* (rev.PhD diss., Yale 1977) (Wiesbaden)

Behrens, H. (1978) *Enlil und Ninlil*, Studie Pohl: Series Maior 8 (Rome)

Benito, C.A. (1969) *'Enki and Ninmah' and 'Enki and the World Order'* (Dissert., Univ. of Pennsylvania, Ann Arbor)

Berlin, A. (1979) *Enmerkar and Ensuhkešdanna* (Philadelphia)

Biggs, R.D. (1967) *ŠA.ZI.GA. Ancient Mesopotamian Potency Incantations* (New York)

Bing, J.D. (1977) 'Gilgamesh and Lugalbanda in the Fara Period', *Journal of Ancient Near Eastern Societies* 9

Bing, J.D. (1984) 'Adapa and Immortality', *Ugarit Forschungen* 16

Black, J. and Green (in preparation) *Gods, Demons and Symbols of Ancient Mesopotamia* (provisional title) (British Museum Publications)

Böhl, F.H.Th. (1959) *Welt des Orients* 2

Bonnefoy, I. (ed.) (1981) *Dictionnaire des mythologies*, 2 vols (Paris)

Bottéro, J. (1975) 'Les noms de Marduk, l'écriture et la logique en Mésopotamie ancienne', in de Jong-Ellis (ed.) *Essays on the Ancient Near East in Memory of J. Finkelstein* (Hamden)

Bottéro, J. (1985) *Mythes et rites de Babylone* (Paris)

Bowman, C.H. and Coote, R.B. (1980) 'A Narrative Incantation for Snake Bite', *Ugarit Forschungen* 12

Brandon, S.G.E. (1963) *Creation Legends of the Ancient Near East* (London)

Bruschweiler, F. (1989) *Inanna la déesse triomphante et vaincue dans la cosmologie sumérienne* (Leuven)

Buccellati, G. (1973) 'Adapa, Genesis and the Notion of Faith', *Ugarit Forschungen* 5

Buccellati, G. (1982) 'The Descent of Inanna as a Ritual Journey to Kutha?' *Syro-Mesopotamian Studies* 4

Burrows, E. (1932) 'Problems of the abzu' *Orientalia, Neue Serie* 1

Burstein, S.M. (1978) *The Babyloniaca of Berossus* (Malibu)

Cagni, L. (1969) *L'epopea di Erra* (Rome)

Cagni, L. (1977) *The Poem of Erra* Sources and Monographs, Sources and Monographs of the Ancient Near East 1/3 (Malibu)

Caquot, A. (1958) 'Le dieu 'Athtar et les textes de Ras Shamra', *Syria* 35

Caquot, A. (1959) 'La divinité solaire ougaritique', *Syria* 36

Caquot, A., Sznycer, M., Herdner, A. (1974) *Textes ougritiques, I. Mythes et légendes*, Littératures anciennes du Proche-Orient, Vol. 7 (Paris)

Caquot, A., Sznycer, M. (1981) *Ugaritic Religion* (Leiden)

Carroué, F. (1981) 'Geštinanna à Lagaš', *Orientalia* 50

Cassuto, M. (1962) 'Baal and Mot in Ugaritic Texts', Israel Exploration Journal 12

Cassuto, V. (1951) *The Goddess Anat. Canaanite Epics of the Patriarchal Age* (Jerusalem)

Castellino, G.R. (1976) 'The Šamaš Hymn: A Note on its Structure', in *Kramer Anniversary Volume* (Alter Orient und Altes Testament 25) (Neukirchen-Vluyn) Vluyn)

Cohen, M.E. (1981) *Sumerian Hymnology: The Eršemma* (Cincinnati)

Colpe, C. (1969) 'Zur mythologischen Struktur der Adonis, Attis- und Osiris-überlieferungen', in W. Röllig (ed.) *Lišan mithurti*, (Alte Orient und Altes Testament 1) (Neukirchen-Vluyn)

Cooper, J.C. (1977) 'Gilgamesh Dreams of Enkidu: The Evolution and Dilution of Narrative', in *Essays of the Ancient Near East in Memory of J.J. Finkelstein, Memoirs* (Connecticut Academy of Arts and Sciences, vol. 19)

Cooper, J.C. (1978) *The Return of Ninurta to Nippur* (Rome)

Cooper, J.S. (1980) review article of Behrens, Enlil and Ninlil, *Journal of Cuneiform Studies* 32

Cooper, J.S. (1981) review article of Römer's Gilgameš und Akka, in *Journal of Cuneiform Studies* 33

Dalley, S. (1989) *Myths from Mesopotamia, Creation, the Flood, Gilgamesh and Others* (Oxford, New York)

Danmanville, J. (1962) 'L'iconographie d'Ištar-Šaušga en Anatolie ancienne', *Revue d'Assyriologie* 56

De Jong Ellis, M. (1982/83) 'Gilgamesh's Approach to Huwawa: A New Text', *Archiv für Orientforschung* 28

Deighton, H.J. (1982) *The Weathergod in Hittite Anatolia* (Oxford)

Del Olmo Lete, G. (1981) 'Le mythe de la Vièrge-Mère 'Anatu', *Ugarit Forschungen* 13

Dhorme, P.E. (1949) *Les religions de Babylonie et de l'Assyrie* (Paris)

Dietrich, M. and Lorentz, O. (1980) 'Die Bannung von Schlangengift', *Ugarit Forschungen* 12

Dijkstra, M. (1979) 'Some Reflections on the Legend of Aqhat', *Ugarit Forschungen* 11

Dossin, G. (1934) 'Le dieu Gibil et les incendies de la végétation', reprinted in *Receuils Georges Dossin*, Akkadica Supplementum 1 (1983)

Draffkorn-Kilmer, A. (1971) 'How was Queen Ereškigal tricked?', *Ugarit Forschungen* 3

Draffkorn-Kilmer, A. (1972) 'The Mesopotamian Concept of Over-population and Its Solution as Reflected in the Mythology', *Orientalia* 41

Draffkorn-Kilmer, A.D. (1976) 'Speculations on Umul, the First Baby', in *Kramer Anniversary Volume* (Alter Orient und Altes Testament 25) (Neukirchen-Vluyn)

Draffkorn-Kilmer, A. (1982) 'Word Play in Gilgamesh', in Veenhof, K.R. (ed.) *Zikir Šumim, Festschrift für F.R. Kraus* (Lieden)

Draffkorn-Kilmer, A. (1987) 'The Symbolism of Flies in the Mesopotamian Flood Myths and some further Implications', in Rockberg, F. and Halton (eds.), *Language, Literature and History: Philological and Historical Studies* presented to E. Reiner (New Haven)

Dressler, H.H.P. (1979) 'Is the Bow of Aqhat a Symbol of Virility?', *Ugarit Forschungen* 7

Driel, van G. (1969) *The Cult of Aššur* (Van Gorcum Assen)

Driver, G.R. (1956) *Canaanite Myths and Legends* (Edinburgh)

Dussaud, R. (1938) 'Les combats sanglants d'Anat et le pouvoir universel de El', *Revue Hittite* 118

Edzard D.O. and Wilcke, C. (1976) 'Die Hendursanga Hymne', *Kramer Anniversary Volume* (Alter Orient und Altes Testament 25) (Neukirchen-Vluyn)

Eissfeldt, O. (1951) *El im ugaritischen Pantheon* (Berlin)

Falkenstein, A. (1948) review of Kramer's *Sumerian Mythology*, *Bibliotheca Orientalis* 5

Falkenstein, A. (1951) *Compte rendu de la Deuxième Rencontre Assyriologique Internationale* (Paris)

Falkenstein, A. '*Tammuz*', *Compte Rendu de la Troisième Rencontre Assyriologique Internationale* (Leiden)

Falkenstein, A. (1963) 'Sumerische religiöse Texte. Ein Lied auf Šulpa'e', *Zeitschrift für Assyriologie* 55

Falkenstein, A. (1965) 'Die Anunna in der sumerischen Uberlieferung', in *Studies in Honour of B. Landsberger*, Assyriological Studies 16 (Chicago)

Falkenstein, A. (1966) *Die Inschrifen Gudeas von Lagasch* (Rome) (*Analecta Orientalia* 30

Falkenstein, A. (1968) *Der sumerische und akkadische Mythos von Inanna's Gang zur Unterwelt* (Leiden)

Falkenstein, A. and Soden, W. von (1953) *Sumerische und akkadische Hymnen und Gebete* (Zürich, Stuttgart)

Farber, W. (1989) review of Kinnier-Wilson's Etana, *Journal of Near Eastern Studies* 48/2

Farber-Flügge, G. (1973) *Der Mythos 'Inanna und Enki' unter besonderer Berücksichtigung der Liste der m e*, Studia Pohl 10 (Rome)

Foster, B.R. (1977) 'Ea and Şaltu' in de Jong Ellis, M. (ed.), *Essays on the Ancient Near East in Memory of J.J. Finkelstein* (New Haven)

Frazer, Sir J. (1964) *The New Golden Bough* (ed. Th. Gaster)

Friedrich, J. (1930) 'Die hethitischen Bruchstücke des Gilgameš-Epos', *Zeitschrift für Assyriologie* 39

Friedrich, J. (1949) 'Der churritische Mythos vom Schlangendämon Hedammu in heth. Sprache', *Archiv Orientalin* 17/1

Friedrich, J. (1949) 'Churritische Märchen in hethitischer Sprache', *Zeitschrift für Assyriologie, Neue Folge* 15

Galter, H.D. (1981) *Der Gott Ea/Enki in der akkadischen Überlieferung* (Graz)

Gardiner, A.H. (1932) 'The Astarte Papyrus', in *Studies presented to F.H. Griffiths*

Garelli, P. (1960) *Gilgameš et sa légende* (Paris)

Gaster, T.H. (1939) 'Baal is Risen: An Ancient Hebrew Passion Play from Ras Shamra-Ugarit', *Iraq* 6

Gaster, T.H. (1950) *Thespis: Ritual, Myth and Drama in the Ancient near East* (New York)

Gese, H., Höfner, M., Rudolph, K. (1970) *Die Religionen Altsyriens, Altarabiens und der Mandäer* (Stuttgart)

Gibson, J.C.L. (1978) *Canaanite Myths and Legends* (2nd ed., Edinburgh)

Ginsberg, H.L. (1946) *The Legend of King Keret: A Canaanite Epic of the Bronze Age* (New Haven)

Goedicke, H. and Roberts, J.J.M. (eds) (1975) *Unity and Diversity* (Baltimore, London)

Gonnet, H. (1987) 'Institution d'un culte chez les Hittites', *Anatolica* 14

Gordon, C.H. (1949) *Ugaritic Literature: A Comprehensive Translation of the Poetic and Prose Texts* (Rome)

Grabbe, L.L. (1976) 'The Seasonal Pattern in the Myth of Ba'lu', *Ugarit Forschungen* 8

Gray, J. (1949) 'The Desert God' Aṯtr in the Literature and Religions of Canaan', *Journal of Near Eastern Studies* 8

Gray, J. (1957) *The Legacy of Canaan Supplements to Vetus Testamentum V*; re-edited 1965 (Leiden)

Gray, J. (1964) *The KRT Text in the Literature of Ras Shamra: A Social Myth of Ancient Mesopotamia* (2nd ed., Leiden)

Gray, J. (1969) *Near Eastern Mythology* (London, New York, Sydney, Toronto)

Greengus, S. (1979) *Old Babylonian Tablets from Ishchali* (Istanbul)

Groneweg, B. (1981) 'Philologische Bearbeitung des Agušaya Hymnus', *Revue d'Assyriologie* 75

Gurney, O. (1977) *Some Aspects of Hittite Religion* (Oxford)

Güterbock, H.G. (1946) *Kumarbi, Mythen vom churritischen Kronos*

Güterbock, H.G. (1951, 52) 'The Song of Ullikummi, Revised Text of the Hittite Version of a Hurrian Myth', *Journal of Cuneiform Studies* 5, 6

Güterbock, H.G. (1954) 'The Hurrian Element in the Hittite Empire', *Cahiers d'Histoire Mondiale* 2

Haas, V. (1970) *Der Kult von Nerik* (Rome)

Haas, V. (1976) 'Die Unterwelts- und Jenseitsvorstellungen im hethitischen Kleinasien', *Orientalia* 45

Haas, V. (1979) 'Remarks on the Hurrian Ištar-Sawuska of Nineveh in the second millenium BC', *Sumer* 35

Hall, M.G. (1986) 'A Hymn to the Moon-God, Nanna', *Journal of Cuneiform Studies* 38

Hallo, W.W. (1969) 'The Cultic Setting of Sumerian Poetry', *17ième Rencontre Assyriologique Internationale*

Hallo, W.W. (1975) 'Towards a History of Sumerian Literature', in *Sumerological Studies in Honor of Thorkild Jacobsen, Assyriological Studies* 20 (Chicago, London)

Hallo, W.W. (1984) 'Lugalbanda Excavated', in *Studies in Literature from the Ancient Near East dedicated to S.N. Kramer*, American Oriental Series 65 (New Haven)

Hallo, W.W. and van Dijk, J.J.A. (1968) *The Exaltation of Inanna*, (Yale Near Eastern Researches 3) (New Haven, London)

Hallo, W.W. and Moran, W.L. (1979) 'The First Tablet of the SB Recension of the Anzu Myth', *Journal of Cuneiform Studies* 31/2

Hartner, W. (1965) 'The Earliest History of the Constellations in the Near East and the Motif of the Lion-Bull', *Journal of Near Eastern Studies* 24

Hawkins, J.D. (1981) 'Kubaba at Karkamiš and Elsewhere', *Anatolian Studies* 31

Hecker, K. and Sommerfeld, W. (eds) *Keilschriftliche Literaturen, Ausgewahlte Vorträge der 32. Rencontre Assyriologique Internationale, Münster 1985* (Berlin)

Heidel, A. (1942) *The Babylonian Genesis* (Chicago)

Heidel, A. (1954) *The Gilgamesh Epic and Old Testament Parallels* (2nd ed., Chicago)

Heimpel, W. (1981) 'A note on "Gilgamesh and Agga"', *Journal of Cuneiform Studies* 33

Heimpel, W. (1982) 'A Catalogue of Near Eastern Venus Deities', *Syro-Mesopotamian Studies* 4/3

Heimpel, W. (1986) 'The Sun at Night and the Doors of Heaven in Babylonian Texts', *Journal of Cuneiform Studies* 38/2

Helck, W. (1971) *Betrachtungen zur grossen Göttin und den ihr verbundenen Gottheiten* (Munich, Vienna)

Hermann, W. (1968) *Yarih und der Preis der Kutarat-Göttinnen* (Berlin)

Hermann, W. (1969) 'Astart', *Mitteilungen des Instituts für Orientforschung*, Berlin 15

Hillers, D.R. (1973) 'The Bow of Aqhat: The Meaning of a Mythological Tale', (Alter Orient und Altes Testament 22) (Neukirchen-Vluyn)

Hinz, W. (1972) *The Lost World of Elam* (London)

Hruška, B. (1975) *Der Mythenadler Anzu in Literatur und Vorstellung des alten Mesopotamien* (Assyriologica II) (Budapest)

Hutter, M. (1985) *Altorientalische Vorstellungen von der Unterwelt* (Göttingen)

Ichiro, K. (1979) *Deities in the Mari Texts* (Ann Arbor)

Jacobsen, Th. (1946) 'Sumerian Mythology: A review article', *Journal of Near Eastern Studies* 5

Jacobsen, Th. (1953) 'The Myth of Inanna and Bilulu', *Journal of Near Eastern Studies* 12

Jacobsen, Th. (1970) *Towards the Image of Tamuz* (Cambridge, Mass.)

Jacobsen, Th. (1973) 'Notes on Nintur', *Orientalia* 42

Jacobsen, Th. (1976) *Treasures of Darkness* (New Haven, London)

Jacobsen, Th. (1984) 'The Harab Myth', *Studies in Ancient Near Eastern Societies* 2/3

James, E.O. (1965) *The Cult of the Mother Goddess*

Jastrow, M. and Clay, A.T. (1920) *An Old Babylonian Version of the Gilgamesh Epic on the Basis of Recently Discovered Texts* (Yale Oriental Researches IV, 3), (New Haven)

Jean, C.F. (1931) *La religion Sumérienne* (Paris)

Jean, C.F. (1950) 'Le dieu An à Lagash', *Revue d'Assyriologie* 44

Kammenhuber, A. (1955) 'Die protohattische Bilingue vom Mond der vom Himmel gefallen ist', *Zeitschrift für Assyriologie* 17

Kammenhuber, A. (1975) 'Die hethitische Göttin Inar', *Zeitschrift für Assyriologie* 65

Kapelrud, A.S. (1969) *The Violent Goddess. Anat in the Ras Shamra Texts* (Oslo)

Katz, D. (1987) 'Gilgamesh and Akka: Was Uruk ruled by Two Assemblies?' *Revue d'Assyriologie* 81

Kienast, B. (1965) 'Igigu and Anunnakku nach den akkadischen Quellen', *Studies in Honour of B. Landsberger, Assyriological Studies* 16 (Chicago)

Kienast, B. (1973) 'Die Weisheit des Adapa von Eridu', in Beek, M.A., Kaufman, A.A. et al. *Symbolae Bibliae et Mesopotamiae, Francisco Mario Theodoro de Liagre Böhl Dedicatae* (Leiden)

Kienast, B. (1985) 'Überlegungen zum "Pantheon Babylonicum"', *Orientalia* 54

Kinnier-Wilson, J.V. (1979) *The Rebel Lands.* Cambridge Oriental Publications 20

Kinnier-Wilson, J.V. (1985) *The Legend of Etana: A New Edition* (Warminster)

Kinnier-Wilson, J.V. and Landsberger, B. (1961) 'The fifth Tablet of Enuma Elish', *Journal of Near Eastern Studies* 20

Klein, J. (1981) *Three Šulgi Hymns* (Ramat-Gan)

Komoroczy, G. (1964) 'Zur Deutung der altbabylonischen Epen Adapa und Etana', *Neue Beiträge zur Geschichte der Alten Welt* I

Kramer, S.N. (1944) *Sumerian Mythology* (New York)

Kramer, S.N. (1945) 'Enki and Ninhursag: A Sumerian Paradise Myth', *Bulletin of the American Schools of Oriental Research* Suppl. Studies 1

Kramer, S.N. (1949) 'A Blood-plague Motif in Sumerian Mythology', *Archiv Orientani* 17/1

Kramer, S.N. (1951) 'Inanna's Descent to the Netherworld', *Journal of Cuneiform Studies* 12

Kramer, S.N. (1952) *Enmerkar and the Lord of Aratta* (Philadelphia)

Kramer, S.N. (1953) 'Inanna and Bilulu', *Journal of Near Eastern Studies* 12

Kramer, S.N. (1960) 'Death and Netherworld according to Sumerian Literary Texts', *Iraq* 22

Kramer, S.N. (1963) *The Sumerians* (Chicago)

Kramer, S.N. (1969) *The Sacred Marriage Rite* (London)

Kramer, S.N. (1969) 'The Dumuzi-Inanna Sacred Marriage Rite: Origin, Development, Character', *17ième Rencontre Assyriologique Internationale* (Leiden)

Kramer, S.N. (1971) review of Wilcke's Lugalbanda, *Acta Orientalia* 33

Kramer, S.N. (1976) 'Poets and Psalmists', in Schmandt-Besserat, D. (ed.) *The Legacy of Sumer* (Malibu)

Kramer, S.N. (1980) 'The Death of Dumuzi: A New Sumerian Version', *Anatolian Studies* 30

Kramer, S.N. (1982) 'A Sumerian Prototype of the Mater Dolorosa', *Eretz Israel* 16

Kramer, S.N. (1982) 'Lisin, the Weeping Mother Goddess. A New Sumerian Fragment', in *Zikir Šumim. Assyriological Studies Presented to F.R. Kraus* (Leiden)

Kramer, S.N. (1983) 'The Sumerian Deluge Myth. Reviewed and Revised', *Anatolian Studies* 33

Kramer, S.N. (1984) 'Ninurta's Pride and Punishment', *Aula Orientalis* 2

Kramer, S.N. (1985) 'Bread for Enlil, Sex for Inanna', *Orientalia, Nova Seria* 54

Kramer, S.N. (1987) 'By the Rivers of Babylon: A balag Liturgy of Inanna', *Aula Orientalis* 5

Kupper, J.R. (1961) *L'iconographie du dieu Amurru* (Brussels)

Labat, R. (1959) 'Les origines de la formation de la Terre dans le poème babylonien de la Création', *Analecta Biblica* 12

Labat, R., Caquot, A. and Sznycer, M. (1970) *Les religions du Proche-Orient asiatique* (Paris)

Lambert, M. (1961) 'La littérature sumerienne à propos d'ouvrages récents', *Revue d'Assyriologie* 55

Lambert, M. and Tournay, R. (1969) 'Enki et Ninhursag: A propos d'un ouvrage récent', *Revue d'Assyriologie* 43

Lambert, W.G. (1957/8) 'An Unpublished Fragment of the Tukulti-Ninurta Epic', *Archiv für Orientforschung* 18

Lambert, W.G. (1960) *Babylonian Wisdom Literature* (Oxford)

Lambert, W.G. (1964) in *The Seed of Wisdom: Essays in Honour of T.J. Meek*

Lambert, W.G. (1965) 'A New Look at the Babylonian Background of Genesis', *Journal of Theological Studies* 16

Lambert, W.G. (1967) 'The Gula Hymn of Bulluṭsa-rabi', *Orientalia, Nova Seria* 36

Lambert, W.G. (1969) 'A Middle Assyrian Medical Text', *Iraq* 31

Lambert, W.G. (1971) review of Weiher, *Der babylonische Gott Nergal, Bibliotheca Orientalis* 30

Lambert, W.G. (1975) 'The Historial Development of the Mesopotamian Pantheon. A Study in Sophisticated Polytheism', in Goedicke, Roberts (eds) *Unity and Diversity* (Baltimore)

Lambert, W.G. (1982) 'The Hymn to the Queen of Nippur', in *Zikir šumim, Assyriological Studies presented to F.R. Kraus* (Leiden)

Lambert, W.G. (1984) 'Studies in Marduk', *Bulletin of the School of Oriental and African Studies* 47

Lambert, W.G. (1985) 'The Pair Lahmu-Lahamu in Cosmology', *Orientalia* 54

Lambert, W.G. (1986) 'The Reading of the Divine Name Šakkan', *Orientalia* 55

Lambert, W.G. (1987) 'Gilgamesh in Literature and Art: The Second and First Millennia', in Farhas, A. (ed.) *Monsters and Demons in the Ancient and Medieval Worlds* (Mainz)

Lambert, W.G. (1987) 'Goddesses in the Pantheon', *Comptes rendus de la 33ième Rencontre Assyriologique Internationale, Paris 1986* (Paris)

Lambert, W.G. and Millard, A.R. (1969) *Atra-hasîs, The Babylonian Story of the Flood* (Oxford)

Lambert, W.G. and Walcot, P. (1965) 'A New Babylonian Theogony and Hesiod', *Kadmos* 4

Landsberger, B. (1926) *Islamica* 2

Laroche, E. (1947) 'Hattic Deities and their Epithets', *Journal of Cuneiform Studies* 1

Laroche, E. (1948) 'Tešub, Hebat et leur cour', *Journal of Cuneiform Studies* 2

Laroche, E. (1960) 'Koubaba, déesse anatolienne, et le problème des origines de

Cybèle', in *Elements orientaux dans la religion grecque.* Coll. Strasbourg (Paris)

Laroche, E. (1963) 'Le dieu anatolien Sarruma', *Syria* 40

Laroche, E. (1984) 'Les dieux du paysan Hittite', in Douceel, R. and Lebrun, R. (eds) *Archéologie et religions de l'Anatolie Ancienne* (Homo Religiosus 10) (Louvain-la-Neuve)

Laroche, E. (1986) in Hoffner, H.A. and Beckman, G. (eds) *Kanissawar, A Tribute to Hans G. Güterbock* (*Assyriological Studies* 20) (Chicago)

Lebrun, R. (1980) *Hymnes et prières hittites* (Louvain)

Lebrun, R. (1984) *Ebla et les civilisations du Proche-Orient Ancien* (Louvain)

Lewy, H. (1965) 'Ištar and the Bow-star', *Studies in Honor of B. Landsberger* (*Assyriological Studies* 16)

L'Heureux, C.E. *Rank among the Canaanite Gods* (Ann Arbor)

Limet, H. (1971) 'Le poème epique "Inanna et Ebih", Une version des lignes 123–182' *Orientalia, Nova Seria* 40

Lipinski, E. (1965) 'Les conceptions et couches merveilleuses de Anat', *Syria* 42

Lipinski, E. (1972) 'The goddess Aṯirat in ancient Arabia, in Babylon and in Ugarit', *Orientalia Lovaniensa Periodica* 3

Loewenstamm, S. (1972) 'The Killing of Mot in Ugaritic Myth', *Orientalia* 41

Loewenstamm, S. (1979) 'Zur Götterlehre des Epos von Keret', *Ugarit Forschungen* 11

Lokkegaard, F. (1953) 'A Plea for El the Bull and other Ugaritic Miscellania', *Studia Orientalia Pedersen dicata*

Lokkegaard, F. (1956) 'The Canaanite divine Wet-nurses', *Studia Theologica* 10

Macqueen, J.G. (1959) 'Hattian Mythology and Hittite Monarchy', *Anatolian Studies* 9

Macqueen, J.G. (1980) 'Nerik and its "Weather-god"', *Anatolian Studies* 30

Margalit, B. (1980) *A Matter of 'Life' and 'Death'* (Neukirchen-Vluyn)

Margulis, B. (1972) 'The Kôsarôt/ktrt: Patroness-saints of Women', *Journal of the Ancient Near Eastern Societies* 4

Millard, A.R. (1964) 'Gilgameš X: A New Fragment', *Iraq* 26

Montgomery, J.A. 'The Conflict between Baal and the Waters', *Journal of the American Oriental Society* 55

Moran, W. (1971) review of Lambert and Millard's Atra-hasîs, *Biblica* 52

Moran, W. (1987) 'Some Considerations of Form and Interpretation in Atra-hasis', in Rockberg, F. and Halton, (eds) *Language, Literature and History, Philological and Historical Studies presented to Erica Reiner,* American Oriental Series 67 (New Haven)

Moor, J.C. de (1971) *The Seasonal Pattern in the Ugaritic Myth of Ba,lu according to the Version of Illumilku* (Neukirchen-Vluyn)

Moor, J.C. de (1986) 'Athtartu the Huntress', *Ugarit Forschungen* 17

Moor, J.C. de (1987) *An Anthology of Religious Texts from Ugarit* (Leiden, New York, Copenhagen, Köln)

Morrison, M.A. and Owen, D.I. (eds) (1981) *Studies on the Civilization and Culture of Nuzi and the Hurrians in Honor of E.R. Lacheman*

Müller, H.-P. (1983/4) 'Mythos als Gattung des archaischen Erzählens und die Geschichte von Adapa', *Archiv für Orientforschung* 29

Neu, E. (1974) *Studien zu den Bŏghazkŏy Texten* 18

Oberhuber, K. (1963) *Der numinose Begriff ME im Sumerischen* (Innsbrucker Beiträge zur Kulturwissenschaft, Sonderheft 17)

Oberhuber, K. (ed.) (1977) *Das Gilgamesch Epos* (Darmstadt)

Oden, R.A. (1981) 'Transformations in Near Eastern Myths: Cpn. 1–11 and the Babylonian Epic of Atrahasis,' *Religion* 11

Oldenburg, V. (1969) *The Conflict between El and Ba'al in Canaanite Religion* (Leiden)

Otten, H. (1942) *Die Überlieferung des Telepinu Mythos* (Leipzig)

Otten, H. (1950) 'Die Gottheit Lelwani der Boğhazköy Texte', *Journal of Cuneiform Studies* 4

Otten, H. (1950) *Mythen vom Gotte Kummarbi* (Berlin)

Otten, F. (1953) 'Ein kanaanäischer Mythos aus Boğazköy, *Mitteilungen des Instituts für Orientforschung*, Berlin 1

Otten, F. (1953) 'Kanaanäische Mythen aus Hattusa-Boğazköy', *Mitteilungen der Deutschen Orientgesellschaft* 85

Otten, F. (1973) *Eine althethitische Erzählung um die Stadt Zalpa* (Wiesbaden)

Patai, R. (1965) 'The Goddess Asherah', *Journal of Cuneiform Studies* 24

Perlman, A.L. (1978) *Asherah and Astarte in the Old Testament and in Ugaritic Literature*, Berkeley University Ph.D. Diss.

Pettinato, G. (1971) *Das altorientalische Menschenbild und die sumerischen und akkadischen Schöpfungsmythen* (Heidelberg)

Picchioni, J.A. (1981) *Il poemetto di Adapa* (Budapest)

Pomponio, F. (1978) *Nabû, Studi Semitici* 51 (Rome)

Pope, M.H. (1953) *El in the Ugaritic Texts*

Pritchard, J.B. (1950) (ed.) *Ancient Near Eastern Texts Relating to the Old Testament* (Princeton)

Pritchard, J.B. (ed.) (1975) *The Ancient Near East II* (Princeton)

Reiner, E. (1961) 'The Etiological Myth of the "Seven Sages"', *Orientalia*, N.S. 30

Reiner, R. (1974) 'A Sumero-Akkadian Hymn to Nanâ', *Journal of Near Eastern Studies* 33

Reisman, D. (1976) 'A "Royal Hymn" of Išbi-Erra to the Goddess Nisaba' (Alter Orient und Altes Testament 25) (Neukirchen-Vluyn)

Ringgren, H. (1973) *Religions of the Ancient Near East* (London)

Roberts, J.J.M. (1972) *The Earliest Semitic Pantheon* (London, Baltimore)

Römer, W.H.Ph. (1965) *Sumerische Königshymnen der Isinzeit* (Leiden)

Römer, W.H.Ph. (1969) 'Eine Hymne mit Selbstlob Inanna's', *Orientalia* 38

Römer, W.H.Ph. (1969) 'Einige Beobachtungen zur Göttin Nini(n)sinna auf Grund von Quellen der Ur II Zeit und der altbabylonischen Periode' (Alter Orient und Altes Testament 1) (Neukirchen-Vluyn)

Römer, W.H.Ph. (1980) *Das sumerische Kurzepos Gilgameš und Akka* (Alter Orient und Altes Testament 209) (Neukirchen-Vluyn)

Römer, W.H.Ph. (1982) 'Ein Eršemma-Lied für Iškur (CT 15, 15–16)', in *Zikir šumin, Assyriological Studies presented to F.R. Kraus* (Leiden)

Rosengarten, Y. (1971) *Trois Aspects de la Pensée Religieuse Sumerienne* (Paris)

Rosengarten, Y. (1977) *Sumer et le Sacré. Le jeu des préscriptions (me) des dieux, et des destins* (Paris)

Roux, G. (1961) 'Adapa et le vent', *Revue d'Assyriologie* 55

Rundle Clark, R.T. (1959) *Myths and Symbols in Ancient Egypt* (London)

Saggs, H.W.F. (1986) 'Additions to Anzu', *Archiv für Orientforschung* 33

Sasson, J.M. (ed.) (1984) *Studies in Literature from the Ancient Near East dedicated to S.N. Kramer* (American Oriental Series 65) (New Haven)

Sauren H. (1969) 'Besuchsfahrten der Götter in Sumer', *Orientalia* 38

Sauren, H. (1978) 'Le sacré dans les textes sumeriennes', in Ries, H. et al., eds *L'expression due sacré dans les grandes religions. Vol. I* (Louvain-la-Neuve)

Schmidt, W. (1963) 'Baal's Tod und Auferstehung', *Zeitschrift für Religion und Geisteswissenschaften* 15

Schnabel, P. (1923) *Berossus und die babylonisch-hellenistische Litteratur* (Leipzig, Berlin)

Schott, A. and Soden, W. von (1958) *Das Gilgamesch-Epos neu übersetzt und mit Anmerkungen versehen von A. Schott, durchgesehen und ergänzt von W. von Soden* (Reclam's Universalbibiliothek, 7235/35a; Stuttgart); latest edition 1982

Seux, M.J. (1976) *Hymnes et prières aux dieux de Babylone et d'Assyrie* (Paris)

Siegelovà, J. (1971) *Appu-Märchen und Hedammu-Mythos (StBoT 14)*

Siegelovà, J. and Otten, H. (1970) 'Die Hethitischen Gulš-Gottheiten und die Erschaffung der Menschen', *Archiv für Orientforschung* 23

Sinioons, R.E. (1974) 'The Mesopotamian flood stories, a comparison and interpretation' *Numen* 21

Sjöberg, A.W. (1960) *Der Mondgott Nanna-Suen in der sumerischen Überlieferung* (Uppsala)

Sjöberg, A.W. (1973) 'Nungal in the Ekur', *Archiv für Orientforschung* 24

Sjöberg, A.W. (1976) 'In.nin.ša.gur₄.ra: A Hymn to the Goddess Inanna by the en-Priestess Enheduanna', *Zeitschrift für Assyriologie* 65

Sjöberg, A.W. (1976) 'Hymns to Ninurta with Prayers for Šusin of Ur and Bursîn of Isin', (Alter Orient und Altes Testament 25) (Neukirchen-Vluyn)

Sjöberg, A.W. and Bergmann, S.J. (1969) *The Collection of the Sumerian Temple Hymns* (New York)

Soden, W. (1936) 'Die Unterweltsvision eines assyrischen Kronprinzen', *Zeitschrift für Assyriologie* 43

Soden, W. (1955) 'Gibt es Zeichen dafür daß die Babylonier an die Wiederauferstehung Marduks geglaubt haben?', *Zeitschrift für Assyriologie* 51

Soden, W. (1966) 'Babylonische Göttergruppen: Igigu und Anunnaku, Zum Bedeutungswandel theologischer Begriffe', *Compres rendu de la onzième Rencontre Assyriologique Internationale*

Soden, W. (1966) 'Die Igigu Götter in der altbabylonischen Zeit', *Iraq* 28

Soden, W. (1976) 'Bemerkungen zum Adapa-Mythos', (Alter Orient und Altes

Testament 25) (Neukirchen-Vluyn)

Soden, W. (1985) *Einführung in die Altorientalistik* (Darmstadt)

Sommerfeld, W. (1982) *Der Aufstieg Marduks. Die Stellung Marduk's in der babylonischen Religion des zweiten Jahrtausends v.Chr.* (Alter Orient und Altes Testament 213) (Neukirchen-Vluyn)

Spronk, K. (1986) *Beatific Afterlife* (Neukirchen-Vluyn)

Spycket, A. (1960) 'La déesse Lama', *Revue Assyriologique* 54

Stefanni, R. (1969) 'Enkidu's Dream in the Hittite "Gilgamesh"', *Journal of Near Eastern Studies* 28

Steinkeller, P. (1987) 'The Name of Nergal' *Zeitschrift für Assyriologie* 77

Szabo, G. (1971) *Ein hethitisches Entsühnungsritual für das Königspaar Tuthalia IV, und Nikkalmati, Texte der Hethiter* (Heidelberg)

Tallqvist, K. (1932) *Der Assyrische Gott, Studia Orientalia* 4/3

Tallqvist, K. *Akkadische Götterepitheta* (Helsinki)

Thureau-Dangin, F. (1921) 'Rituel et Amulettes contre Labartu', *Revue d'Assyriologie* 18

Tigay, J.H. (1982) *The Evolution of the Gilgamesch Epic* (Philadelphia)

Urbin-Choffray, T. (1983) 'Déesse-mère, in *Dictionnaire des Religions* (Paris)

van Buren, E.D. (1934) 'The god Ningizzida' *Iraq*

van Buren, E.D. (1943) 'Mountain Gods', *Orientalia, Nova Seria* 12

van Dijk, J. (1953) *La sagesse suméro-accadienne* (Leiden)

van Dijk, J. (1966) 'L'hymne à Marduk avec intercession pour le roi Abi'ešuh', *Mitteilungen des Instituts für Orientforschung* 12

van Dijk, J. (1975) 'Incantation accompagnant la naissance de l'homme', *Orientalia, N.S.* 44

van Dijk, J. (1976) 'Le Motif Cosmique dans la pensée sumérienne', *Acta Orientalia* 28

van Dijk, J. (1976) 'Existe-t-il un "Poème de la Création" Sumérien?', *Kramer Anniversary Volume* (Alter Orient und Altes Testament 25) (Neukirchen-Vluyn)

van Dijk, J. (1983) *Lugal ud me-lám.bi nir.gál. Le récit épique et didactique des Travaux de Ninurta, du deluge et de la Nouvelle Création I–II* (Leiden)

Vanel, A. (1965) *L'iconographie du dieu de l'orage dans le Proche Orient ancien jusqu'au VIIe siècle avant J.C.* (Paris)

Vieyra, M. (1957) 'Ištar de Ninive', *Revue d'Assyriologie* 51, 2

Walker, C.B. (1983) 'The Myth of Girra and Elamatum', *Anatolian Studies* 33

Watson, P.L. (1971) *Mot, God of Death, at Ugarit and in the Old Testament,* Yale University Ph.D Diss. 1970 (Ann Arbor Microfilms)

Wegner, I. (1981) *Gestalt und Kult der Ištar-Sawuška in Kleinasien* (Alter Orient und Altes Testament 36) (Neukirchen-Vluyn)

Weiher, F. von (1971) *Der babylonische Gott Nergal* (Alter Orient und Altes Testament 2) (Neukirchen-Vluyn)

Weiher, F. von (1972) 'Ein Fragment des Gilgameš-Epos aus Uruk', *Zeitschrift für Assyriologie* 62

Wilcke, C. (1969) *Das Lugalbandaepos* (Wiesbaden)

Wilcke, C. (1987) 'Die Schwester des Ehemannes(*erib*)', *XXXIIIième Rencontre Assyriologie Internationale*, Paris 1986 (Paris)

Wilhelm, G. (1988) 'Neue akkadische Gilgamesch-Fragmente aus Hattusa', *Zeitschrift für Assyriologie*, N.F. 78

Wohlstein, A. (1976) *The Sky-God An-Anu* (Jericho, New York)

Wolff, H.N. (1969) 'Gilgamesh, Enkidu, and the Heroic Life', *Journal of the American Oriental Society* 89

Wyatt, N. (1980) 'The Relationship of the Deities Dagan and Hadad', *Ugarit Forschungen* 12

Xella, P. (1973) *Il mito di ŠHR e ŠLM* (Rome)

Young, D.W. (1979) 'The Ugaritic Myth of the god Hōrān and the Mare', *Ugarit Forschungen* 11

Zijl, P.J. van (1972) *Baal: A Study in Connection with Baal in the Ugarit Epics*, (Alter Orient und Altes Testament 10) (Neukirchen-Vluyn)

Abbreviations

RLA   Reallexikon der Assyriologie (Berlin, Vols I–VI)

SRT   Chiera E, Sumerian Religious Texts (Upland 1924)

Vbot   Götze, A. Verstreute Bogazköi-Texte (Marburg 1930)

WdM   Wörterbuch der Mythologie, Vol. I *Götter und Mythen im Vorderen Orient* (ed. H.W. Hausig) (Stuttgart 1965)

INDEX

Note: Numbers which appear in italics are references to illustrations.

189

1. Egyptian stela showing the Syrian goddess Anat seated on a throne. While emphasizing her femininity by a tight robe, it also shows the goddess' violent aspect, as she brandishes a mace and her shield. After Cassuto, The Goddess Anat (1950).

2. Horse's head-piece in ivory with a representation of a nude Syrian goddess, probaby Astarte. She carries a papyrus plant and above her is a winged disc. Such details are typical of the Egyptianizing style of the period. From the palace of Nimrud. 8th century BC. British Museum.

3. Stela of Shamshi-Adad V (823–811 BC). The king pays homage to the gods of the nation, represented by their symbols. The horned crown denotes the supreme divine ruler of the pantheon, in this context, the Assyrian national god Aššur. The winged sun disk stands for Šamaš, the crescent moon within the disk for Sîn, the forked lightning for the weather-god Adad, and the eight-pointed star is the symbol of Ištar in her astral aspect as the planet Venus. British Museum.

4. The Assyrian national god Aššur, here within a winged sun-disc, holding a bow. Neo-Assyrian.

5. Stone stela from Ras Shamra, the ancient Ugarit. The image is known as 'Baal au foudre', and thought to represent the Syrian weather-god, Baal-Hadad. He is shown as a young god, with long locks and a pointed beard, wearing a short kilt into which a dagger is thrust and a horned, peaked cap. The lightning-bolts, especially the one he grasps with his left hand, resemble plants, perhaps to emphasise the connection between fertility and the rain-heralding thunder. The waves indicate Baal's control of the sea. The small image of a man in the background is probably that of the unknown commissioner of the stela. Mid-second millennium BC. Louvre.

6. Terracotta of a seated goddess flanked by two palm-trees. The two birds may represent geese, animals sacred to Baba. The excavator, Sir Leonard Woolley, suggested that images such as this were worshipped in small wayside chapels and private shrines in the city of Ur. Old Babylonian Period. British Museum.

7. Terracotta of an unidentified Babylonian god. Old Babylonian period. British Museum.

8. The Babylonian god Marduk with his emblematic animal, the *mušhuššu* dragon, clasping the rod and ring. His dress and tiara are replete with celestial symbols. From a piece of lapis-lazuli found at Babylon. 9th century BC.

9. Terracotta reliefs of Babylonian gods with a martial aspect. From Ur. Old Babylonian Period. British Museum.

10.(*opposite*) Boundary stone of Nebukadrezzar I (12th century BC). Boundary stones were set up to document publicly the donation of land-grants by the king. The inscriptions evoke a number of gods to guarantee the donation as well as to persecute anyone who dares to act against it. The gods are further presented through their symbols, not all of which can be interpreted. In the top register is the astral triad Sun (Šamaš), Moon (Sîn) and Venus (Ištar). The 'great gods', Anu, Ellil and Ea, are summarily represented by horned crowns set on pedestals. In the third row, there is another row of peldestals or altars, this time identified by symbolic objects and animals. The first on the left, a stylus and the *Mušhuššu*-dragon, represents Nabû, the second features the emblem of Marduk (akkadian *marru*), probably an old agricultural rather than martial implement, and the third altar, with the scroll-like symbol (thought to symbolise swaddling bands), stands for one of the Mother-goddesses. The symbols on the fourth register are rather obscure, except for the mace that ends in two antithetical lion-heads, which is sometimes associated with Nergal, and the vulture headed staff typically symbolising the warrior-god Zababa. In row five there is a figurative representation of Gula, the healing deity, accompanied by a dog, her sacred animal. Next to her is a scorpion-man, Girtablulu. In the bottom register on the far left is a pronged lightning supported by a bull, the symbol of Adad, the weather-god. The scorpio belongs to the goddess Išhara, who is identified with this zodiac constellation. The tortoise is often associated with Ea (who is also included in the divine triad on register two) and the lamp on the upper right corner is the emblem of Nusku. British Museum.

11. Babylonian terracotta. Masks of demons were popular for warding off evil influences. The bared teeth and skin folds are characteristic of this demon who is generally known as Humbaba. From Ur. Old Babylonian Period. British Museum.

12. In the royal palaces of Assyria, demonic beings or spirits, usually depicted with human bodies and animal heads kept danger at bay. These two lion-faced genies are from the palace of Ashurbanipal at Nineveh. Ca 645 BC. British Museum.

13. Babylonian terracotta fragment of the demon Pazuzu with his snarling muzzle and lion-paws. From Ur. Old Babylonian Period. British Museum.

14. Orthostat relief from the palace of Arslantepe. A Hittite queen is offering libations to Ištar in her martial aspect, standing on her lion. 10–9th century BC. Museum of Anatolian Civilizations, Ankara.

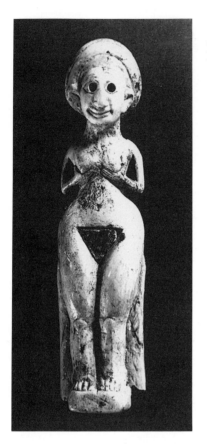

15. Ivory statuette of an unidentified female deity. From Kültepe. 9th century BC. Museum of Anatolian Civilizations, Ankara.

16. Statuette of a Hittite god in bronze. From Dövlek. Ca 1500 BC. Museum of Anatolian Civilizations, Ankara.

17. Relief of a procession of Hittite warrior-gods, brandishing swords. From the rock-sanctuary of Yazılıkaya, near the ancient Hittite capital Hattusa. 1250–1220 BC.

18. Orthostat relief from Alaça Hüyük, showing a royal couple conducting a ritual before a divine image in the shape of a bull. 14th century BC. Museum of Anatolian Civilizations, Ankara.

19. Stone relief of the goddess Kubaba holding a mirror and a pomegranate, symbols of magic and fertility. From Karkamish. 9th century BC. British Museum.

20. Terracotta relief of a goddess in the traditional pose of intercession and greeting. From Ur. Old Babylonian Period. British Museum.

21. Terracotta figurine of a seated woman possibly representing the mother-goddess, embracing a child. From Çatal Hüyük. 7–6th millennium BC. Museum of Anatolian Civilizations, Ankara.

22. Terracotta statuette of a seated woman supporting her breasts, a gesture typical of deities associated with fertility; several such figurines were found in grain bins in the granaries of this neolithic town. From Çatal Hüyük. 7–6th millennium BC. Museum of Anatolian Civilizations, Ankara.

23. One of the many Babylonian terracotta reliefs of nude women with strongly emphasized pudenda. From Ur. Old Babylonian Period. British Museum.

24. Libation cup of steatite, dedicated by Gudea, ruler of Lagash, to his god Ningišzida. The symbolism on this vessel combines the ancient auspicious motif of entwined serpents with an apotropaic demonic being, eagle clawed, winged and with a feline body. The creature holds a long staff, the meaning of which is obscure, and wears a horned cap. He was probably closely associated with Ningišzida himself. Ca 22nd century BC. Louvre.

25. Sumerian limestone plaque. A priest in archaic ritual nudity offers a libation to a seated goddess. The stylised scale-like 'mountains' suggest that she may represent Ninhursag, 'the lady of the *hursag*', the stony foothills to the north of the alluvial plains. Such plaques were offered to the gods and mounted on the temple walls by means of large metal nails, driven through the central hole. From Lagash. First half of the third millennium BC. Louvre.

26. King Nabû-Polassar of Babylon worships the Sun-god Šamaš in his shrine at Sippar. The Sun-god sits on a throne supported by minor deities and holds his ensigns of authority, the rod and ring. Above his head are the symbols of the Moon, the Sun and Venus. Before the shrine is an altar with a large sun-disk. A priest of the Sun-god leads the king and the procession is completed by an interceding 'Lama'-type goddess. The actual tablet was recovered several times by later Babylonian kings who made copies of the original scene. Emblems of astral deities, the moon-crescent, the sun-disk and the eight-pointed star of Ištar, represented the deities in cultic as well as secular proceedings. They were fashioned of precious metals, often gold and silver, and mounted on special stands. Attached to a temple facade, they pronounced the divine occupant of the sanctuary. 9th–7th century BC. British Museum.

28. (*opposite*) The Elamites were greatly influenced by Mesopotamian culture, and the iconography of the stela closely resembles that of the more famous monument of Hammurabi which contains the collection of legal precepts known as the 'Code' of Hammurabi. This stela had in fact been taken to Susa during an Elamite raid on Babylon. The main difference between the two images, stylistic considerations apart, is that the Babylonian god is characterised by the traditional device of luminous rays emanating from his shoulders, whilst the Elamite god is designated by the solar disk. 18th century BC. Louvre.

27. Elamite stela from Susa, with the seated Sun-god Nuhhunte and an Elamite king. Mid-second millennium BC. Louvre.

29. Terracotta relief of an unidentified Sumerian goddess from Ur. The figure of the deity is surrounded by six eight-pointed rosettes which are usually typical Inanna-Ištar. She is wearing a large head-covering, an elaborate garment and holds two bottle-shaped objects. Old Babylonian Period. British Museum.

30. Terracotta relief of a divine couple embracing. From Ur. Old Babylonian Period. British Museum.

31. Terracotta relief of a goddess, seated on a throne which resembles the facade of a temple. From Ur. Old Babylonian Period. British Museum.

32. Terracotta relief of a 'nude hero' with a flowing vase. The *aryballos* or flowing vase is an ancient symbol for the precious gift of water, tantamount to life itself in the arid climate of southern Mesopotamia. It can be held by gods or goddesses. The nude, bearded hero shown here, has been associated with Enki/Ea and his six sons. From Ur. Old Babylonian Period. British Museum.

33. Bronze figurine of a seated goddess from Ras Shamra (Ugarit). The slim and youthful goddess cannot be identified with any certainty. She wears a tight robe which exposes her breasts and a snake is coiled around her shoulders. On her head is the horned cap, the symbol of divinity. Middle of 2nd millennium BC. Louvre.

34. The Anatolian Storm-god astride his bull, holding a bolt of lightning. From Arslan Tash. 8th century BC.

35. Monumental stone relief of a Hittite warrior god. From the King's Gate at Boğazköy. 14–12th century BC. Museum of Anatolian Civilizations, Ankara.

36. One of the few myths that can be identified with any certainty on cylinder seals, is the story of Etana who ascended to heaven on the back of an eagle. The scene is pastoral, set within a sheep corral, indicated by the reed-fences on either side. Several figures are busy tending animals or preparing dairy products. This is plausible, since Etana is reputed to have been a shepherd before he became king of Uruk. Etana himself is already seated on the eagle who is about to carry him to heaven. His dogs and his wife are looking up as he takes off. Akkadian. Berlin Museum.

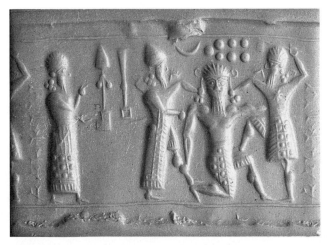

37. One of the rare scenes representing an episode from the Gilgameš-epic, the slaying of the demon Humbaba. Gilgameš is the more elaborately dressed figure on the left, wearing a crown and a long robe. His companion, Enkidu, has put his right foot on Huwawa and lifts his arm to deliver the fatal blow. An attendant figure, who does not participate in the main scene, stands on the far left. There are several symbols used as in-fills, the *marru* of Marduk, the stylus of Nabû, the crescent of Sîn and the seven 'dots' of the Pleiades or Sibitti. These are thought to have originally been stones for the casting of lots in oracles. Neo-Assyrian. C 750–650 BC. British Museum.

38. The worship of Ištar. The goddess, fully armed with bows and arrows, quivers, mace and daggers, stands on her emblematic animal, a crouching lion. The scene is flanked by fruit-bearing date-palms and filled out by antithetically grouped rampant gazelles. Neo-Assyrian. C 750–650 BC. British Museum.

39- On this seal from the Akkadian period, the water-god (Enki/Ea) is seated on the far right. Streams of water emerge from his shoulders wherein fish swim. Before him stands a scorpion-tailed 'bird-man', tethered by a rope held by two attending gods. The scene is completed by a bearded god who shoulders a bunch of vegetation. This is one of many representations of mythological subjects which have no known parallel in a written source. British Museum.

40. The Sun-god Šamaš, holding his rod and ring, is here seen seated in his boat which is propelled by divine figures at each prow. The celestial symbols of Sun and Moon float above the god and two kilted priests offering libations flank the scene. Two deities guard the stream on which the barge is travelling. Old Babylonian Period. British Museum.

41. In this 'introduction-scene', a goddess presents a worshipper to the deified king Ur-nammu, who sits on an elaborate throne, while a second goddess, in a different type of dress is in attendance. Third Dynasty of Ur. British Museum.

42. This seal-impression assembles several deities. The inclusion of the altar points to a scene of worship. The second figure from the left presents an offering of a gazelle to the war-goddess (Inanna/Ištar) on his right. Then follows a goddess holding a vessel overflowing with water. Facing the other way is a bearded god, cloaked with a lion's pelt and carrying a club in his right hand, and maybe a sling in the other. Branches of vegetation sprout from his shoulders. Opposite him stands a female vegetation goddess, clasping some plant in her left hand. Akkadian. British Museum.

43. This beautiful seal, which belonged to a scribe, shows the Sun-god emerging from the *kur*, here represented by tall mountains. The Sun-god (Utu), with flaming rays behind him, brandishes a serrated sword. Above him, to his right, hovers a winged and martial goddess (Inanna/Ištar), weapons emerging from her shoulders. In her left hand she holds some kind of bundle, which may represent a bunch of dates. On his left stands the Water-god (Enki), one foot on the mountain. Fish swim in the streams of water that spring from his shoulders. A crouching bull represents the Weather-god. Next to the Water-god stands his vizier Isimu, who has two faces. On the right, beside the inscription stands a warrior-god, accompanied by a lion. Akkadian. British Museum.

44. Such combat scenes were very popular during the third millennium BC. They used to be associated with Gilgameš, but they may refer to a quite different tradition which has no known literary parallel. A nude hero is grappling with a bull-man on the left, his partly clothed companion tackles another to the right. The scene is further complimented by a predator (here a lion) attacking a domestic animal (the bull). Akkadian. British Museum.